29 PALMS

29 PALMS

AN AMERICAN ODYSSEY FOR TRUE LOVE

BY HAWKE SMITH

© 2021 Vikare Publishing LLC

All Rights Reserved

Dedicated to my father

Robert Thomas Smith

Who never stopped daring to love

TABLE OF CONTENTS

CHAPTER I: DANCIN' IN THE DARK 1
CHAPTER II: SMOKESTACK LIGHTNING 5
CHAPTER III: WAITING FOR A GIRL LIKE YOU 33
CHAPTER IV: RUN THROUGH THE JUNGLE 46
CHAPTER V: THE PROMISE 58
CHAPTER VI: DON'T FEAR THE REAPER 65
CHAPTER VII: LONG COOL WOMAN 80
CHAPTER VIII: BLACK MAGIC WOMAN 98
CHAPTER IX: DANGER ZONE 115
CHAPTER X: GOING UP THE COUNTRY 130
CHAPTER XI: DRAGGIN' THE LINE 130
CHAPTER XII: NIGHTCALL 164
CHAPTER XIII: ALWAYS & FOREVER 176
CHAPTER XIV: I CAN'T FIGHT THIS FEELING 186
CHAPTER XV: RACING IN THE STREET 195
CHAPTER XVI: BREAK ON THROUGH 203
CHAPTER XVII: KICKSTART MY HEART 213
CHAPTER XVIII: I WANNA KNOW WHAT LOVE IS 226
CHAPTER XIX: RAMBLIN' GAMBLIN' MAN 240
CHAPTER XX: CAN YOU HEAR ME KNOCKING 247
CHAPTER XXI: HELLRAISER 256
CHAPTER XXII: IS THIS LOVE 273
CHAPTER XXIII: SHOOT TO THRILL 286
CHAPTER XXIV: NO EASY WAY OUT 295
CHAPTER XXV: WELCOME TO THE JUNGLE 313
CHAPTER XXVI: BLINDED BY THE LIGHT 334
CHAPTER XXVII: THRILLER 350
CHAPTER XXVIII: MORE THAN WORDS 362
CHAPTER XIX: UNDER THE BRIDGE 374
EPILOGUE: LIFE IS BUT A DREAM 384

CHAPTER I: DANCIN' IN THE DARK

In a way, I was running away: away from the clouds, away from the storm, away from the pain. Away from crying in the rain. I was running away, but at least I was runnin' toward something. The storm still raged, and the shadows of my heart still chased me, but today it was all behind me, and there, the sun rose before me. There was the road. I finally had someplace to go.

I took the keys to a little, blue Nissan Frontier from the Enterprise agent and waltzed my way out the door toward my brother Pavin's car. He was damn near half asleep waiting for me to come out. He didn't like the idea of getting woke up at 7 a.m. at all, but he never wanted to get woke up no matter what time it was.

I tapped on his car window and said, "Gonna need you to pop the trunk there, pal."

My brother rolled his eyes and hit the button. After I got my red duffel bag out, I walked back over to him and said, "Well, friend, it looks like this is it. We're at the end of the line now. It's been a good run, ain't it?"

My brother replied, "Stop fucking with me, man. I don't even know what you're talking about." He rubbed his eyes and continued, "Whatever, though. Have fun, bro. I'll see you in a few days."

After we gave each other the sweetest brotherly hug goodbye, it didn't take him long to crawl his way back into the driver's seat of his car. I waved him goodbye and said, "Ok, big guy! I love ya now, ok?!"

Pavin just shook his head and said, "Whatever, man—I love you too."

He pulled off, and it was time for me to get off—on the road, that is. The Frontier I rented wasn't the fanciest ride I could've picked for my trip, but it was damn near guaranteed to get me from point A to B, and that's all I needed. I still couldn't believe I was actually about to set off—finally, *a new direction*. I hadn't felt like I was going anywhere for a while, if ever really, but it was the worst when my ex started keeping my kids from me.

They both have blonde hair and blue eyes, just like me. I think they'll grow to be tall like me one day too. Don't get me wrong; they're both their own person, but they've always reminded me a lot of myself when I was a little boy. Nobody could overlook that even if they tried.

I did all I could to get to see them again, but the courts and the caseworkers weren't helping me with a thing. They didn't care if I got to see my kids or not. It got to the point I couldn't even focus at my job anymore. So when my boss gave me the option to furlough out for a couple of months because of the Covid, I was more than ready for the break. It didn't help too much, though. I started drinking a lot a couple of weeks back, around the beginning of May, and it pretty much turned into an all-out binge. I just didn't care anymore. My purpose was gone. If it weren't for family, I would've been a goner. That's the thing. You really gotta be thankful for those warriors who come to help you in the middle of a storm. Not everybody has that.

None of them could fix me, though. That was my job to do. I wasn't sure how to do that—still not to tell you the truth, but when this beautiful girl I know said to me, "Hawke, have you ever thought about taking a solo trip just for you," it all just clicked into place.

Her name is Brooke. She was used to taking trips by herself all the time because she was an outsider in a way just like I was. It seemed so impossible for me to take the journey I wanted to at first because of my job and everything, but with the pandemic hitting the US in the way it did and furlough coming to my rescue, now was the best time more than ever to take a trip—sort of. I figured, *I have two months off work, so why not go to Georgia for the weekend?* It was set just like that. What did I have to lose?

I sat behind the wheel of the Frontier and turned the ignition. *I gotta bring those old tunes back for this adventure,* I thought. So I hit play on my eighties playlist. I got a sixties and seventies playlist too, but the eighties songs always make me feel like my dad is with me when they go blaring through the system. Anything that can bring just a part of him back feels magical to me.

With that, I damn near shot out of the Enterprise's parking lot blasting the classic song "Paradise City." It was time to get the hell out of Mobile, Alabama. Here I was on the road, and it was happening. When I finally set out toward the morning sun, I tried not to expect much on what was to come, but in my heart, I hoped to encounter that true love story I've always wished for. I thought to myself, *Who knows who I might meet along the way? And maybe, just maybe, I'll find that one girl for me, and my dreams really will come true.* That dream for true love has been alive for me ever since I was a little boy.

Back then, the stories I enjoyed the most were the ones where the hero gets the girl. That's always when the happily ever after moment happens—when the knight in shining armor finds his true love. People say things like happily ever after or true love don't exist, and it's all just a part of some fairytale, but I'm the type of guy who asks the why to everything. Why can't true love be a real thing? And if happily ever after doesn't exist, what's really the point to all this? I get things will never be perfect with anybody, but your heart knows what it wants, and when you find what your heart really wants—you'd run down just about any obstacle you come across just to get to it. Like one of the heroes of old, but the most beautiful thing about it all is you wouldn't have to do it all alone anymore.

I damn near even made a promise to myself I wouldn't make the trip about finding the one. I'd just take things as they came no matter what crossed my path, but that isn't really what happened. While I was running all of the possibilities over in my head, that all-too-familiar voice came—the one that always comes when I need it most, and it said *You're going to come across so many beautiful things along the way; you just wait and see. Just take what you can out of as much beauty that you can. Witness and feel it in your heart. I promise it'll do the trick just right.* I'm not too sure what that voice is. I've wondered a lot if it's my dad coming back to talk to me, but it feels like something even greater than who he was, or maybe it's just something he's a part of now. In my heart, I have to say I think it's both.

CHAPTER II: SMOKESTACK LIGHTNING

I figured I'd make my first stop in Savannah, Georgia. It seemed like everything pointed me toward there for some reason. I kept seeing pictures, ads, movies, and even ran into a few people telling me to check it out. It just seemed right, and on top of that, it was only about a seven-hour drive from Mobile. That's not too far—practically a nice afternoon cruise to me.

I came into Savannah at the dawn of a Friday night on May 22 in the summer of 2020. The sun had just started to set right over the interstate where I had booked a hotel room. Speaking of that, it wasn't what I had expected at all from the beautiful pictures I saw of it on booking.com. Online, it looked like it had a vast and glimmering swimming pool almost sure to have a few supermodels lying out around it, but in person, the pool alone made me want to scream. The water was murky like a swamp, and I'm almost glad the water was as dark as it was because I was pretty sure from the looks of it *something*—perhaps some long-forgotten creature—lived at the bottom of it. I didn't stick around to find out. *No supermodels to find here*—I thought—*only death in the water.*

I tried not to let the swamp get to me, but I was literally in a city where I didn't know a soul, and I had no idea where the hell I should go first. Then an angel put a sign right across the road. It started with an H, just like heaven. The supermodels weren't too far away after all. Hooters it would be then.

After checking into the motel I had gotten duped into paying for, I went to the Hooters across the street, donning a lovely blue and gray pinstripe dress shirt that was pretty fancy—if I must say so myself—to make my debut in Savannah. As soon as I walked into the restaurant, I could almost smell the garlic parmesan wings I would order getting cooked up already and the beer, of course, too. I couldn't smell it, but I could already taste it. *Get that handle ready, girl,* I thought. *It's Miller time.*

Before I was even seated, I started looking around to see if I could spot a chick who would make me feel those fireworks of butterflies within me, and to my luck, it didn't take long for that to happen. It wasn't a magical moment or anything when I saw her, but I could feel a familiarity with this girl. The best way I can put it is there seemed to be something lonely in her eyes, and I could feel that more than ever at the time.

She had long, flat blonde hair falling across her petite shoulders, and she had these beautiful, brown, doe-like eyes too. She was beautiful, and she made me feel beautiful from how she smiled at me when I came up to talk to her. I tried approaching her in a relaxed way even though I was nervous, but I think I pulled it off when I said, "Hey, there. How you doin'? What's your name?"

She looked me up and down while she swung her arms in a light way back and forth. She pointed to her name tag and replied with a little laugh, "My name's Zoe, and I'm doing alright; how are you?"

I leaned up against the wall with my arm, trying to strike a sexy pose, I guess, and replied, "I'm doing great. I just drifted into town—that's the kind of stuff I do. I've never been here before. You got any idea where all the fun is happenin' tonight?"

Zoe kept staring into me with those big, brown eyes of hers. They shimmered a little bit in the light as her smile grew larger, and she replied, "Well—um—there probably isn't going to be much goin' on here later, but you could always go downtown. I'm new here, so I don't know, but downtown is where I'd start."

Hmmm, downtown, of course, I thought. I flashed a smile right back at Zoe and replied, "Yeah, that's what I figured. Maybe you could go downtown with me later. Can I get you on Snap?"

Zoe replied as she showed me her Snap code, "Yeah, sure. That's me, but I probably won't be able to make it downtown tonight. I gotta close later."

What a bummer. Just my luck. I replied, "Well, ok. I'll be in town for the weekend, so—you got me on Snap now . . . If you wanna hit me up tomorrow or something, you can."

She told me she would and smiled as she walked back to her tables. It sucked, but honestly, I was just afraid to go downtown by myself. I could end up getting lost, my ass kicked, drugged, you name it. The worst could happen, but the best could just as easily. With that said, I was bound and determined to make my way down there anyway. I didn't have it in my head to sleep with her or anything. I just wanted to have a night out on the town with a pretty girl I had just met and thought maybe we could get lost in a good time, you know? I hit her up later on, but she left me on read. It wasn't a surprise. I've been left on read so many times; if Bloody Mary was a man, that's who I'd be. Minus the ghoul part, I'm not a creep after all.

On the way downtown, I got a lot of info from the Uber driver about the town. He told me the Barrelhouse or B&D Burgers would be the place to start. He went on and on about all the beautiful women in Savannah; he kept saying stuff like, "Very, very beautiful women here—right here in the big city. I can see that the American women here—everywhere—very, very big breasts. Everywhere my friend. You will see them everywhere."

I didn't care to tell you the truth. I was just out to have a good time. I wasn't trying to have any more kids yet or anything. I don't size women up that way anyway—most of the time. I don't care how big their breasts are. A girl who knows what she wants and knows how to carry on a good conversation is good enough for me. I love stuff like that.

When I escaped all the breast gibberish, I stepped out of my Uber and was met with an overwhelming feeling of being completely lost. Sure, I knew where I was, but I didn't even have a crew to hang with.

You see, it's typically my brother's job to find folks to start a fire with. I might be the older brother, but he's the one who usually does all of the talking, and on any night I've gone out in Mobile, I was just along for the ride and sort of followed his lead.

My brother knows just about everybody and doesn't give a shit what comes out of his mouth. I, on the other hand, am usually the quiet type. I'm an awkward person, and most of the time, I don't even know what to say to people. I stood there on the sidewalk, really wishing I had brought him with me, but then I thought, *Well, you're just going to have to learn to do the talking for yourself now, aren't you?* True as that might've been, I was still full of fear over just the thought of it.

I started taking in the downtown area immediately. I noticed it wasn't as jam-packed as downtown Mobile on a Friday night, and I wondered if it was just the town or because of the Covid. Across the country, the news always spouted off about Covid-19 or, in Trump's words, "the Chinese virus" or the "Kung-Foo flu." I hoped the new restrictions weren't going to ruin my time in Savannah.

It wasn't that I didn't see the virus as a threat, but I didn't understand why everyone's lives were expected to stop because of it. Every day you leave your house, you're at the mercy of a risk that could involve something terrible happening. It could be a car wreck, getting your ass kicked, or maybe catching herpes; who knows? Anything could happen. You're always at risk of something, and that's the way I chose to handle the virus, like any other risk. I wanted to live my life as I always have, regardless of all the dangers out there. That's why, after a short spell of thinking and looking around, I decided to march my way toward the Barrelhouse to get my first drink in Savannah.

When I approached the Barrelhouse, a vast line stretched down the sidewalk. I didn't look forward to standing in line at all because I had a hell of a lot of anxiety I really needed to drown with a few shots and a beer, but it gave me a little more time to take in the atmosphere.

As I looked around, I could tell Savannah was truly a city blending the modern era with the old perfectly. At the time, I wondered if those nights back in the day were a lot like that very night. I started imagining drunk folks in their top hats and big old corseted dresses hanging halfway out of carriages rumbling down some old, dark road after leaving a good-old-fashioned southern party. Savannah was always sort of known for its parties, and I intended to wage a hell fest of my own as soon as I got into the bar.

I stood there getting lost in my thoughts like I always do until a feminine-sounding voice broke them, and it said, "Oh, you're handsome. You have a beautiful face."

I got the feeling that voice talked about me, so I spun around to see who it was, but then the voice spoke again behind me and said, "Yeah, I'm talking about you."

When I turned back around, there was a little, blonde, probably 140-pound gay dude standing right in front of me with a big smile on his face. I thought, *Oh man, here we go again. Why do gay dudes always hit on me?* I broke the awkward silence of shock when I said, "Who me?"

Blondie threw his arms up with a smile and said, "Yeah you. You're absolutely gorgeous."

It's always kind of awkward when it happens. I replied, "Oh—well, thanks, man. Appreciate it."

Blondie rushed back off into his group of girlfriends after I said that. They started giggling and everything. I started to get so nervous. I even looked down at my wrist to look at a watch that wasn't even there. *Why do I always get myself into this kind of shit?* The line just couldn't move fast enough.

It's not that I minded the fellow complimenting me—I love compliments. They always make me feel really good no matter who they come from, but I didn't want to break the poor little lad's heart. My boat just doesn't sail that way. It didn't matter, though, because the bouncer let me in just in time before things started to get even more awkward.

When I walked into the Barrelhouse, it seemed like it had an old-style flair, just like the rest of the city. The lights over the stage appeared to paint a violet hue across the brick walls and the old-fashioned light bulbs hanging across the ceiling. It sort of sucked there wasn't a band there, but they had some Kanye playing, which seemed fine enough to me.

After I ordered a Blue Ribbon from the masked bartender, I stood propped up against the bar with my drink and started to scope out the crowd.

The Uber driver was right. There were a lot of beautiful women in Savannah. To my left at the table across the bar, there was this stunning brunette laughing and talking with a friend. I usually observe a smile and someone's body language more than anything. She seemed pretty friendly; she didn't seem like a prude or anything, but then her boyfriend Andre the Giant came up to her and brought her another drink, so that was a no-go. I didn't have any plans of getting snapped in half, so I looked onward.

Blonde but mean, she's yelling at that guy; another pretty brunette, but too many friends are with her. Then all of a sudden I spotted the one—a beautiful redhead. Chicks with red hair just light my soul on fire, and I don't have a clue why. There's just something about them, and this one looked kind of dangerous. She wasn't wearing any makeup or anything, just a rocker tank top with some tight, ripped-up jeans. She had a few tats as well, and that really gets me too. She had rebel painted all over her. *Just my type of girl*, I thought, but I needed more liquid courage to prepare myself for the approach.

I started taking shot after shot without a care in the world. *Goodbye, Mr. Jekyll, and hello, Mr. Hyde*, but all of a sudden, a bouncer materialized out of thin air right beside me as soon as I started to get riled up and said, "Hey, buddy, you gotta stay in your seat. We can't let people run around in here because of the Covid."

That was one hell of a buzz kill. How could I go over there and talk to that beautiful red-headed rebel if I couldn't move? I looked back toward where she was, but she was gone. I couldn't spot her anywhere. I thought to myself, *Damn, I missed my shot.* It didn't matter anyway; I couldn't even move around, but then I figured, *Well, nobody can stop me from running around outside.* After all, I had a city to explore, so I headed toward the smoke shop down the road because what's really a beer without a smoke?

Outside the smoke shop, I saw a sign advertising dabs, edibles, roll-ups, kratom, you name it, I guess the whole gang was in there, and I thought to myself, *Damn, maybe that's why everyone seems so friendly around here; they're all blown out of their minds. I wish I could join in, but the piss man at work could get me if I get called back, so I better not.*

The piss man will do everything he can to make sure Joe Whoever doesn't have too much of a good time over the weekend. Regardless, it seemed like my type of place, but as soon as I walked in, I was almost struck dead in my tracks. I spotted this lovely looking French girl with dark brown hair and even darker eyes and quite the slender figure to match. I wondered what the hell she could've been doing working at a smoke shop because she looked like she could've been a model or something. In pure crowned Blue Ribbon bravery, I went up to her immediately. I had to find out who this beautiful woman was.

I walked up to the counter and tried to get some words out of my mouth, but I just stood there with my jaw open. I couldn't speak a word. *Don't embarrass yourself,* I thought. The French girl flashed one of the brightest smiles I'd ever seen—I mean, her teeth damn near glowed—then she said, "Can I help you?"

Say something, dumbass. You look so stupid right now, I thought, but all I managed to say was, "Yeah—umm—what do ya have back there?"

The French girl pushed herself away from the counter laughing and said, "I have a lot back here. What are you looking for?"

For you to take me back to France with you, I thought, but I couldn't say that. I laughed a little while I blushed and said, "Well—ummm—cigars—do you got any black-n-milds?"

The French girl replied in excitement, "Well, of course, I do! Are you new around here? I've never seen you in here before."

Marry me, I thought. This chick was beautiful—too beautiful—that's why it was so hard for me to talk to her, but I had to answer her back. The words I brought up felt like a hundred pounds, but I brought them up anyway. "Yeah—I mean—I guess you could say that. I just sort of drifted into town, you know—" I could feel myself blushing so hard my cheeks felt like they were gonna pop, but I continued, "I don't know too much about this place really. Are you from here?"

The French girl continued to smile as she played with her hair a little bit and said, "No, I'm from France. I'm sort of new here myself. Just trying to get a start in a new town, you could say. What brings you to Savannah?"

I started to calm down a little bit by then. I didn't feel like snatching my cigars and running away anymore, but I couldn't stop blushing.

"I just sort of came here on a whim, I guess. I came all the way from Alabama—so I don't know—I guess I'm just hangin' out."

The French girl's eyes glowed back at me when she said, "Oh, ok. On an adventure then, it sounds like fun. Well, you have a good time in Savannah, and come back to see me now."

That made me smile even more. She wanted me to come back and see her. I took my cigars and pulled off a cool, "Don't worry; I will."

She watched me walk out, and all I could manage back was a little awkward wave. Soon afterward, the shots really started kicking in.

I was damn near buzzed to the tee and skipping down the sidewalk with a cigar in one hand and a beer in the other. That's the thing about Savannah; you can damn near go anywhere with a drink.

I started to feel a tinge of newfound freedom in the air. Here I was in a city where nobody knew who I was at all, and if I wanted to, I could be whoever I wanted to be. I could be Steve the stockbroker, Gary from the yacht club, or even some up-and-coming Hollywood playboy who just drifted along with my newfound fortune going wherever I pleased. I was nobody here, but I could be anybody. I didn't have to worry about what anybody thought. I could literally run naked in the streets, and nobody back home would have a clue about it at all. It was nice not to worry about judgments for a change. After all, it's not like I'd see any of these people again anyway.

I continued onward with my stroll and couldn't help notice all of the town squares I kept running across. They seemed to be so intricately designed, and in each of them, it seemed like there was a surprise waiting in the middle. Some of them had statues or beautiful fountains, which were my favorite. The squares started to get boring, though, and I needed another drink. So I figured I'd go back to the Barrelhouse for another. The big-guy bouncer would just have to chill out for a few. I didn't care.

After I ordered another drink, the bartender said, "Yep, card's been declined."

I shook my head and said, "There's no way in hell that's impossible."

After a few more attempts, the bank card wouldn't work at all, and I started to panic a little because it began to look like I done and got myself stranded.

Eventually, I got it all figured out, though. After a furious conversation with the bank's customer service center, I found out I went way past my limit after renting a truck and booking a few spots. Thank god for cash. I just so happened to have enough to catch a ride back to my splendid motel room.

Once I got back to the "glorious" motel, I was ready to get some sleep. The bank fucked me again. With shoulders slumped and my head down, I started walking down the motel hallway back to my room. I only took a few steps before I stopped dead in my tracks.

A bloodcurdling scream came from down the hall, screeching its way across the wallpaper all around me. I panicked immediately and pressed my back up against the wall. I tried as hard as I could to get my breath under control so the killer wouldn't hear me. I couldn't pinpoint which room the screeches from hell came from. All I could do was stand there and think, *I should've never taken this trip. Here I am, already in some shitty motel where there's probably some lunatic on the loose going from room to room and just picking people off.*

Then came an even louder scream. "Oh, fuck me with your big fat dick!"

I never thought I'd feel so relieved to hear those words in my life. My shoulders relaxed, and I started to calm my breathing back down to normal. The faster my legs moved, the closer I got to the sound, but my room was just within reach. The action had to be happening right across the hall, of course—*just my luck*.

My hands scrambled with the room key as a big thud hit the door across the hall. It was loud enough to make me drop the key altogether. It was a terrible time to bend over, but I'm fast—perhaps one of the fastest men in the world, you see, especially after the sound of a whip came. *Click. Saved by the bell.* I turned the door handle toward safety and slammed the door immediately.

It was kind of funny after I was safe in my room. I mean, they were really overdoing it over there like they were shooting a porno or something. I couldn't believe it. I just smiled and shook my head as I climbed under my lonely covers. I tried my best to muffle it all out with my pillow, but nothing helped. After about an hour, they stopped, but that morning, I guess they hit reset, and it was time to play again. Right then and there, I decided I needed to get the fuck out of there. I wasn't going to deal with another night of BDSM radio, or whatever the hell they had going on over there. I'd figure it out later, though. It was time to head out for my trolley tour.

I felt tall when I handed the driver my ticket. Not just because I am, but I pulled the cool act off pretty well. You see, I usually get nervous around people because I don't have a whole lot of confidence in myself. I'm always worried about what they could be thinking about me, but not today. I wasn't playing me. I was a confident movie star from Hollywood. I even tried to dress like one too. I probably overdid it a little with my bright-blue silk dress shirt and white khakis, but that's the only thing that would match my black snakeskin dress shoes. I wasn't playing around; I tried to dress to impress.

The air smelled sweet like roses and dandelions as the warm summer wind blew through the air while the trolley bus moved along. I could feel the sun in a cloudless bright-blue sky raining down upon me, forcing a smile to bloom across my face. There was peace in the presence of everything for a change. *Delightful,* I thought. *Today is going to be a good day.*

The first thing we did on the tour was make our way around to all the squares I'd seen the night before. They were much more beautiful in the daylight. The luxurious fountains cascaded clear, crystalline water into the sky, raining its way back down upon the wishes of those who had passed through before. They looked so magical, almost like they really could grant a desire if you truly believed in it.

When we reached one of the squares, the trolley driver asked all of us passengers if it looked familiar. It did in a way, but I wasn't sure until the driver said, "I'll give you a hint. It was in a movie where it all began with a feather flying in the sky. Does anybody know who it landed on?"

A guy in the back said, "Forrest Gump."

The trolley driver replied, "That's correct. That's the same square that Forrest Gump started his journey in the movie. The bench isn't there anymore, but the square ain't going anywhere."

I could feel my cheeks starting to blush. I thought to myself, *Wow, how cool is that. That's where Forrest started telling his story. I wish I could tell a story like that one day.* The thought of it just seemed so impossible at the time.

The houses in the historic district I saw along the tour were captivating, especially the Mercer House. A lot of them were two-story brick, but the most beautiful ones to me were the ones with the balconies and large columns in front of them. I guess experts would call the architecture Greek Revival or Victorian, maybe; I don't know. All I do know is, without a shadow of a doubt, those homes were monuments to stories, and that's all I needed to fall in love with them. My favorite house out of them all was the Sorrel-Weed House, though. It was supposed to be the most haunted of them all in Savannah, so of course, I had to go in there.

None of the homes looked alike in the historic district of Savannah, but the Sorrel-Weed House stood out like a gem across the scenic landscape ushering me back in time. Its Greek Revival architecture was something to behold, and even the bright-orange hue of the place with its dark-green shutters seemed like it tried to send some sort of symbolic code I couldn't hope to interpret; there was something about the windows, though. It was like they could see. In a way, it felt like the house knew I was there. I stood at the doorstep and said, "Well, I ain't came in yet, honey, but here I come."

When I walked into the garden of the home, I couldn't help but notice it was built up to look a lot like the squares. In the garden, I didn't just see my tour group and the bright, beautiful flowers all around. I saw something else in my mind.

I started having this scene play through my mind of a lovely looking woman with dark hair kneeling by some flowers and at peace tending away to her garden. She wasn't trying to pass the day away but approached every minute she could with love. She smiled and seemed so content with what she did. The scene wasn't strange to me. It happens some places I go. Most of the time, I just figure it's my imagination, but in some cases, I'm not really sure.

When the tour went inside the house into the basement, a scene started playing through my mind involving a bunch of little kids running around with laughs and giggles bouncing across the underground walls. They ran off to find a hiding spot in a game of hide-and-seek from what it looked like. One of them was this little boy in an old white shirt and dress pants kneeling in a corner with his hands cupped over his mouth to keep himself from laughing. It looked like he was having a lot of fun. They all looked happy, but the vision kind of made me sad.

Through the basement and onward to the first story, I didn't feel anything malevolent there at all—that is until I got in front of the stairs to the second story. It was roped off, and you weren't allowed to go up there, and honestly, I was glad you couldn't. There was something about those stairs. Something *dark*. I could just feel it. I didn't have any desire to know what was up there.

The rest of the home was beautiful, though. I loved it in there. Each room was adorned with a soft-orange color to its walls, and they were spacious enough to have held one hell of a party back in the day. The ceilings were high with hanging chandeliers, that made you want to dance for some reason. Who knows, maybe it was because I was in the piano room? It felt like a real home, though. Those old houses just get me every time. I felt excellent there, but I kept thinking about those kids I saw playing in the basement. It made me think of my own a lot.

I started to wonder what my kids could've been up to. Maybe they played a game of hide-and-seek of their own like those kids. There was no way for me to know. I just really hoped they weren't staring down the road waiting for Daddy to pull in like I used to when I was a little boy. The difference between my little boys and that lost little boy I used to be was this Daddy wasn't gone yet, and this Daddy was going to come back. I just hoped they knew that in their little hearts.

I started settling back into my despair again, even until that evening. When I sat in the middle of the bustling city market, with live instruments ripping through the air, I was surrounded by people, but I couldn't feel anymore alone. I sat on a bench, mixed drink in hand, and people watched a little bit.

The first thing I noticed was this couple sitting out in the warm evening sun having dinner together. They looked to be around my age, and they seemed so happy with one another. The woman at the table stared back into her lover's eyes with such a warm and compassionate look that was returned right back to her. I sat there and wondered if I'd ever find somebody to look at me like that, because as far as my twenty-seven years had gone, I never had. Sure, I had a long-term girlfriend in the past, but it was just one girlfriend, and we never got on the same page about anything. The recipe for love just wasn't there.

To me, true love is the only thing that matters. I've never cared about becoming a millionaire with a big house and fancy cars. No. All I've ever wanted was maybe a lovely old farmhouse surrounded by acres of rolling creeks, meadows, and trees. I've always had a vision of standing on the porch of an old farmhouse like that, watching the sun go down with my true love in my arms, watching the day go away, and preparing for the next. A moment like that would make all the sorrows in life worth it to me.

As I daydreamed along, my thoughts were halted by a, "Wow, look at you!"

I looked around through the crowd from my lonely park bench and spotted a group of three girls approaching me, and I stammered, "Who-who, me?"

One of them had braces with bushy brown hair, and she replied, "Yeah, you! Your outfit is so put together! Oh my god! The headband, down to the plaid shirt, and your eyes are so pretty!"

I was dumbfounded. Here I sat on a bench getting all in my feelings, and here comes this group of girls out of nowhere. It felt awkward but I said, "Wow, thanks. You look really good too. Y'all want to get some drinks?"

We walked around downtown Savannah that Saturday night and had ourselves a lot to drink—too much. I just couldn't believe out of everybody in the crowd they had noticed me and wanted to hang out with me of all people. I've never really felt like a first choice before.

That day took such a huge turn from the despair I had sunk into earlier, and now I found myself laughing and making jokes with a group of new friends. I almost couldn't believe it. As I talked with each of these girls individually, I couldn't get a word in at all just about. Of course, that's usually how it is when you're talking to someone buzzed out of their mind (I couldn't blame them; I was too), but I didn't even care. It was fun to have people to talk to. When we each relaxed our legs on a park bench after parading around the whole downtown district, a couple of girls approached us, and things started to get a little weird.

I don't recall completely how this all started due to my high level of intoxication at the time, but these two brunettes approached two of the girls I hung out with and started talking to them. They stood there for a minute—talking and whatnot; they seemed friendly enough, but then all of a sudden, one of the brunettes turned her ass toward us and then *bang*. Just like that, an ass was in everybody's face. I bounced back in surprise on my park bench, laughing, and said, "What the fuck is going on?" Then it got even crazier.

Two of the girls I was with started making out with the brunettes.

I just sat there jaw agape. I couldn't believe it; shit started to escalate quickly. Then one of the brunettes broke her kiss with one of the girls and bounced right in front of me like a tiger. I sat there as she kneeled to rest her hands on her knees to where her eyes could meet mine. She just stood there for a few seconds, not saying a thing. She beamed the most sinister gaze through those brown eyes of hers. All I could muster was, "Uhhhhh—Hi—"

Then, without any warning, she slapped and clawed both of her hands into my hair and jammed her tongue right down my throat. When she finally let go of me, I just sat there feeling like a helpless squirrel. I knew that couldn't have been the first time she did that to someone. I thought to myself helplessly, *I might just have to find the rest of her victims and start another Me Too Movement over this shit.* It was just plain ridiculous, and I felt so violated. I didn't have any more time to think, though. Another impending attack was coming.

The second brunette started to stomp toward me and said, "My turn."

I immediately jumped up from that bench and caught her right in her stride. I put my hands on her hips and pulled her in for a kiss. Her friend might've caught me off guard, but tonight there wasn't going to be any fool me twice. I went in for it, and I took it. She wasn't a great kisser, to be honest, so I did all I could to get it over with quick, but afterward, she still stood there staring me down like some sort of ravenous wolf or something. Kind of unsettling, to tell you the truth.

Once our group kissing match ended, the battlefield hadn't cleared yet, and we all stood there talking with one another for a little while. I'm not sure what the brunette girls' names were. I can't remember unfortunately. I guess I'll call the first one attacking me (you know, crouching tiger, hidden dragon) Angie, and the second one I'll just call Gloria or something, I don't know. She was the flasher.

Angie kept her piercing gaze on the group of girls I hung out with, not saying much at all, and Gloria did most of the talking. I didn't say much. I was still in shock over it all. Gloria kept eyeing me down as she looked back and forth from the girls to me, and she said, "So what are you guys doing tonight? We're tryin' to party."

The bushy-haired girl who called me out earlier, her name was Sarah, said, "Hell yeah! That's what we're trying to do. Where ya'll going to? The Barrelhouse?"

Gloria spun her head back toward me even though I hadn't even said anything; as she rocked her hips back and forth, she replied, "Mmmmm—no. We have a room right down the street. We got bottles, booze—some mollie. We got some mollie if you want that."

Gloria cut her eyes at me and looked me up and down. A sinister smile started to crack across her face as she continued, "Why don't we finish what we all started? What do you say?"

I wasn't going to say a damn thing. These chicks were crazy, plain and simple. I almost got murdered the night before—or at least I thought I had for a minute. I didn't trust them at all. Gloria's gaze stayed glued on me as her fierce eyes widened. She tilted her head toward the side and said, "Hmmm? What do you say, hippie boy? You wanna party?"

Hippie boy? What? I'll admit she got me with that one. Hippies are cool, and the sixties are cool; that's why I dress the way I do sometimes, but I didn't know what I was supposed to do. I had to say something, so I shot back in the coolest way I could, "What do you mean, what do I say? Hell yeah! Let's do it!"

I looked back toward the other girls I was with earlier and said, "What about ya'll? We gonna party or what?"

Sarah looked sort of nervous at first, but her friends seemed down for it. *Oh, the peer pressure. How it gets you to commit to unspeakable things you usually wouldn't do.* It didn't take Sarah's friends long to talk her into it. Right away, Gloria said," Ok, then let's do it."

Everybody started following Gloria around the corner to her hotel room, but then I stopped and said,"Oh, wait a minute—Wait—Shit, my bad. I still gotta close out my tab at the bar. You know what—I'll just meet you up there in a minute."

Gloria stopped in her tracks and strolled back over to me. She got in close—too close. Close enough to put her hand right over my stomach. She tried to sound all seductive when she said,"Well, you're coming up right? The party wouldn't be the same without you."

She got to me a little bit by touching on me. People never really touch me, and it always feels so good to me when they do. I just didn't feel right about any of it at all, but I lied anyway to work my way out of her snare. My face began to heat up a little bit from her touch, and she could see that. Maybe that's why she believed me when I said, "Of course I will. I don't wanna miss out on a good time with you."

She put her hand up my shirt and dug her nails into my chest as she scratched her way down my torso. She looked me in the eyes and said,"No, you don't. You can believe that."

I took a few steps back toward the bar away from her, but I still smiled and said,"I'll be there. I'm telling you. I just gotta close this thing out real quick. What room you in?"

Gloria stared at me intently and replied," Room 214. You better be there."

She was still close enough to touch me. I couldn't get away from her, and Angie popped up right by me too out of nowhere. I didn't even notice how close she had gotten—very, very sneaky. Angie's sinister gaze penetrated me like a bolt of lightning as they all began to walk away; she brushed her shoulder up against me aggressively and said, "Be there."

Alright, Jeepers Creepers. Where the fuck did you get those eyes? I wondered in my thoughts. *These girls are psycho; there's no way I'm going up there. I'm fine with not getting turned into a lampshade.* The whole situation was unsettling. Nothing like that had ever happened to me before. Even if they were normal, I still wouldn't have went.

It might sound strange, but I've never been into that kind of thing. I mean, that's a dream come true for most dudes, —five chicks, one guy, you could make a movie out of that—but that type of scene just wasn't for me.

It wasn't because I have a holier than thou attitude when it comes to orgies either; I wish I didn't have a mental block when it comes to those types of things because life would be a lot more free without it, but I can't help it. It's just who I am. Plus I don't really care about sex anyway. I mean, of course I like it and everything—it's the best feeling in the world—but if there isn't a connection there, I don't want to do it. In a way, I hate sex, but I'd love to make love. I've never really done anything like that before.

After I escaped every man's fantasy, I walked back down to the smoke shop where I knew the beautiful French girl worked. She met me with a smile and a hug as I walked in, like she was just waiting for me to show up again. It made me feel amazing a girl as fine as her was that happy to see me. She greeted me with, "Look who it is! Back again. I was hoping you'd come back to see me. You look like you've been getting into some trouble tonight."

I had a pretty good buzz going, so I didn't feel nervous at all to talk to her. I laughed and replied, "You don't know the half of it. I don't try to get in trouble, you know . . . It just always finds me."

She flashed her glowing smile back at me and said, "Hmmm, I don't believe that. You're a trouble maker; just admit it." She playfully pushed my shoulder as she penetrated me with those dark eyes of hers and ever-glowing smile.

I laughed back at her and said, "I guess you got me then. I'll admit I've been known to start a fire or two, but I never really plan on it." Her smile grew even bigger as she made her way back behind the shop counter.

Absolutely beautiful, I thought. I couldn't believe it. Was she actually flirting with me? I wasn't used to all the attention I got in Savannah at all. Girls in Mobile practically treated me like I didn't even exist, but not here. People actually seemed to like me—like I was special or something. It made me feel that way anyway.

The French girl leaned up on the counter toward me and said, "A few fires, huh? Now I can believe that. How do you like Savannah anyway?"

I blushed again. I could feel it, but I was too drunk to care. I told her, "I love it. Folks seem to know how to party around here, but I'm trying to turn it up a notch, you know what I mean?"

The French girl laughed again. I loved the carefree spirit she seemed to have. She went to grab something from behind the counter and said, "Oh, you wanna turn it up a notch? You should try this."

It was a little package, like something a stacker would come in. All I could read on it was purple pill. I asked the French girl, "Purple pill? What the hell is that thing gonna do?"

She raised her eyebrows and said, "It'll get you right, I promise. Just take it and find out. You like starting fires, right?"

Is she testing me? I thought to myself. She didn't know who she was talking to. I took up her challenge immediately.

"Well, ok then. I don't care. Give me two of those little purple dandies right there."

She looked shocked more than ever. Then she started laughing again and said, "Two? Nobody's ever taken two of those together before."

I threw my money on the counter and said, "Just taking one feels too much like going halfway, and I'm the type of guy that likes to go all the way."

She grabbed another one and said with a smile, "Well if you say so, troublemaker."

I unwrapped both of the purple pills immediately and took both of them right in front of her. Her jaw dropped, and she let out a giggle, "You're crazy!"

I was pretty sure I had proved my point that no little purple pill was going to scare me. When I started walking back out of the smoke shop, I said, "Yup, guess I am, but I'm a fun crazy guy; there's a difference."

She kept on laughing at me, and honestly, it started to make me a little worried because I couldn't get rid of the feeling this chick knew I had pretty much fucked myself. Through her laughs, she said, "Don't get into too much trouble tonight! And come back to see me!"

I walked out of the store and thought to myself, *Well, I'd sure like to get into trouble with you, but I'll do just fine by myself.* I did wish she wasn't working, and later on, I regretted not having the courage to ask her what she was doing later, but that night, I didn't have too much of a care in the world. I made my way back into the Barrelhouse, ordered a shot with a mixed drink, and not too soon after, the jaws of the wolf clasped all around me, and everything faded to black.

I woke up the next day in some unknown hotel room. I had no idea where I was. *Did I get a hotel room last night?* I thought, *Where is this place?*

For all I knew, I could've been in Cancun or something. I've woken up and not known where I was quite a few times, but that hadn't happened for a while. *What did I do last night? Did I get this* room, or *is it someone else's*? I wasn't sure at all, but I at least had to look out the window to find out where I was.

As I slowly opened the blinds, I hoped there wasn't some sort of dystopian nightmare taking place outside I had something to do with. I was in downtown Savannah still. I could see the city market down below. *Thank god*, I thought, but I still wasn't completely relieved.

While I looked through the shades, I checked for all possible signs of a manhunt going on out there. I didn't see any cop cars or fire trucks, but as I reached for the doorknob to the room, I started to worry about some deputies or somebody heading my way. It could've been a possibility for all I knew. I had to be brave, though.

I jerked the door open and peered down toward both ends of the hallway. *No cops*, but then I thought, *Wait, wait, wait. What if there are a group of lesbians stomping around downtown out for my blood because I made out with one of their girlfriends like the time I went on that cruise?* Then I started to figure my worries were just ridiculous, and if I did anything crazy the night before, I guess I'd find out eventually.

An Uber picked me up outside of the mystery hotel, and I headed back toward the motel to get a shower. I found a room key in my pocket from the mystery hotel, which I thought was weird because I didn't even know it was in there. I had to call them up to get to the bottom of it all.

The operator picked up and said, "Hotel Indigo, how may I help you?"

I went on to say, "Uhhhh, yeah, hi. I was calling to inquire about a possible hotel reservation I may have made the prior evening. It should be Room 220 under Hawke Smith." I always try to talk like a businessman when I'm on the phone with a stranger. You know, gotta sound professional.

I could hear the operator starting to click away at the keyboard over the phone. *This may have been a bad idea,* I thought, but I hung in there for a response.

The operator came back with, "Oh yes, Mr. Smith. You came in late last night and booked a room for two nights with us. When I relieved Renae this morning, she kept talking about what a sweetheart you were. Is there anything that I can do for you today?"

That's my room I was in? Thank god, I almost thought I did something rather naughty last night. And I was being a sweetheart? Uh oh, I know who that was, I thought. *It was my drunk alter ego, Dorian Gray. You see, I am a sweetheart deep down inside, but when Dorian Gray comes out, he's just a sweetheart to everyone— especially girls. He can be a rather sly dog to tell you the truth.* I replied to the operator, "No, I think I'm good. I just wanted to confirm everything."

"Well, you have a good day then, Mr. Smith."

"Ok, I will, you too."

It seemed I was all in the clear. Hopefully, anyway.

After I got cleaned up, I wasn't sure what to do with the rest of the day, but after running through a few Google searches, I figured I'd go to this place called Wormsloe. Live Oak Avenue looked so beautiful from the pictures, and on top of that, there seemed to be a lot of history to the place. *Beauty and history—who could pass that up,* I thought. So after dropping my stuff off at the Indigo, I made my way toward the magnificent oaks.

Live Oak Avenue is truly one of the greatest wonders of nature to behold in America, at least from my perspective. As I walked along between those beautiful rows of oak trees, it seemed like they just went on forever. The afternoon sun beamed its way through all the Spanish moss hanging from the enormous, overhanging limbs spanning across the road. It was amazing to look up and see it all, but when I looked down, my footprints were alone. The loneliness in my heart started to tear away at me again. I wished so much in my heart my little boys could've been there with me.

I pictured this vision in my mind of how beautiful it would've been to hold each of their hands in one of mine as we strolled down Live Oak Avenue together. My oldest son, Robbie, would look up and go, "Wow, Daddy. These trees are really big. They almost look like monsters—I'm getting scared."

Then I'd say back to him, "You don't have to worry about any monsters because I'm here to protect you, just like Superman."

My youngest one wouldn't say a thing yet. He's just a few months shy of three, and it was almost like I could see my little Azariah staring up at me with that big smile of his. That vision brought a lot of happiness to my heart just from the hope it could become a reality someday, but it also took me back to the walks I'd have as a little boy with my own father.

Those walks my father and I used to take played out the same way my vision of the walk with my boys had. My father seemed as tall as a giant back then and as strong as one too. I remember thinking he looked like a G.I. Joe with his "high and tight" flat-top haircut, making him look like Iceman from the movie Top Gun. I mean, after all, my dad was once an enlisted Marine, and he told me they fought to protect people, just like all of my favorite superheroes did in the comics we used to read. I always felt so small and helpless when I was by myself, but when I walked alongside him, I felt so tall on the inside.

I remember on one of our walks, I looked up at him with a big proud smile on my face, but he didn't notice right away I was staring at him. He looked like he was so deep in his thoughts. Even just being a little kid, I remember seeing so much sadness in his eyes. I'd always wonder what he could've been thinking about and why he seemed so sad. *Is it because him and Mommy don't live together anymore?* Eventually, he caught me staring at him, though, and as soon as he looked down at me, his sadness seemed to rush away with a smile, and he said, "So what do you wanna do today, Billy Bob?"

He had all sorts of funny nicknames for me, and Billy Bob was one of them. I just kept on smiling up at him and said, "I don't know, Daddy. You wanna know something, though?"

He knelt a little and said, "What's that?"

I can remember getting a big grin on my face then because I knew what he'd do next. I just wanted to make him feel better, so I told him, "I love you."

He picked me up in his big arms and said, "Well, you do? I love you too. Always and forever, right?"

I hugged his neck and said with a giggle, "Always and forever, Daddy. Hey, I know what I want to do now! We can fly my kite, Daddy! Do you wanna take me to fly it?!"

He was never too busy to take me. On my father and I's kite flying adventures, it seemed like there wasn't a gray cloud in the sky, just an open field filled with grasshoppers under a bright blue sky. I remember running through the fields with him laughing as I'd let the string roll off my kite. During times like that, I could almost swear it felt like we soared just as high as my kite. It felt that way with the type of joy I had beating in my heart from just being there running alongside him. Eventually, the string on my kite would run out, though, and I'd get so upset about it and cry, "Why can't it go higher, Daddy? Why does the string always have to run out?"

He'd say something like, "The string has to run out sometime; it's not going to last forever." Looking back, I don't care about that string anymore, but I do wish those types of days would've lasted forever. I wish our time together would have lasted forever.

    I didn't do much with the rest of my time in Savannah. It was the third night of my stay in town, and honestly, I was ready to move on to my next destination. I wanted to get away from the hustle and bustle of the city to find some peace of mind in the Blue Ridge Mountains. I asked a girl who was a good friend of mine about a month and a half ago to go with me to the mountains for an escape I felt like both of us needed. We never went, though, because she backed out for whatever reason like she had before. She was always the most wonderful person to talk to, but every time she started to open up to me, the doors would always close right back up again. Not ever in a mean way, but in a gentle way because gentle was just a part of who she was.

    I hadn't talked to her since then because I knew she wasn't interested in a relationship with anyone, but I couldn't help myself in texting her then to let her know I'd finally taken the solo trip she had encouraged me to go on months ago. So I texted that most beautiful girl, Brooke, who I met at the start of the year, just as the roaring twenties came rolling back in.

CHAPTER III: WAITING FOR A GIRL LIKE YOU

The night I met Brooke, we went to a little club not too far from downtown Mobile. Anytime I go to this specific bar, that eighties song "West End Girls" starts playing in my head because the place is called West End, after all. *Call the police; there's a madman in town*, I thought to myself, as I started making my way up to the entrance bent on getting fueled off Blue Ribbon bravery.

Of course, once my brother and I made it past the bouncers, the song in my head wasn't playing in the club. It was some sleepy guy mumbling and fumbling over his words about something. I couldn't understand the words at all. The only thing I understood was the routine. It was time for my brother to split off and find our crew for the night and time for me to grab the fire to get it all started.

After I got the drinks, I couldn't find my brother anywhere. So I figured he had to be out back on the deck. It was hell making it out there through the packed crowd, but I made it well enough without spilling a drop.

At first, I noticed my brother standing out there amped up for the night and talking shit like always, but as a few people started to move their way back inside, I saw this girl sitting on a barstool all by herself. She didn't notice me, but I was caught right up in the wind. I felt awestruck. I'm not going to lie; my eyes just danced all over her. Everything about her was wonderful.

She had long, golden blonde hair seeming to flow like a waterfall down to her shoulders. *Who is this mystery girl?* I thought to myself. When she looked up from her drink, she turned her head toward me and revealed a set of golden brown eyes that glowed in perfect contrast with the rest of her. I started to feel so nervous, but I couldn't panic even if I wanted to. I was as stuck as a stone, and when she smiled at me, I felt like I was just going to die right there. At that moment, my brother, Smokey Joe in the corner, and everyone else outside just disappeared in a flash. In a matter of seconds, that could've been the rest of eternity for all I cared; nobody else was there. It was just her and me. It felt like I'd been struck by lightning or something.

I scrambled to pull myself back together as best as I could. Honestly, I had to feel around on my face to make sure my jaw was still there because, there for a minute, it felt like the thing had dropped right on the deck. I didn't know what to say to her at first. I was still trying to process this alien feeling I had never felt before. I didn't want to approach her with me being all nervous and everything, you know? The more I watched her, though, the more I just couldn't fight it. I had to say something at least.

My brother kept talking and talking, though. I kept thinking, *dude, shut the fuck up, please. I have to think of what I'm going to say to this girl right here.* Eventually, Pavin screamed, "Alright! Alright! Who wants some fuckin' shots?! Come on! Come on! Who wants it?!"

I knew this would be my chance. I could just offer her a drink; that'd be my way in. I went up to her and said, "Hey there, what's your name?"

The beautiful mystery girl's eyes widened and popped a little at me, and she said, "Hey, my name's Brooke. What's yours?"

God, she's so beautiful, I thought. I tried not to look her in the eyes because I was afraid I'd end up losing my soul in there or something. I wasn't sure what to say still, but I came back with, "My name's Hawke—you know, like the bird. Hey, you know my brother's about to go back in and get some drinks; you want one?"

My thoughts started to race. *God, I'm so stupid. What is this, Sesame Street? 'Hey, there, my name's Hawke like the bird. Weee, look at me. I can fly.' What was I thinking?* But she didn't seem to care much. She told me what she wanted to drink, and I had my brother go in and get it so I could finally talk to her. It looked like she was all by herself, so I had to ask, "So what are you doing? Just hanging out all alone?"

She looked as sweet as ever, sitting there on that barstool by me. She just kept on smiling when she said, "Yeah, I am. I just wanted to come out for a few drinks. I don't mind going out by myself. I don't have too many people to hang out with."

A loner just like me. Besides my brother, I didn't have anybody to go out with either. It seemed so impossible to me. *How in the hell could this girl—this wonderful woman from heaven—not have anybody to hang out with?* It all seemed so unreal. I tried to stay casual and all nonchalant with her as best as I could. I didn't want her to realize she completely captivated me.

I came back at her with, "Well, to tell you the truth, I don't have that many people to hang out with either. I mean, there's my brother—I go out with him every once in a while. Things usually get pretty crazy and all, but we have fun. Most of the folks in Mobile seem sorta cliquey to me really."

Brooke let out a light little laugh and said, "Yeah, your brother seems like a lot, but I know what you mean. I don't really like Mobile either. It's like everybody is the same around here. That's why I like to travel so much. It's an escape for me."

She's a traveler, I thought. I always dreamed of being a traveler ever since I was a little kid. Back then, I'd just travel away in my mind through all of my books. I could go to ancient Britannia or Norway and live among my ancestors for a time. I could go anywhere I wanted to in my head, but it had always been a dream of mine to see it all in person. There's just always been something so romantic about traveling, and my heart skipped a beat when Brooke told me she had that kind of dream too.

There it went. I blushed again; I could feel it. I asked her, "You like to travel? I've always dreamed of doing things like that. Where's the place you wanna go the most?"

I could tell she was excited to talk to me about it. She just lit up when she said, "Yeah, I do, but I don't know. I want to see a lot of places—there's a whole world out there to see, but I'd love to go to Iceland someday. It just looks so beautiful up there with the snow and everything." She laughed and said, "We don't ever really get any snow here."

She was a dreamer. I could tell it from the start. It always seemed like to me in today's world nobody has any dreams, or if they have one, they just give up on it before it even starts to come true, but not her. I could tell her spirit was determined. I could just feel it. I replied, "Don't forget about the northern lights! Man, those things are so beautiful. It's like a painter just took his brush and moved it across the sky or something. It looks like there's just magic in the air up there, you know?"

She started batting her eyelashes a little as her cheeks got red, and she said, "Oh no, I didn't forget about them. They're the most beautiful things, though, aren't they? Where's a place that you've always wanted to go?"

While Brooke talked, I kept getting lost in the way her lips moved. When I finally looked into her eyes, it got even worse. I fell completely into them. I was there physically, but my mind stumbled into a trance. I could feel an intense and innocent nature coming from within her speaking back to my own inner child. Like that little boy would've wondered back then if this was a magical moment, I couldn't help but do the same. Was this the start of a dream, or maybe it would just blow away with the wind? *No, that would be terrible*, I thought, *so you better not mess up.*

Suddenly, my brother barged his way back onto the deck and thrust the drinks at me and said, "There you go; drink up, pussies."

You motherfucker, I thought. If looks could kill, my brother would've been dead on the spot. I just took the drinks from him and handed Brooke hers. I couldn't believe him. He walked back toward the chick he had been talking to damn near right away. I guess he got the picture. I let out a deep breath and just shook my head. I looked back to Brooke and said, "Well—sorry about that. My brother can be a real asshole sometimes."

Brooke busted out laughing and said, "No, you're fine. So what were we talking about?"

When we talked even more, it just seemed like we clicked in a way that if anybody had watched us, they would've sworn the both of us knew each other forever. While we talked more about Iceland, I could only imagine her and me lying under the northern lights with one of the grandest wonders of the world flowing above us. I imagined it all so easily. Her and me escaping a town we both saw as dreadful and just going wherever we wished. We both thought everyone was the same in Mobile, and nobody ever wanted to step outside of the box to give it a go at something. Everybody around us seemed to be stuck in a never-ending pattern of going to work and looking forward to the weekend just to do the same thing all over again. Right then and there, listening to her talk so vividly about her dreams, I knew we could fly together.

    Brooke even knew a few people in the party clan my brother had rounded up for the night, so I didn't have to worry about her feeling uncomfortable hanging out with a bunch of people she didn't know. I just felt so lucky we got to hang out all through the night. Which was easier said than done for me because all I wanted to do was talk to her. I just didn't care about anything else. I kept my distance, though, because I didn't want to seem like I was hanging all over her or was being a weird clinger type of a guy breathing down her neck, but when I'd see her not talking to anybody, I'd go in for as much as I could. It took every ounce of me not to try to kiss her. I wasn't sure how to make my move, so I kept backing off. By the end of the night, she was wrapped up with all the other girls.

    We were all damn near wasted by that point. It ended up being around six in the morning, and we were all still doing our thing at the Laughing Lizard. I sat there at the bar staring off into my drink, wondering if it would ever be the time to make my move, but then all of a sudden, Brooke came up to me. She beamed right at me with those dazzling eyes of hers, and somehow deep down inside, I knew if she kissed me, I'd lose myself to her forever, but I didn't even care—I just let myself go. She grabbed ahold of me in a kiss that could've lasted a lifetime. I thought, *Wow, this feels real— This is real.* All the bad things just disappeared. I stood there awestruck, locked within time just like I was when I first laid eyes on her. The sad thing is she had to go home and get ready for work, but she didn't want to leave without kissing me.

When I watched her go, I already couldn't wait until I got to see her again. I stayed enamored by the kiss she had given me. In my heart, I knew it was the first kiss that ever felt real to me, and it was the type of kiss I desired above anything else. Other guys tried to hit on her while we were out of course, but she didn't give any of them the time of day. Out of everyone, she chose me to give a kiss to, and it just made me feel so special inside. I couldn't believe my vision for a perfect night out really had come true. I don't care what anyone thinks; to me, magic has to exist because every word she spoke and that kiss she gave me was just full of it. It meant the world to me. It really did.

I thought about Brooke for days after I met her, but I still tried to wait and bide my time before asking her out on a date. You see, I didn't want to break any of the "unwritten rules" our generation has when it comes to communication. I'm talking about the rules that say you shouldn't text a girl too soon or you'll look desperate, or you shouldn't wait too late because that means you don't care—those kinds of rules. Luckily for me, she asked me on a date first. She wanted to go to New Orleans with me for the day over the weekend. After she asked me, my imagination just flooded with the possibilities of romanticism that could take place. I couldn't wait to show her who I truly was outside of the bar scene because, in most cases, I'm caught up in playing a character instead of being myself, but with Brooke, I wasn't afraid to drop the veil of my mask at all. The sad thing is, though, we never actually went to New Orleans together because it ended up raining all weekend.

Eventually, I got her to go on a date to a Chinese sushi restaurant she wanted to try out. When I saw her walking up to my truck for our date, I started to wonder if all of it was even actually happening. It was like I was caught up in some sort of illusion. I thought to myself, *How could a girl like this want anything to do with me?* I mean, I'm half nuts and I'm real bad news, but she didn't seem to care. There she was, walking out of her house looking just so ordered and well put together.

I didn't open the door for her even though I wanted to. I was glued to my seat, stuck there staring at her. My mind rambled everywhere. *Do I look crazy? Am I staring too much? What am I going to say? What if I stutter or say something stupid? I'm going to mess this up; I just know it,* but when she opened the door, my mind settled instantly. Everything about her looked happy, and she made me happy. I thought to myself; *You got this if you believe that you do. Just stop freaking out. She's cool, your cool, everything is cool. So be cool.*

The conversation between us as I drove to the restaurant just recapped the night when we met, but I dared not tell her yet exactly how I felt when I had first saw her. I didn't want to move as fast as my heart was. I thought it would be best to take things as slow as possible so we could develop into something special because if you don't build a foundation first, it'll eventually collapse all around you. I knew that to be true for a fact.

Brooke only being twenty years old was the only thing bothering me initially, but I knew people my age that acted like they were younger than that, so it didn't seem like a big deal to me. It's always been about the maturity level in a person from my perspective, and Brooke seemed to be even more mature than I was, so I decided to just go with it anyway.

When we had dinner together, she surprised me with the subtle level of assertiveness she had in her character that I hadn't managed to pick up on before. She was a girl who knew what she wanted and exactly how she wanted it. The funny thing is she seemed to know the menu so well—even though she'd never been there before. Honestly, I just sat there feeling like a dumbass because I didn't even know where to start.

I didn't order exactly what she had at first, but since this place served small dishes, on maybe the second or third round, I just gave in and got the same thing as her. What I picked by myself was completely out of my taste, and I seemed to prefer the same types of things she did all across the board. There was one point during the dinner when I took a sip of my water, and some of it ran down my chin—I was so embarrassed. I thought, *There you go screwing this all up. You're across from her droolin' like some kind of fool; now she's going to think you're stupid.* Luckily, it didn't bother her at all, or maybe she didn't even notice; who knows?

When we headed back to my truck after dinner, I acted like a gentleman and opened the door for her like I should've before. I just had a different level of respect for her, especially since she wouldn't go home with me on the first night we met. If she had, I would've completely doubted my inner feelings about people for the rest of my life. The force inside of me assured me she wasn't that type of girl and I was so glad she wasn't.

When we pulled back up to her house, my heart sunk because our date had ended, and it was time for her to go. I could've stayed up all night talking with her. It would've been so wonderful lying with her under the stars in some park somewhere and have her tell me more about all the dreams she had. That's the type of moment I've always lived for. She had to work in the morning, though, so as bad as I wanted her to stay with me, I had to let her go. I opened the door for her as she got out, and I got another kiss out of her, lifting my sunken heart right back up. The kisses I got from her were the addictive kind. The kind where two stars end up clashing, and there's just fireworks everywhere. When she walked back inside, I pulled off, feeling like the luckiest guy in the world. It made me regret even more what I did to myself about a week before I met her because if I wouldn't have woken back up, I would've never met her at all.

It all occurred on another night when I found myself steeped deep in the well of loneliness again. It was around the time my ex started keeping my kids from me. On top of all that, a girl I spent the past couple of months talking to had decided to ghost me out of nowhere.

Rebecca and I spoke from the time we'd wake up till the time we'd fall asleep day after day. She seemed utterly head over heels for me, and she made me feel like I was the type of guy somebody could actually want. She showed so much interest in what I had to say, which was a significant change for me because every other girl acted like they didn't find me interesting at all. Not her, though. She was somebody that wanted me, and I wanted her, but out of the blue one day, she didn't want me anymore. I had someone to talk to for all of that time, but then all over again, I didn't have anyone to talk to. My phone was as dry as a desert. My entire life felt that way.

Under the dark sky on that night, I stood there contemplating the stars and how far away they all seemed. They reminded me a lot of how out of grasp my little boys were and how far away love seemed to be. I sat out there damn near guzzling a handle of Crown down while I faced the darkness and tried to come to grips with how empty everything felt. Then, after a while, I started going through my phone and looking at all the pictures I had on there of my boys.

They looked so happy, and I did too. While I scrolled through, I eventually came across this video I took of me holding the baby and swinging on the swing set with him at the park. His little cheeks were pressed up so high showing his tiny teeth. He started laughing while he tried to push the camera away. In the video, I said, "Smile, Azariah. I got ya on camera."

He wouldn't look at the camera, though. He just kept looking up at me, and the way he looked at me—he looked at me like I was just the most incredible person in the world to him. *He felt so safe in my arms. He did,* I thought, *but now my arms are empty. Those little boys of mine think the world of me. But why? I can't even protect them. I'm a failure.*

I dropped my phone and landed on my knees. I couldn't watch the video or look at any more of their pictures. I just sat there in the dark outside and cried. *When is this all going to be over? I've tried and tried. I've done everything I could for those little boys, but none of it even mattered. They're gone now, and it doesn't feel like they'll ever be back. Everything I've ever loved the most seems so far away from me, and there's no way for it to get any better.* I just kept thinking and thinking. *I don't even have any friends. It's like everybody out there hates me for some reason. I've held my heart out to so many, only for them to just throw it right back in my face. It's like crying in the rain. You're just left there holding your heart wondering why nobody wants it,* and then you begin to wonder, *Is this heart of mine worth anything? I've always thought that it did—that it had to be. That all the tragedies and the heartaches all meant something. I always believed it all had to be for something—it all had to mean something,* but at that moment, nothing meant anything. I was nothing.

I looked back down at my empty arms as I cried, but then I started to run my fingers across them. I could see my veins sticking out—even out there in the dark, and I began to wonder. *What if it did end? What if it all could just go away? I'm not any good to anybody anyway. I don't even belong here. I've never belonged here.*

I wanted it all to end right then and there. That's how deep the rivers of pain run sometimes. You eventually feel completely flooded by it until you can't bear it anymore. You just want to drain it so it'll all just go away. But I didn't want it all to go away.

I knew that if I tried to kill myself, the pain wouldn't be the only thing that would go away. Everybody I loved would go away forever too. I'd leave this place and go to wherever or whatever comes after and leave them all behind. I'd leave my boys behind, and then they would really be gone forever. I didn't want them to grow up without a father.

That's one of the most terrible things a kid could ever go through. You just lay in your bed at night holding a picture of a person that's never going to come back. You cry yourself to sleep every night and only hope that maybe—just maybe—you'll get them back in a dream. I didn't want that to be my boys. I had to keep on fighting. I got up out of the yard and lifted that handle of Crown to let it run down my throat until I couldn't take it anymore. I went into a rage after that. I started screaming and punching the side of my house, but with each punch, things began to dim and darken even more until everything went black.

When I woke up the next day, I wasn't even sure where I was at first. It was like everything; the whole world came back with a gasp as soon as I lifted my head from the hardwood floor. I was still in my house at least, so that made me feel better. I went to push myself up the rest of the way off the floor, but my arms started to hurt, and my hands slipped in something. The slip almost sent my face crashing back into the floor; *What the fuck is that all over the floor? It's all over me.* I didn't know what it was until I got up and turned on the light.

There was blood. Smeared all across the floor. I looked down at my throbbing arms, and then I knew. I knew I blacked out and tried to do what I fought not to. There were large gash marks on each of my arms running down from wrist to elbow. The blood that came out of them started to dry up for the most part and looked like they were scabbing over. *What the fuck did I do to myself last night?*

I dropped back down to my knees and started to come apart all over again. I put my face in my hands and just let it all go. I couldn't believe I had tried to do it. *I guess I'm really not worth anything now*, I thought as my tears rained down across the blood-soaked floor. I was so ashamed of myself. I was ashamed for what I had done, but I hurt even more by having to face another day. Deep down, a part of me wished it would've worked, but in my heart of hearts, I was so glad it didn't. I don't know how long I sat there and cried, but I never went to the hospital. I didn't want to face the shame. The cuts didn't look deep enough for stitches anyway, so I just wrapped my arms up in gauze, bought a few extra-long sleeves at the store, and cleaned everything up. Nobody knew a thing.

The night I met Brooke, around a week later, I wore a long sleeve shirt to cover my bandages up. That would've been a dead giveaway to everyone. I didn't want anyone to think I was a weak person for what I did. While I talked to her that night, I kept making sure my bandages didn't pop out from under my sleeves. It would've been bad enough for others to find out, but I figured if she would've seen my arms, she would've rejected me completely. It was one of the lowest moments of my life until I laid eyes on her that night; she was the brightest sunshine. She became my sunshine through the darkness.

CHAPTER IV: RUN THROUGH THE JUNGLE

When I prepared to leave Savannah, I couldn't take the break of silence between Brooke and me anymore. Even though she was just a friend, she was someone I could always empathize with. It's not that family ever made me feel alone, but they seemed to never understand where I came from. Not Brooke. She always had the perfect things to say, and she never failed to make my day. So I just had to tell her what I thought about her. At least a little anyway.

I went all-in from the heart and texted her, *You're more of an inspiration to me than you will ever know. You inspired me to get out of my comfort zone and take this whole trip.*

I just woke up. I'm glad I can inspire someone. It means a lot that you feel that way about me. I sometimes feel like I could vanish and no one would even notice.

That's one of the many ways we could empathize with one another because I've felt the same way a lot of times, so I replied, *I think that way a lot too. Sort of like an invisible man, lol. Honestly, you're the most beautiful and bright person I've ever met. It's not just your looks; it's your whole attitude toward life. I've never encountered anything like it.*

You have a soul unlike so many in Mobile I've ever encountered. Do you know how much I would love to drop everything and just wander with you? Like, that's what I feel like I'm made to do with my life. I want the life of waking up and saying, "Where to next?" And when I run out of money, doing little side jobs to get me to the next destination.

I wanted her to meet up with me on my journey more than anything. *I really wish you could come along too. Most of our conversations have been about traveling, and now every time I travel, I think about you. You should just tell your job see ya later and hit the road with me. It really does mean a lot that you notice I'm different and still talk to me, though. I feel so out of place here a lot of the time. Like a stranger in a strange land.*

She went into how she couldn't just leave her job, which I understood in the end, but I had to try to get her to come along anyway. I would've loved to give her the chance to go on a trip she always dreamed of. She's the only person who made me feel like somebody could travel the country, the world even if they wanted to that much in their heart. I wanted to wake up with her every day and say, "Where to next," just like she would've loved. I imagined us just going wherever we felt like and talking about everything that happened to the sunset. Like a dream, I wanted it to be a reality. Brooke couldn't join me, but I pushed onward anyway to the most remote area of the Blue Ridge Mountains I could find, and I was going to be staying in this old log cabin.

At first, I couldn't find the cabin I'd be staying in at all. The GPS drove me nuts because it would pop up with "arrived at destination," but there was no destination in sight, just a bunch of mountains and fields. I kept driving up and down the road throwing my hands up the whole time. I screamed to myself, "Well, where the fuck is it at?!"

Then I saw it. Through the trees, I spotted a narrow dirt road leading back into a thick green forest darkening as it stretched further and further back into the trees. The damn road was barely visible at all. I started thinking to myself, *Ok—well—isn't this how every scary movie starts?*

I was literally out in the middle of nowhere, with barely a signal to go off of, and here I drove into a "wrong turn" type of situation. The dirt road seemed to go on forever and none of it felt right at all. I was halfway expecting Freddie to pop out and say, "I'm your new nightmare."

It wouldn't have been much of a shock because it damn sure was a new nightmare, alright. I was pretty sure I was far enough from any town, though, to have to worry about getting caught up on Elm Street with a guy that had knives for fingers.

After what seemed like an eternity, the cabin started to come into view. I put the truck in park and took a deep breath. My heart plunged into fear when I got out of the Frontier.

The outside of the cabin reminded me a lot of the cabin from the movie *Evil Dead*. I hoped and prayed in my head the cabin wasn't haunted or anything as I slowly reached for the doorknob.

When I walked inside to look around the death den, I have to admit it looked pretty modern. It had a flat-screen TV, a renovated kitchen, and a granite walk-in shower to boot, but there was something off. The first red flag I noticed, besides the creepy hidden dirt road, was there weren't any blinds at all in any of the windows. *I definitely can't walk around in here naked,* I thought. *Who knows, maybe Michael Myers will take that as his cue to come in here while I have my back turned and give me his sick idea of a nice shave.*

I tried the best I could to stay calm by telling myself, *The worst that could happen usually never does.* There's still that "usually," though, and I didn't want to end up in the paper. I almost had my cool back, but then I saw a picture of some old dudes hanging on the bedroom wall. They all looked like some rich "good old boys," and what do rich good old boys do when they're together? They hunt.

I thought, *What if those old dudes got bored of hunting animals, and they set this place up so they could get some thrills out of huntin' people?* I could see it all then. Me in the dark, running naked through the woods, dodging rifle bullets as cackles ripped through the air from a group of sick fucks screaming, "Almost got him, Charlie. Almost got the son of a bitch."

Then his buddy would reply with something like, "Don't worry, Daryl; we'll get him. Cover my right, John."

I couldn't take thinking about the possibility of it all, so I put the picture in a drawer. I tried my best to forget I had ever saw it, but now that I was finally in my cabin, I started to get a little hungry. After all, I'd been on the road all day.

When I pulled up to the Marina Restaurant of Blue Ridge Lake, I was damn near starving. I hadn't eaten all day up to that point, which was something I was used to. To tell you the truth, I usually force myself not to eat anything until nighttime because I'm afraid of turning into a fat guy again.

Being a fat kid in high school didn't do me any good back then, and I had enough troubles as it was getting a girl to notice me back home, so gaining weight was a risk I didn't want to take. However, being a recovering ex-fat-guy who's been a good boy all day gave me the freedom to get me some loaded nachos, and I was damn ready for them too.

While I sat at the Marina bar with nacho cheese all over my face, I couldn't help notice how all the locals were with one another. Folks would just pop in out of nowhere and automatically know everyone there. You could see different people going from table to table just acting as friendly as ever with one another. That might sound like your typical bar scene, but this was different. It all looked like one big family to me, and I just thought it was so wonderful that even though I was the outsider at the bar, I never felt unwelcome or caught any kind of scorn from anybody. I was met with smiles from everyone. Even though I was too nervous to talk to anyone, it all just seemed so magical to me.

After I got done eating, I stood at the edge of the lake and admired the beautiful vision in front of me. The surrounding, broad, rugged mountains hosted waves of dark and light greens reflecting themselves across the bright blue waters circling their way around. It looked like a meeting place for titans lying within a giant well of whispering wisdom blowing through the rippling winds flying their way across the lake.

I was almost at peace for a moment, but the more I looked at Blue Ridge Lake, the more it made me think of Crystal Lake. *Chhh-chhh-chhh-hahaha.* I could almost hear Mrs. Vorhees saying, "Jason was my son; he was my little boy, and you let him drown."

It sounded so real I damn near answered back. I started thinking, *Yep, Jason Vorhees's machete is going to end up giving me another ass crack right across my face later on. I can just see it now.* I shook my head as I stared into the lake and thought, *Why did I ever watch those movies with my Uncle Gary growing up? I'm just a mess right now.*

After all, I'd never been out that far by myself, and even if my fears were ridiculous at the time, they sure seemed legitimate. I took a few deep breaths and said to myself, "You're going to be ok, man. You got this. You're as brave as a lion and as strong as an ox. You can—"

"Who you talking to, buddy? The fish or what?"

I turned around to face a completely puzzled man standing there with a fishing pole in one hand and a tackle box in the other. I wasn't sure what to say at first because he caught me off guard, but I just went with what came first and replied, "Uh—well, I guess I was. Yeah, I was talking to myself."

The man pushed his eyebrows down a little, which made him look even more confused than before. He said, "Huh. Well, that's how it all started off with my brother. Now he's sittin' in the looney bin staring out of a window eatin' crayons."

I thought, *What an odd thing to reveal to a stranger. Wonder if that shit runs in the family?* Pretty embarrassed by that point, I started to walk away, but then I spun around and asked, "Is he still there? I mean—well—I'm sorry to hear that and everything, but—uh—he didn't escape or anything, right?"

The man started to carry his way on and said, "Nope. At least, I don't think he did. Have a nice day now."

At least he didn't think he did? Oh god. Why do I get myself into shit like this? I tried to shake it all off by telling myself it would all be ok, and it was for at least a little while anyway. That feeling wiped entirely away after the sun went down.

When I faced the shadows of the dark dirt road leading back to the cabin, I figured it led to my final doom, but I had nowhere else to go, so I didn't have much of a choice. I took a deep breath and started to drive my way slowly through the forest of nightmares. I was so terrified. After replying to a text from Brooke earlier, I had to get her opinion on it all. It was just a big mess.

When Brooke saw my Airbnb on Snap, she texted me about how nice it was, and I replied, *Hopefully I don't end up in a wrong turn kind of situation*

That's still very nice! I love the inside!!! Don't think negatively, lol.

Following her advice, I really tried not to. I replied, *I'm not, lol; there's always one scary movie that pops in my head everywhere I go. I don't have to worry about running into a highway phantom during the day, so that's good, lol.*

I sure hope not, lol; where exactly is the cabin?

I replied, *It's near Morganton, Georgia, and it's right up in the Blue Ridge Mountains. I'm going to the Smokys next.* Then I showed her pictures of the loft I rented three thousand feet up in the air.

That looks amazing. I'm so happy for you. My heart is definitely full for you.

Now I wasn't stupid enough to take that like she was in love with me or anything. Of course not. We were just friends, but it did make me feel great inside she felt that happy for me. I came back with, *Thank you, that means a lot. It's only been a couple of days, and I'm starting to feel more confident, and I'm not as anxious about talking to people I don't really know anymore.*

We continued to text for a little bit, and it felt so great because it seemed like she was finally opening up to me, so I had to ask her if she wanted to meet me up in the mountains. *I was thinking if you want to get out of Mobile next week, you can meet me where I'm at if it isn't too far. I'll probably go further up the Blue Ridge Mountains toward the Smokys if you want to come.*

Yeah, if you aren't too far away, I wouldn't mind.

I could feel so much joy welling up inside of me over having the chance to see her again, but I was scared of getting my hopes up just for her to back out. *Would the Smokys be too far? There's no pressure if you decide not to last minute. That's fine. I just figured I'd throw that out there because I know you like escaping Mobile any chance you can get, lol.*

The Smokys are pretty far for me from Mobile just for the weekend. It's 8 ½ hrs away. Ocoee is 6 ½, though.

Initially, I thought she was talking about Ocoee, Florida, which would've been over 500 miles in the opposite direction to where I was headed, but I didn't even care. *That would work out fine. I'd like to see the azalea gardens anyway; they look really nice.*

Okay, then I'll look into it. Your Airbnb is so nice. I wish I was there with you.

I wanted her to be there so much. *I wish you were too. I'm going to get scared out here. A lot of red flags. Lol, I'll be able to handle it, though.*

We continued to talk about the cabin I was in and how much on the verge of pissing myself over every little noise I heard outside. Well, I didn't go into that descript of a detail, but I was about there with my anxiety. After talking with Brooke, I had enough of my fears. I told myself, *Fuck it. I'm going out there, and I'm going to walk all the way down that dirt road. If I die, I die, I guess.*

I opened the door to the cabin as slow as I could before I stuck my head out into the pitch-black ether surrounding me. The bugs around the porch light were the only thing in sight, as far as I could tell. Then the real question came. Was there an inbred hillbilly running around with some sort of ax out there somewhere? *So what if there is*, I told myself. *If it's my time to go, I guess it's that time then.*

I walked slowly toward where the dirt road began to narrow. Of course, I had my flash turned on while I walked along, and after a little ways down, I started to feel like there was nothing to be afraid of at all. *Like some scary movie shit is going to happen out here? That just sounds stupid.* Then I got cocky and turned the flash off on my phone. The shadows swallowed me up completely.

I couldn't even see the trees or the road anymore. The woods were so thick the moon couldn't even penetrate past the treetops. Then an owl hooted above me. It almost seemed like the thing tried to scare me. *What an asshole for an animal. That thing is just trying to scare me, but it's just an owl. No big deal,* but then something from out of the thick brush darted out and stomped its way onto the road.

My flash was still off, and I couldn't see the porch light on the cabin anymore. Some sort of terrifying shriek followed the stomp. I tried to fumble through my erratic breathing and sweaty palms to get my flash back on. I didn't have a clue what could've been making those terrible screams out there like that. *Was it human?* No, it definitely wasn't human. It sounded like mad beasts on the prowl. It could've been the gallu demons howling out there for all I knew; coming to drag Dumuzid back into the underworld. *Not tonight, you wild beasts*, I thought.

I ran as quick as I could back to the cabin. I didn't want to know what it was to tell you the truth. I tripped on a root running across the road and fumbled myself into the dirt. The shrieks sounded like they were getting nearer by each call. *This shit is a scary movie now, and here I am, tripping through the woods like all the other dumbasses you see in a scary movie.* I flipped myself up off the ground and bolted toward the only light I could make out. *Thank god, there's the cabin.* I damn near jumped at the doorknob and turned it as quick as possible. *Safety finally.*

After I got the door slammed shut and locked back into place, I placed my back up against the wall to try and catch my breath. While I came out of complete panic mode, I thought to myself, *Well, I guess I pissed the owl off enough for him to call on one of his friends. Whatever that thing was.* Then I started to realize the whole time I stayed at this super creepy cabin, I never gave a second thought to all the wild beasts that could've been runnin' around out there. *What the hell was that thing?* I didn't want to know, honestly. Whatever it was sounded completely raving mad.

While I settled myself back down, I figured I'd watch a movie, and after having the complete shit scared out of me in the woods, I thought a good old-fashioned horror movie couldn't scare me any more than that. I flipped through Netflix for a little while, thinking, *Thank god, they have Netflix because those hunting magazines on the table ain't gonna do a thing for me.* I settled for the old classic horror flick *Evil Dead* because, after all, the cabin reminded me a lot of the one from that movie. So I figured why not? It's always been one of my favorite movies since I was a little kid. I didn't like the movie at all the first time I watched it with my dad. I'm still shocked to this day he let my little five-year-old self even watch it.

Maybe it was his new wife Christina that wanted to watch it, and he put it on to make her happy; who knows? Even though I didn't like the movie initially, it's still one of the few memories I have left of him to cherish. I keep all the memories I have left of my father deep within my heart—especially the ones with my father and Christina.

My father fell into his times of loneliness time and time again, just like I have. I think that's why I can remember seeing that longing expression on his face he used to get sometimes. I still see that look a lot. When I look in the mirror, I see him all over again and wonder why he seemed so sad, but then I realize it's not him. There's no way he could be there. It's just me staring back at myself. It usually happens when I'm brushing my teeth or something. It's in those kinds of moments when you're not wearing a mask that you get a good picture of what's going on inside. It seemed like all of my dad's loneliness went away after he met Christina, though.

Christina was someone he felt like he could love and give his all to. I could tell his heart was full with her when he'd stand there with a big smile on his face and hold her. Sometimes he'd stare deep into her eyes and run his fingers through her hair, and you could definitely tell it when those two started joking around. They'd be pushing each other around, and Christina would say, "Stop it, Rob. You don't even wanna get me started."

Christina always had this crazy-sounding, energetic laugh that would make you want to share along in whatever made her happy by laughing along with her. The first time I met her, I fell in love with her completely. She was twenty years old at the time and was this super-crazy, energetic redhead that would just sort of dance her way around and make everybody happy. She would always find time to play with me, and she would always give me more hugs and kisses than I could ever handle. We used to sit outside of her and my dad's apartment, and she'd hold me while we waited for my father to get home from work. One time while she held me, I told her, "I want to stay here with you and Daddy forever. I always feel safe with you."

She wrapped her arms around me after I said that. It felt so good to me when she would do that. Like everything was ok, and it would stay that way no matter what happened. She knelt her head down close to my ear and said, "Can you feel my arms around you? Pretend that they're an angel's wings. They're always going to be here to protect you."

I sunk deep down into her arms after she said that. *My angel*, I thought, *I'm a really lucky little boy to have my own angel.* I held one of her hands in both of my little ones, and said, "You wanna know something? I really love you."

Her arms pressed tighter around me, and she said, "Awww, I love you too. Always and forever, right?" I laid my head across her shoulder and said, "Always and forever. I'm never going to stop loving you." That's one of the moments that could've lasted forever, but nothing ever does.

CHAPTER V: THE PROMISE

I woke up the following day in the cabin after somehow drifting off to sleep regardless of my fears of their being a window peeper outside. After that first night, I wasn't too scared of the place anymore, and to tell you the truth, I started to love that quiet little cabin out in the middle of nowhere: no car horns, no light pollution, just me, the trees, and the beasts. When I walked outside to breathe in the fresh mountain air, it had a rejuvenating feel to it that cured whatever felt terrible inside of you, if only for a moment. I wanted to see if I could get more of that feeling from the nature surrounding me, so I decided to go waterfall hunting in the mountains.

It might've been a dark and cloudy day, but the forest felt like such a wonderful place to be. Through the wind and the rain, everything just felt so vibrant and full out there, as if the wind at my back pushed me toward something masked and hidden throughout the hanging limbs and thickness of the brush all around. It was like following a song toward something I'd never seen before. Toward nature's own treasure, a one-of-a-kind thing beckoning its call through the trees by the casting of its falling waters. The only thing making me want to stop following that song in the forest was Brooke loved waterfalls too, and if she really could make it to see me in a few days, I'd rather follow that song with her so we could see the waterfall for the first time together.

When I finally reached the falls, they were just breathtaking. Even though it wasn't the massive waterfall with a little cave behind it that I had pictured in my head, it still held a lot of magic to it. As the sparkling indigo water bounced off the rocks, it formed a mist-like vapor enshrouding me within the presence of something I couldn't quite explain. It felt glorious and unknown; like a beauty unfounded. Brooke popped into my mind immediately.

She might not have been there with me, but I still wanted to share the moment with her in the only way I could, so I took a picture of the falls for her. When I made my way back to where service was, Brooke got the picture, and she loved it just like I thought she would. She texted, **That's so beautiful! My favorite waterfalls are the ones you can get soaked under.**

She started to get excited about coming to the mountains to see me and sent me an Airbnb listing for this bungalow she had found, but apparently, she had forgotten about something. **But you know what I remembered, I have a hair apt Saturday morning. I don't expect you to wait around for me. I would say I can do it the following weekend, but I really don't want to hold you back. So just keep me updated on where you are!**

Even though I was disappointed she wasn't coming, I thought the text was kind of funny. *Sorry I was driving and the roads* are really twisty around here, lol, but that's a really nice Airbnb. You have a knack for finding the good ones too, I see. Are you really going to not come to the mountains because of a hair apt? Lol, it's ok; I understand. I'll be somewhere around here or there, so we can still link up somewhere when it's a good time for you.

Well it's hard to get into salons right now, and it's the only one I could get before my trip to Vegas, so I've gotta take it, lol. And my mom's bday is Saturday, so the family is probably doing something for that. The cabin is beautiful, though. I really like it. Like I said, just keep me updated on your whereabouts, lol.

I thought to myself, *Really, a hair appointment, man? Come on.* It made me laugh, to say the least. Just Brooke being Brooke. I should've known. I didn't plan on being in Georgia too much longer anyway. I figured I'd just see her when I got back to Alabama. That's until I found out the furlough for my job had been extended for another month. I was ready to run through the hills naked after I got the "oh, so terrible" news, but right before I started to strip my clothes off, I figured I'd text Brooke and let her know. *Just found out today I don't have to go back to work until August, lol. I guess I'll just try to hit every state. I'd really like to see the New England states; my grandpa lives there, so I could stop to check in on him.*

What a dream, I would love to get that call. Your view is amazing! I wish I could join.

Of course, through my wild imagination, I hatched an escape plan for her so she could join me. *You could always fake your own kidnapping or something so you could leave for a while, and when you decide to go back, you'd get your job back because they'd feel sorry for you, lol. I mean, it could work. I could pay a French guy to call and act like a kidnapper so it would be a believable story, lol.*

I wish, lol, but I want you to promise me something.

Wondering what kind of promise I was about to make, I replied, *What's that?*

Don't stop. Go where your heart tells you to until August. Conquer your fears, achieve your goals, and follow your dreams. Let your heart embrace the journey.

Her words of encouragement filled my heart with so much joy, and it almost felt like we shared a dream. I replied, *That's going to take a lot of spending money, lol, but I'll try to go as far as I can, lol. I'm going to try to embrace this journey as much as I can. It's helping me a lot. It hasn't even been a week, and I've felt better than I have in the past year or so.*

Find side jobs you can do for extra cash, lol, but yeah, of course, as long as you have money, lol. I don't want you broke and lost, lol.

I had to think awhile about her words. You see, I was joking about hitting every state. The trip was just supposed to be a week-long getaway from all my troubles back home, but the more I thought about it, the better the idea started to sound. Brooke seemed more engaged in talking with me than she'd ever been.

Sure we talked off and on as friends for a while, but it always seemed like she held back so much with what she'd say, almost like she was afraid to get close to me. She'd been hurt before by somebody, that was obvious, but who hasn't?

Nevertheless, I wanted to do everything I could to show her I was different from everyone else. If I had to walk the country, if not the whole world, for her to fall for me, I knew deep down in my heart I would. I had to tell her how I felt in my heart when I texted her later on and said, *I have to let you know that you inspire me in a lot of ways. You've encouraged me a lot to get out of my comfort zone, and I really do believe if I would've never met you, I would've never done anything like this. There's plenty of pretty girls out there, but there really aren't any that are truly beautiful on the inside too like you are. It's really* a phenomenal thing to truly be beautiful on the inside and the outside. You pull it all off in the most natural way too. I've seen a lot of amazing spectacles, but you're at the top of the list. You really are.

I believe everything has a reason or purpose, so us meeting wasn't just a coincidence. I'm so happy you found a part of yourself during this trip. I've never been told I have a beautiful soul, so that means more to me than you'll ever know. You doing this journey just makes my heart full for you and shows me that my dreams can be a reality and will be one day. I can't wait, but right now, it's your turn, and I hope you take full advantage of it.

Her words lifted me even higher, but I wanted her to make me a promise too. *You have to make me a promise now, though. I plan on sharing this whole journey with you through pictures as much as I can so when you take your journey, just do the same. Pictures aren't just pictures to me. What a person chooses to take a picture of shows what is truly beautiful to them. It would help me learn more about you if you did. I want to know what you find beautiful with your own eyes.*

Well, I definitely will send you pictures. That's a year away, so I hope you still remember me by then ;) Don't stop sending yours though. I love seeing people embrace their free-spirited side.

The thought of ever forgetting about her seemed impossible to me. *I don't think I could ever forget about you. No matter what happens. I'm twenty-seven years old, and I've texted with a lot of girls over the years. You're an unforgettable type of person to me because you're phenomenal with the way you look and the type of attitude you approach life with. You don't need to be a big "success" as the world defines it as. You're a success all on your own because you've been through so much in life that you didn't allow destroy you. You don't have to be anything but you, and you'll do just fine. It's like the sun and the moon. No matter what they do, they shine, and you're going to shine because your just like that.*

I needed that. Your soul is so unique. You have a way with words too. Maybe you can find some book ideas while you're on this journey?

It was like, on that day, Brooke filled me to the brim with so much inspiration. The idea of writing a book was always something I really wanted to do. I just didn't know what to write about, but just like that, Brooke pointed it all out. One of the best ideas I've ever come across. If you don't have a story, go out and make one. I loved the sound of that.

Once I got tired of taking in the scenery of all the rolling hills across the Blue Ridge Mountains, I made my way back to the cabin.

That night in my hidden abode, I couldn't get my mind off Brooke and all of what she had said to me that day. I was so glad she showed so much interest in my journey. She responded back to me with a kind of enthusiasm that's really hard to find in other people. I only wished she could've been there with me. I wrote in my journal that night about her like I had so many other times before. This is what I wrote:

I've been talking to Brooke a lot during this journey, and even though I've met a lot of beautiful women on this trip, none of them amount to her. She's just the most beautiful woman I've ever come across inside and out. I just wish that I could share this trip with her in person so we could really be together in it. We're just so much alike, and there's so much that I want to give to her. I just think she's afraid. I think when she starts to get feelings, she pulls away. I'd never hurt her, and I'd do everything I could for her to realize the extent of how beautiful I think she really is. Only time will tell, but I hope time will bring us together rather than apart.

I passed smooth out while I wrote, but I needed the rest anyway. After all, I had to get ready for the Smokys, and I couldn't wait to be elevated three thousand feet in the air in the little loft I planned to stay in.

CHAPTER VI: DON'T FEAR THE REAPER

When I looked in the rearview mirror of the Frontier as I drove away from the cabin, I was already starting to miss it. I started thinking about how scared I had been to stay there on the first night, but you know what? None of my fears mattered after a little while. I was scared over nothing.

Then that all-too-familiar voice came to me and said, Yes, it's true anything could happen, but the worst usually doesn't. Probability typically rules everything. The biggest problem is just finding what is more probable than the other. I thought to myself, Maybe that's why dating is so hard now. You lose yourself in the probability that this person wants you, only to find out, out of nowhere, they never did. The likelihood of finding something true is the hardest to measure. I ended up getting completely lost in my thoughts on my way toward the

Smokys, but when I finally got to the loft I'd be staying in, I couldn't believe the view.

    The loft was literally on top of a mountain. The place was decorated in modern art, with the black-and-white modern style furniture to boot. When I walked outside to take in the view from the balcony, I felt so high on life. Songbirds started to hum little tunes as I stood out there, and I thought to myself, *Three thousand feet up on top of a mountain, it doesn't get much higher than this.* I could even see the whole town of Gatlinburg from up there. I couldn't believe it. Even though I could've just sat up there taking in that magnificent skyline, the little town below called to me. So I figured it was time for me to check out Gatlinburg.

    Gatlinburg wasn't anything new to me because I'd been there before on a weekend trip I had taken when I was a kid with my aunt, uncle, and cousins. It was different in a way, though, because I got a chance to walk around this time. There were so many attractions just waiting to suck you in everywhere you went, and the place was filled with damn tourists. I mean, I guess I was sort of a tourist too, but I didn't have a fanny pack on or anything like the rest of them. I was kind of in shock from how many people were there because of the virus going around and all, but I chalked it up to everyone adopting the same view I had; you can't let it stop your life. There are risks with everything after all.

    While I walked down the street, noticing all the attractions for kids seeming to abound from corner to corner, I started thinking about how much fun mine would've had in a place like that. We'd go try out all the different candies from the store you probably couldn't find anywhere else. I could've got on a few rides with them and watch them light up with those big smiles of theirs; it would've been wonderful. I started wondering to myself why I never took them there when I had the chance.

It's like when I always had them around, I got used to having them around, and at that moment, I realized I should've taken more advantage of the time I had with them. It's just so easy to fall into the same tired work routine and never think about stepping outside of the box. So I sealed that lesson within myself in a promise to take advantage of every minute I had with someone I love from that moment forward because out of nowhere, they could be out of your life for no reason at all. You'd think I would've learned that a long time ago.

After walking around Gatlinburg and taking different pictures of some of the odd little shops they had, I decided to get some dinner somewhere. The name of the place escapes me, but they had some of the most incredible garlic parmesan wings I'd ever had, and the Mountain Lite beer there kicks Mountain Dew to the curb.

While I sat at the bar, my loneliness started to sink in again. I kept picturing how nice it would've been for Brooke to be there with me. I knew she was probably bored to death in Mobile; there's only so much you can do there. I didn't want to blow her phone up every day, but I couldn't help but text her.

I'm in Gatlinburg now. I'm about to ride on the trolley through everything. I'll try to get some pictures of it. This is even better than the Blue Ridge Mountains.

Gatlinburg is very beautiful. I told you you'd love it. Tennessee is where I belong, lol.

I didn't understand the love she had for Tennessee; really, it was nice, but I had to ask, *Tennessee is your favorite then? I like Gatlinburg, but you can tell it's a major tourist trap, lol.*

As a resident most likely, yes. I don't like harsh winters, but I don't like hot ass summers either. Tennessee offers a median; although the west is very pretty, and I wouldn't mind the sights,

Tennessee is most likely where I'll move when I want to start my stationary life.

I wondered if she'd ever been to Clarksville; it's a town I've always liked. What's your favorite town here? Clarksville is a nice little town in Tennessee. I always liked staying there with my cousins when I was a kid. A lot of Jehovah's witnesses there, though, and they are very forceful, lol.

I don't think I have a favorite yet. I've only been a few times, so I haven't explored much. I've been to Gatlinburg, Chattanooga, Nashville, and Ocoee River.

I've always wanted to see the ins and outs of Nashville myself, but I figured I'd include that in another trip down the road. Maybe she and I could visit Nashville together. She'd already been there, so she would know all about it. I figured that'd be pretty fun, but then I remembered the pictures I'd taken up in the room of the hell of a grand view I saw up in the loft earlier. So I sent her some pictures of it, and texted, *I hope the sun is out tomorrow to get some better pics. My room is literally on top of a mountain.*

Gosh, that view is amazing.

I replied to her with a few poetic thoughts I had rattling around in my head. *It is; wait until you see all of this with your own eyes. When I was looking out over all that, it feels like there really isn't an end to anything at all. That everything just keeps on going. The shades and the colors change, but it all still goes on. It all just finds a way to stay beautiful from one horizon to another no matter what.*

She didn't reply to that. I found it kind of funny, though, because when I go with a really poetic reply, I feel like people don't know how to respond to it, or they don't care to. Passion is lacking everywhere.

I carried on with my Mountain Lites until this strange dude came out of nowhere, and we struck up a conversation about traveling. Apparently, he was doing the same thing I was. He just couldn't handle Netflix anymore, he said, which I could understand all the way, but then he said something else, "Yeah, man, I was starting to get super depressed and everything sittin' at home until one day I woke up with a gun in my mouth, and then I thought out of nowhere: Hey, you know what? Maybe I should take a trip somewhere?"

Immediately I thought, *Wow, that was pretty open. You had a gun in your mouth and figured you'd just go on a trip instead of blowing your brains out? Interesting.* I was shocked, and I'm sure my face showed it too. All I could say was, "Yeah—ok, man— I think you made the right choice." Then I gulped my beer, all the while thinking, *Sadly, I can empathize a little bit too much with that.* Afterward, I resumed the rest of my day with a focus on getting ready to hike all over the hills the following day.

I set my alarm to align with the time of sunrise. I took a picture of the sun rising over the mountains and sent it to Brooke. She loved it just like I thought she would. It was the only way I could share the sunrise with her, and it meant a lot to me she appreciated it. I didn't want to keep all that beauty to myself.

Brooke's encouraged me a lot in the past to find happiness within myself and not look for it in others, but I have way too much of a giving nature for that. I feel amazing when I get the chance to make someone else feel happy, and even though it gets me hurt repeatedly, I can't help it. It's just who I am, and the greatest joy I've ever been able to find in this life is the kind shared with others. After I took in the view of that healing sunrise, I started making my way toward the Rainbow Falls Trail, located about halfway up the third highest mountain in the Smokys, Mt. LeConte.

The sign to the trailhead for the mythical sounding Rainbow Falls said it was only a two-and-a-half-mile hike, so I figured, *That's it? This is going to be nothing. I could walk two-and-a-half miles doing a *handstand walk.* So in a short-sleeve purple dress shirt with dress boots to match, I began my ascent. The only thing is, as unprepared I was for the hike, I didn't even bother to take any water with me—big mistake.

Two and a half miles is an easy walk if you're walking across a flat surface, but if it's up a steep incline stomping through mud and across boulders, it turns into a hell of a hike. My fancy purple shirt was drenched in sweat, and I hadn't seen a sign for the trail for what seemed like miles. I passed a guy along the way up the mountain who looked at me like I was a complete lunatic. It didn't bother me much, though. I mean, I had to look pretty crazy just strolling up the mountain dressed to the tee like some Hollywood guy puffing my vape clouds up in the air and everything. While I walked further and further along, I started to get out of breath more and more along the way. I kept pushing myself by thinking, *There isn't going to be any stopping. You're going to become a fatass again if you don't push yourself as far as you can up this mountain. Come on; you can do it!*

Eventually, after my whole body became soaked and I got pretty lightheaded, I told myself to fuck off. I didn't care anymore. I sat down on a boulder for a break. David Goggins, from all the motivational videos I watch, would've been very disappointed.

Sitting there on the boulder finally allowed me to take my attention off my dry mouth long enough to get a sense of where I was at within nature. All I could see were tree trunks shooting up from the dark-soiled Earth all around. Some of the trees were broken, and some of them seemed to stand as strong as iron. I started to remember something I read before talking about the forest having a consciousness of its own. It said if a tree becomes broken or fallen— by lightning or whatever done the deed—all the other trees surrounding it used this network in their roots to push an excess of nutrients toward the fallen member in the forest. I thought that was the most beautiful thing when I read it, and I wondered: if trees could do that for one another, why can't people?

There weren't just trees out there of course. Abounding around as if in a circle, birds flew overhead, spilling their beautiful melodies into the air. I tried to join in with my own little bird noise I used to use all the time back in my middle school days. It used to piss everybody off back then, especially the teachers. It was so funny because, eventually, after tearing their classroom apart looking for some bird, they'd always find out it wasn't a bird at all they were looking for. It was the blonde-headed heathen sitting in the back row of their class doing it all along. The birds out there didn't seem to mind it, though. There was even a little sparrow sitting nearby on a branch watching me and following along with my tune, like he tried to sing along with me in his own little way.

After the sparrow and I's sing-along, I got this feeling to close my eyes. I wasn't sure what for at first, but my instincts were telling me just to breathe—*Breathe in the moist mountain air. Feel it deep within you.* I felt it.

It was a magnificent presence nearly overwhelming me completely. It felt nourishing, caring, and loving. It felt like whatever it was, a spirit maybe, sat down next to me and held me for a time. The warm air felt like a loving embrace from some sort of thing I couldn't see or hear. I think it was there to tell me to hang in there. *Just hang in there. You're not as alone as you think.* It felt like a goddess of some sort or maybe I just wished it was. All I know is, whatever it was, it sure felt like it loved me. After feeling a beauty unknown in my heart, I decided to start my way back up the trail.

To put it more accurately, I didn't start back in the direction I followed. I hadn't seen a sign for the Rainbow Falls in I don't know how long, and I started to think I had gone the wrong way because I couldn't hear any water flowing anywhere, and where a waterfall's supposed to be, you think you'd hear water. So what do I do? I turned right back around. I walked back down the mountain for over a mile until I reached the last sign I'd seen. Low and behold, according to the sign, I'd been going the right way all along. I thought to myself, *I don't want to walk all that all over again—but I'm not going to throw away all this hard work for nothing.* So I made the ascent all over again.

Along the path, my fantasies started to run wild within my mind. I thought about the Cherokee natives who used to roam all around those hills and how cool it would be to somehow run into one out here. I thought to myself, *God, it would be great if a beautiful Pocahontas kind of girl just hopped on the trail in front of me. I'd take her hand, and we'd sprint toward the Rainbow Falls together, and under those magical cascading waters, we would become locked within a lover's embrace tongue tied to the knot. Then we'd just start making love for days. I'd stay in that type of moment forever.*

As I walked further along, I thought, *Forget about Pocahontas, that type of scene just looks so much more right with Brooke,* but then I realized how ahead of myself I had gotten. I reminded myself, *You're just her friend, and she doesn't want anything like that with anybody or probably just not with you because she thinks you're a loser.* Oh the god-awful purgatory that is the friend zone. Sometimes it's a terrible place to be, you know?

When I finally arrived at the Rainbow Falls, it was the type of waterfall I'd always wanted to see. It had crystal clear water rushing off and away, plus it was the type you could walk right under too. A perfect place for a true romantic moment like I'd pictured in my mind earlier. I stood there for a while, caught in awe of all the wonder in front of me. All the hell on the way up had been worth it.

The long hike back down wasn't half as arduous as the ascent up, and while I was on the descent, I passed an older man equipped to the tee like a hiker version of Rambo with all the tools necessary for a hike. He asked, "Are you going to hike up to the top of LeConte?"

I replied in a pretty exhausted voice, "Hell no, man; I'm going home. Good luck with that, though."

I wasn't going home, though. More like back to my truck so I could start toward the old Elkmont Campground where an old ghost town was located. Where some go and never return so I heard. It seemed like the perfect place to go I figured.

When I finally got back to my truck, I hung out for a little while so I could send Brooke a picture of Rainbow Falls. I texted her, *I found your waterfall.*

Yes!!! I dare you to go under.

Unfortunately, I already left the falls and had no intentions of busting my ass in my slick old dress boots. *I already started back down, lol; it was a hell of a hike up there. I'm not even wearing hiking boots; I'm wearing dress boots, lol, had to climb in style.*

Dude, what??? You definitely need some hiking boots if you keep goin' more into the mountains, lol.

By being reminded I was absolutely in the friend zone by her calling me dude, I replied, *Lol, the one person I passed looked at me like I was crazy; I'm just strolling up the mountain with a purple dress shirt on, vaping along the way, lol. To make it even worse, my boots aren't even tied, lol.*

Yeah, I would look at you like you were crazy too, lol.

Speaking in pure bravado fashion, I replied, *I can climb mountains in anything. It wasn't that bad.*

I know you can, but it's not recommended, LOL.

By the time I got her last reply, I was already off and away.

When I arrived at the road leading to the Elkmont Campground, it was all blocked off. I threw my hands up in the air wondering why the road would be closed. *Why is it closed off?* I thought. I asked a passerby what was going on with the road, and he replied, "Yeah, they closed the campground because of the virus. I think you can still take a bike back there; you just can't camp anymore until this all blows over."

I replied quite annoyed, "Really, the road is closed because of the 'vid?"

The friendly passerby said, "Yep. It's bullshit, but I guess there's nothing we can do about it."

I carried on past the roadblock anyway on my hunt for the treacherous Elkmont ghost town lying deep within the woods.

While walking through the light drizzle of rain, I noticed fog seemed to be floating along the route. It reminded me so much of the movie *Silent Hill* because the sky was gray and the road was dark. I tried not to let my fears stop me, though.

There wasn't one other soul in sight to be found anywhere back there, and I started to get bothered by the decision I had made to take a three-mile hike to a ghost town out in the middle of nowhere, with no other people and no cell service. With each step, it seemed to feel more and more like a horrible idea. Then I saw this old, gigantic stone staircase going up a hill off the left side of the road.

The staircase chilled me to the bone on sight. I knew it was all that remained of the old Wonderland Hotel that burnt down back in the early 1900s. I forced myself to make the ascent until I reached the top. There was nothing but a bunch of brush that I could see at first, but I kept feeling this overwhelming, menacing presence as soon as I got up there. It might've been the creepy well in the bushes; who knows? All I know is I didn't feel welcome at the top of those stairs at all, so I rushed down them, hoping I wouldn't fall and break my neck along the way.

There was still no ghost town in sight, at least where my eyes could see. I couldn't remember where it was located. All I knew was it was near the campground and that's where I was. While I walked around the area, the temperature of the feeling I'd got at the top of the staircase escalated way past one hundred and—I don't know, all my hairs were standing on end. I was alone, but it sure didn't feel that way. I lost control of my breath, and my eyes were damn near popping out of my head. I was frozen solid. I didn't want to move, but then I heard the laugh.

This was no regular laugh. It was a long, dragged-out, high-pitch joker kind of laugh. Now it could've just been a person out in the surrounding woods hiking around just like me, or maybe it was the manifestation of some sort of dark, evil presence closing in on me. I didn't think it was someone in the woods because it sounded so close to me I should've been able to see who it had come from. Plus, if it was someone out in the woods laughing like the joker all by themselves, that's not a guy I want to run into anyway, so I figured it was time to get the hell out of there.

While I made my way back up the road, I still tried to look for signs of the ghost town I probably missed along the way, but then I saw a man along the road. He was an older man brandishing an old-fashioned, wide-brimmed hat many of the folks back in the day used to wear. It might've just been me, but his clothes looked old-fashioned too. I mean, who still wears suspenders? When the old man approached me, he spoke with a tone that had an edge of rasp to it, "What brings you out here among these hills, young man?"

There was something off about him, and the guy completely scared the shit out of me. I mean, I was on the verge of pissing my pants. I replied, "Oh, I was just out here looking for the old Elkmont Resort. I just wanted to put my eyes on an old ghost town."

When the man let out a cough and a grin, he said, "An old ghost town, you say? Well, you don't have to look far. It's right over there."

He pointed toward a darkened area in between the trees that lie across the stream. He continued, "That's where I'm headed myself. I could take you to it, you know? Since you're having trouble finding it."

I couldn't shake the feeling this wasn't the average old man I was talking to. There just seemed something incredibly off with him. I started to walk my way back up the road, "No thanks, man, I have a dinner date lined up that I forgot about."

The old man stayed planted in the middle of the road with a wide grin on his face, barely separating his teeth as he spoke, "Ok then. You be safe out there now, boy, ya hear? Safe travels."

Practically running at this point, I shouted, "You too, man!"

Once I arrived back at my Frontier, I kept thinking about the old man back on the road and wondered to myself if he'd been some sort of ghost trapped out there in the woods. He seemed pleasant enough, but I couldn't shake the feeling of something dark lying behind that wide grin of his. I have a picture of someone that looks a lot like him. The strange thing is, it was taken over a hundred years ago, and it didn't look like he was supposed to be in the picture at all. He looked more like a specter of some kind; standing behind my great-great grandmother back in 1903. It chills me to the bone even now. I'd rather not even think about it honestly.

By then, I should've had enough of ghost hunting, but I wasn't quite through yet. I was on the chase now after a legend occurring along the Roaring Fork Motor Trail back in 1909. There was a young girl named Lucy who died in a cabin fire around that time, and according to the legend, after her death, a young man spotted a beautiful, dark-haired girl in a white gown walking barefoot along the road one evening. He asked her if she needed a ride back to her cabin, and she agreed to accompany the young fellow on his trusty steed. Along the way, they had a pretty vibrant conversation, and he found her very charming, I guess. When he dropped her off where her cabin was supposed to be, she either disappeared within the woods after the ride, or he came back later to look for her, and there wasn't a cabin there at all.

    I loved the tale as soon as I read it for the first time, but it brought me a lot of sorrow thinking about the spirit of some young girl roaming the woods and being lost for an eternity in a never-ending search for a home. I've had my own experiences with ghosts or spirits in the past ranging from really vivid ones to ones I can barely remember at all. The worst experiences I had as a kid were with the creeping shadow men that would sometimes appear behind me while I looked into a mirror. I shy away from mirrors to this day because of it, but I hadn't seen any of them for over ten years now, so I wasn't worried too much. I was off to find my new girlfriend.

    When I reached the Roaring Fork Motor Trail, it was around dusk, and it seemed to loom with a dark glow peering through the twigs and tree limbs scattering my line of sight as I drove the Frontier down the road. There were cabins along the way stretching through what seemed like a lapse in time, connecting the old world with the new one, just as it had in Savannah. I went inside each of the cabins along the road and wondered if any of them used to be Lucy's. One of them just so happened to have an attic, and like a complete fool, I poked my head right up into it. Luckily, I didn't see anything or get my head ripped off. It was a pretty stupid thing to do, I'll admit.

I really did hope in my heart to find Lucy out there. Sure, I'd be scared to death at first, but if there were any way I could help her move on to the next stage, I would get ahold of my fear and do what I had to. As crazy as that sounds. I yelled her name out of the Frontier with my windows rolled down so she would hear me. I was just joking around, to be honest. I didn't really think too much of it until I saw some sort of figure in my rearview mirror. It didn't look lady-like at all, more like a misty white silhouette of a human figure. It managed to dart off into the woods as soon as it appeared, and as much as I would've liked to help Lucy's spirit move on, I couldn't be sure that was even her.

In that moment, I was reminded of a time I sat on the porch with my Grandpa Gene St. Clair on my mom's side of the family. Everybody always used to say he was born with a veil over his face and folks back in the olden days used to say that was a sign of a child having one foot in this world and the other in another. He's still a very quiet man, and I knew as a little kid he could see things other people couldn't. There was even this one day he and I sat on the porch together, and out of the clear blue, he looked at me with a cold stare and said, "Hawke, if you ever see a spirit, don't ever follow it because it'll lead you right to your death." I'll never forget that.

I texted Brooke earlier that day after the bone-chilling fiasco at Elkmont, but I never got a reply from her. My overthinking mind started getting the best of me, and I sat there in my "high above it all" loft and wondered if she was tired of me texting her. I got that sense time and time again while we texted back and forth in the months before I went out on my journey. I got scared and allowed my emotions to get the best of me. So I'll admit it, I sat there all in my feelings and decided to write this in my journal:

With all the adventure that I partook in throughout the day, not hearing back from Brooke overtakes it all. We've been talking so much, and without any kind of reason, it seems like she doesn't want to talk to me anymore. It really hurts me a lot because I was starting to think that we were beginning to bond a little bit. Maybe that's why she didn't respond. I don't know. I just wish somebody would just take me for who I am without changing a thing. I wonder so much why it hasn't happened for me yet. I'm nice to people, and I think I have good qualities to share with somebody, but it feels like nobody wants me. I just wish that for once, I could be someone's first choice and for them to be the same to me. I just feel like the last choice a lot of the time to everybody. I'm always the last in line, and I wish it wasn't that way. I do have a lot in my heart to share, and I have things that are special about me too, at least I think I do. I just wish someone would notice that. I just wish somebody would love me.

Maybe I got way too much in my head about it. I just got lost in the fear of her changing her mind about me sharing the trip with her. She was the only person I had to talk to after all, but I couldn't let it bring me down. The next morning, I headed out of the great Smokys toward my next destination. It was a city my father liked a lot, and at some point, he was even thinking about moving there, or so I'd heard. I was off toward the great Queen City, or better known as Charlotte, North Carolina. That morning, I spun the wheels on that little truck of mine and hit play on "Carry on Wayward Son." I was off toward another adventure.

CHAPTER VII: LONG COOL WOMAN

    I decided to book my next stay in a highrise among the glittering skyscrapers of Uptown Charlotte. When I checked into my room, I had to show it off on Snap a little bit. I like to do that a lot, to tell you the truth. Sometimes I go a little overboard on there, especially if I've had a lot of caffeine. That stuff makes me go crazy sometimes.

    I played the song "Uptown" by Billy Joel in the video I took. I felt like the big guy in town—ready to take the place over. The only thing bringing my high down was I hadn't heard a word back from Brooke. I just figured, like everybody else, she got bored of me and decided to go cold. I didn't want to sit in my upscale apartment and think about it too much because I knew it would drag me into a dark hole faster than if I had cinder blocks tied to my ankles. So I started my site seeing around Uptown.

Walking around town felt dull at first after being in the mountains for all those days. It felt like I leaped out of paradise back into all of the bullshit that comes with people in a big city. I became so accustomed to people smiling and waving with kind greetings since the start of my trip, and I even picked up on the habit along the way; only there in Charlotte, people just weren't that nice. I was met with the all-to-familiar scowling, *leave me alone*, kind of look everywhere.

I walked through a bus depot along my walk, and I spotted a group of about five or six guys listening to a boombox Bluetooth speaker. It took me back to all of the 'hood movies that came out in the '90s, and it reminded me of back in the day when you'd see everybody wearing Charlotte Hornets gear everywhere. I mean, I even wore it when I was a kid.

Uptown Charlotte wasn't as up as you might think either. I could immediately see the effects of the pandemic gloss over everything. Many shops and stores were closed, which made that part of the city look more like a ghost town than the one I had looked for the day before. The real funny part to me when it came to Uptown was the "yuppie" kind of atmosphere that seemed to be painted everywhere, and *everyone* seemed to have a scooter. I felt like a poor guy just walking around using my legs like an average person.

I saw all of these avid scooter enthusiasts operate in groups like a gang or something on those corny-looking things. This one guy who had this combover and wore some tight-ass spandex clothes looked like the pack leader. You could just tell it. He done a little trick out in the middle of the road and spun around toward the rest of his gang and said, "Are you ready to lead the way, pal?"

Another guy in the scooter clan slowly rolled his way up to Mr. Combover. Now, this other guy looked like your typical Steve. Now Steve, to me, isn't anybody. It's more like an archetype, I guess you could say—I'll try to explain it.

You see, your typical Steve used to be an all-star in high school and got all the chicks. He was the big man in his prime—king of the castle, some might say, but when high school ended, all of that changed. Steve pretty much lost all of his short-lived fame, and even the girls didn't look his way that much anymore. Mommy kicked him out, but she still does his laundry, and on top of all that, he didn't have anybody left to pick on. He had begun to lose his edge, and he knew it. So he decided to become the manager of a sporting goods store and turn his employees into thralls to push around whenever he desired. He still gets a pretty girl here and there, but he can never be faithful because at the end of the day, he's too much of a piece of shit to ever do any better. That's your typical Steve, the department store manager, and that was the type of fellow about to take charge of the scooter gang.

The typical Steve said, "I should've been leading the way the whole time anyway. I'm the one that used to be captain of the football team. Not you, Brad."

The typical Steve, such a lovable guy. At least they were happy and having fun, I guess. I'm just glad they weren't the violent or more sinister type because I would've been severely outnumbered, and the way they operated those scooters, there wouldn't have been any getting away.

At the end of the day, after trying to find a bar to have an old draft beer in, to no avail, I finally found the perfect little place on the corner called the Cedar Street Tavern. It was one of the few places in the area allowing you to dine in and not have to walk around looking like a surgeon or Billy the Kid due to a ludicrous mask requirement. It appeared to have pretty cedar floors where a cedar roundabout bar lay atop it with the regular pub tables you would see in about any kind of tavern or pub.

 The people working there were wonderful, but the patrons seemed a little different. They were friendly enough, don't get me wrong, but the atmosphere didn't flow together. The people just didn't seem as open and friendly like in Savannah and Blue Ridge. In those places, everyone seemed more like a family, but here I found myself plopped right back into a cliqued-up environment. I started to wonder, *Am I back in Mobile? Well, if that's the case, I might as well just run out in the middle of traffic.* I couldn't stand the thought of ending up in another town like Mobile. Don't get me wrong; Mobile isn't that bad. Mardi Gras is always one hell of a good time, but most people there just make you feel like an outsider. I've never lived in a more depressing town.

 I've just never understood why people are so reserved toward one another. I've tried to ignore that type of vibe before, but it never works out well when you do. Folks will often acknowledge you enough to make you feel like a person; don't get me wrong. Still, when you try to join in with a conversation they're having, you slowly begin to lose your acknowledgment status, and before you know it, you're being completely ignored. It's those moments that really make you feel unaccepted by others. It leaves you walking away thinking, *I came here all by myself, and all I wanted to do was make a few friends tonight. I thought maybe I'd have a few new people to hang out with instead of being stuck with my books all the time. Why do I even try?*

 I decided not to put myself through that. I was already distraught over not having anyone to text or talk to. It wasn't a big deal Brooke didn't reply to me. I just didn't want to keep texting someone if they didn't respond. When you do that, you look needy, and once you start to appear needy, you might as well just throw your phone away or delete the number because it's over with. So I sat there at my little pub table making a pyramid out of Pabst Blue Ribbon cans and people watched my way across the samurai dudes with their man buns and folks wearing capris so tight they would probably split at the seam if they bent over to pick up a quarter. After a while, I headed back to my room hoping tomorrow would bring more magic. Little did I know the next day would bring a hell of a lot of magic with it.

    I awoke the next day with a thirst for some history. I've always loved visiting historical sites because it always feels like to me they still retain a little bit of old-world charm to them. The times when love stories and romanticism just abounded everywhere you looked with the walks in the park, carriage rides, kisses in gazebos, you name it, they all just seemed to take me back to a time I've always felt more at home in. Unfortunately, due to the pandemic, my planned historical tour was canceled because every historical site in the surrounding area was completely closed. Still, Charlotte's historical district wasn't, so I figured I'd just head that way.

    The fourth ward in Charlotte was my favorite part about the city. Like many other places, it provides an avenue to travel back in time to where life was full of meaning and adventure. While I walked upon some of the old brick sidewalks, from left to right, I could see brightly colored houses with the most ornamented and delicate features. No house looked the same as houses today do, and every home I observed invoked a different kind of feeling in a unique way. The most beautiful home in Charlotte's fourth ward was this giant, bright-blue house with what appeared to be a wraparound porch with a tower on top of the roof. It looked like a gothic-style house, but the bright colors it was ordained with brought a unique kind of light to a darker style. I thought to myself; *I sure would like to take that house right there and place it right out in the middle of about thirty or forty acres. That would just be a dream come true.* After I took in the breadth of beauty the fourth ward had to provide, I decided to explore Uptown a little more, but I sort of ran into some trouble along the way.

 At this point of my trip, the whole nation was in an uproar over the death of an innocent man named George Floyd, who lost his life while in police custody. In my opinion, everyone had a right to be mad because all four of those officers contributed to killing an unarmed man. It doesn't matter where you sit with politics at all. Right is right, and wrong is wrong. After all, this hadn't been the first time that'd happened.

 Year after year, we come across stories of people, white and black, practically getting murdered in cold blood by policemen who end up getting off entirely on a paid leave vacation for killing another human being. Not all cops are bad, but the way I see it, the good ones out there need to stand up and get rid of the bad ones because a change needs to come in our nation one way or another. Enough with injustice; let's fight for justice. That was the type of social climate falling upon Charlotte on this hot summer's day, and rightly so.

 The walk from the Fourth Ward in Charlotte to the middle of Uptown took a little longer than I'd thought, so I decided to sit on a nearby bench so I could get caught up on all the antics the folks in Mobile had been up to during the day. Even though I know a lot of people in a distanced way there, I've always loved watching the party posts some of them put on Snap.

 While I went through the latest snaps of one of the most beautiful souls in Mobile, a red-headed bartender named Rachel, I heard shouting come from down the street. At first, I wasn't sure what was going on because I don't pay attention to the news at all. I believe it's designed to mush up the way you think, but here I didn't need the news because it seemed to be marching right toward me. I still have no clue what they shouted; all I know is everyone looked pissed off. I saw DMX, or maybe it was his clone, walking down the street holding a chain that had a pitbull on the other end shout, "This is our motherfuckin' town! We want justice!"

I didn't feel comfortable on that little bench anymore, to be honest. So I decided to hike on down the road away from the protesters.

It's not that I was against the cause or anything, I was for it all the way, but I was afraid of getting attacked for just being a white guy hanging around. Most protests tend to be peaceful, but there are a few cases out there where people have been attacked just for being white, just like black people do in some cases. I get that as it stands right now, America isn't an equal opportunity nation whatsoever. I know this from my personal experiences of being a part of an interracial family. The odds have been weighed against the black man in so many ways across the years. My grandpa, Gene St. Clair, is black, and he used to tell me, "You know, Hawke, when I was growing up in this town, I couldn't have a white woman or a Cadillac," then he'd smile and say, "Now I got both."

That's the type of progress we've made from fighting for what's right for all people, but until the day comes when people no longer say "that black guy" or "this white guy," racism is never going to end because we're the ones who choose to distinguish ourselves as different from one another. We're not any different, and someday, maybe we could all stand up to this system hand in hand and show them we are the same through a common cause.

I decided to walk back to my room on the other end of Uptown after wading my way past all of the protesters starting to accumulate everywhere. Along the way, I ran into this guy probably as tall as Shaquille O'Neal, and he even had a bald head just like his. The man said, "Hey, man, you done looked like you stepped out of GQ magazine, man. I like that outfit."

I not only love it when someone compliments me, but when they do, it always brightens up my day. I start to remember that I'm not a ghost.

I said to the guy, "Thanks, man. A lot of people like it. I try to go in style just about everywhere I go."

Then the man and I started talking about the city and what he thought about it, what I thought about it, and along the way, I'd found out the guy was homeless. He came to Charlotte for work and lost his job due to all of the pandemic layoffs. Now, usually, I would think it was all just a big ruse he pulled to get some money out of me, but the guy didn't seem downtrodden about his circumstances at all. He just walked around with the biggest smile on his face like he would make himself the happiest man in the world no matter what happened. I just saw that as a very special quality for somebody to have. So I did help him out in the best way I could, and I hope he's doing a lot better.

After my encounter with that uplifting guy I had been blessed to come across, I went back to my room for a few hours and played *Mr. Lonely* with my lower lip stuck out. After a while, I jumped up and said, "Fuck this. I'm going to give the Cedar Street Tavern another go." I ironed my clothes and out the door I went.

I entered the tavern with multiple Blue Ribbons on my mind. I even spotted a few folks there I'd seen the night before. The first person I noticed was this chick with dark hair that had huge boobs, I mean, they were probably the biggest I'd ever seen, and I tried not to look, but I couldn't help it; they were just there. Her name was Lex, and I talked to her a little the night before, and she seemed pretty laid back. So I said hi and went to the bar to order my first drink.

Lex had a very impressive friend group, I have to say. Well, the guys in it were practically breathing and huffing all over everybody at the bar, so they weren't. Still, there was an astonishing brunette sitting over there with them. She wore a little red dress, and her skirt hiked itself a little above her knees. She had this cute little smile seeming to be filled with joy. I watched her for a little while from across the bar as I plotted up a plan on how I wanted to approach her until I saw a guy walk up and kiss her. I popped my head back in surprise and shook it. I'm pretty sure if the word *Ew* could pop up on a person's face, that's the kind of the look I had on mine. I thought to myself, *Really, that guy? Come on; you can do a little better than that.* Eventually, the guys in their group got a little too wasted and started driving people out of the bar with their annoying "hands all over" approach they seemed to have with everyone in there. Eventually, I decided to take a break from the horror show and go outside for a little smoke with a Blue Ribbon in hand.

I could tell this other guy outside came out of the tavern for the same reason, and with a cigarette flopping between my lips, I asked him, "What the fuck do you think is up with those guys in there? I saw them literally hanging all over you and your friend."

He said, "Shit, man, I don't know; that shit was really startin' to get on my nerves, though."

He looked a tad familiar, so I replied, "Hey, man, you look like Asap Rocky a lot. What's up with that, man?"

He laughed back, "My name's Stacy, man. I've never had anybody tell me that. I'll have to remember that one."

I busted out laughing and said, "Your name's Stacy?"

Stacy laughed a little bit with me, and he said to his friend, "Yo, my man here thinks my name's funny."

While I was still laughing, I said, "Well, my name's Hawke, so I guess we both got fucked when it comes to names."

We both laughed at that, and we all stood there and talked about everything it seemed like. From the protests, to chicks, and even onward to aliens.

I think I shocked my new group of friends with a few of the ideas I threw at them, but I never really get to talk about my theories with others; I do my brother and my Uncle Josh, of course, but they hear it all the time. Eventually, Stacy and his friends had to go back to Charleston, and right before they left, Stacy said, "I respect what you're doing, man. Traveling the whole country and everything, that shit is crazy."

As he walked away, he shouted, "Hey, man, when you get back home, tell everybody you met a guy named Stacy. Good luck." Note taken, I'll tell a few folks.

After Stacy and his friends left, the guy hanging out with the amazing-looking Italian girl across the bar got kicked out. Lex barged out after him shouting, "Yeah, get your stupid ass out of here and don't show up at my house anymore; your stuff will be out on the porch! Fucking prick!"

The guy practically speed-walked down the road. All that was missing was the "meep meep" noise the old roadrunner used to make. I didn't know what was going on, so I asked Lex, "What the fuck was that all about?"

She started to tell me the gentleman who had just left barged in on her while she was in the lady's room, and he said, "Hey, I've been looking for those big tits everywhere. Bring 'em back out here."

Apparently, I wasn't the only one realizing how huge her boobs were, but with him gone now, it meant the pretty Italian girl in there didn't have a guy that could stand on his own two feet to hang with. So I headed back into the tavern fueled off of Blue Ribbon bravery to make my move.

29 Palms

When I entered back into the Cedar Street Tavern, I was surprised to see the two guys left out of Lex's friend group were somehow miraculously still standing. Lucky for them, a draft didn't blow through the door when I walked back in. That would've sent them toppling over for sure. I saw them, but I couldn't find the Italian beauty queen anywhere. Instantly my thoughts started to race in panic, *Did she leave? Did she go after the guy that was trying to breastfeed earlier? Where could she have gone?*

I started to walk back outside, all disappointed, until I lifted my face a little to meet her smile as she checked me out from her table. I walked, or to tell you the truth, I might've skipped right over to her. I almost tripped over a chair and busted my ass along the way, but I made it nonetheless. I pointed to the chair next to her and politely asked, "Anybody sittin' there?"

The doe-eyed beauty queen replied, "Yeah, you are."

My heart started to do a victory dance in my chest as I sat down. I propped an elbow up on the back of my chair, then lit up another smoke, and said, "Well, hey there, what's your name?"

God, she was penetrating me with those eyes of hers. The beauty queen said, "My name's Lauren. What's yours?"

I took a puff off my smoke and said, "The name's Smith. Hawke Smith. Like the bird, you know? I like to fly a little, if you know what I mean."

Lauren busted out giggling and said, "You're funny. Your name's really Hawke? That's such a cool name. Are you from around here? You don't look like it."

Oh my god, my shoes are untied. We can't have that. No wonder I almost broke my neck, I thought. I instantly tried to fix the problem. I propped my foot up on one knee and said, "Nope, I'm not. I'm sort of a wanderer, you know? I'm pretty much traveling the whole country right now. I'm gonna make my way all the way to California by the end of it all."

Lauren looked really surprised. I guess she had a right to be. Not too many people just travel the whole country off a whim. Lauren replied, "Wow, really? That's amazing. You're traveling all by yourself?"

I put my smoke out and said, "Yeah, pretty much, I guess. Hey, I gotta ask, was that dude that got kicked out your boyfriend or something?"

Lauren didn't hesitate at all. I guess she wanted to set the record straight, "No, not at all; we're just friends. I can't believe he acted like that in there, though. That's usually not like him at all, but he's got a lot of problems. Oh well, I'm still ready to have some fun."

That made me feel even better because I've never liked the idea of trying to mess around with someone in a relationship, but that night, honestly, I didn't really care. I was having a good time, and I wanted to have a good time with this beautiful brunette with her luxurious looks and all. The red dress really got to me. Chicks should wear dresses a little more, you know?

I had to confess I couldn't take it anymore. I told her, "Well, that makes me feel better. I'm not gonna lie; I was watching you from across the bar for a while. You're like the prettiest girl I've seen since I got to Charlotte, I gotta say. You didn't look like you were really having a good time in there with him. To tell you the truth, I was damn near ready to hop across the bar and save you."

Lauren's eyes started to dance a little as a big smile spread across her face. Then she leaned toward me and said, "Well, you can save me now."

While Lauren and I were getting to know each other a little bit more, this bald guy and his buddy came out of the tavern, and they said, "That's bullshit, man; it's last call already?"

I looked at Lauren and mouthed the words; *it's really last call?* She laughed and said, "Yeah, I guess it is."

Damn, coronavirus strikes again. I went into the tavern to order another round of drinks, only to find out last call had just ended and all I could do was close out my tab. When I met the disappointed bald guy and his buddy outside, I said, "Sorry, man, I tried to get you guys some drinks on my tab, but they just shut the bar down."

The bald dude started bouncing up and down as he said, "Screw it, man; we can all just go back to our place up the road; we'll just drink there."

Lauren waited on her blonde friend to arrive, so I stayed with her for a little bit.

When her blonde friend came crossing the street toward the tavern, she almost got clipped by a car, but the car stopped just in time with a honk, and Lauren's friend screamed with a middle finger in the air, "Fuck you, asshole!"

It instantly reminded me of my brother, Pavin, back home. I thought to myself, *Is this a chick version of Pavin? He'd fall in love with this girl if he ever got to meet her.* I even brought up my brother to her later that night, but unfortunately, her boyfriend stood right in front of me while I told her how much my brother would be into her. He said, "Hey, man, she has a boyfriend."

I didn't know, so I said, "Really, who's that?"

"Me, bro—I'm her boyfriend."

Like I said, I didn't know. I replied, "Oh, ok, well, it's nice to meet you then. I didn't even notice you were there, to be honest."

With everyone rounded up, Lauren, her friend, and I followed the once-disappointed bald guy who turned into the happy bald guy and his buddy back to their place.

While Lauren and I walked together through the streets of Charlotte during a full moonlit night, our hands found themselves together as we followed the happy bald guy's pot smoke back to his place. When we got into the elevator, I studied the happy bald guy for a minute and said, "Hey, man, you kind of remind me of Joe Rogan."

The happy bald guy grinned from ear to ear as he laughed in a "huh huh huh" sound and said, "Hell yeah, that's awesome, man!"

Then he elbowed his buddy and said, "Do ya hear that? This guy just said I'm like Joe Rogan."

I instantly took my comment back in my mind as I thought, *You're nothing like Joe Rogan. He would never laugh like that.*

When we entered the apartment, it seemed like a cool enough party pad to me. They had a huge TV with a balcony and all. Lauren's hand suddenly slipped away from mine, and she sat down in this leather recliner. She kept her eyes on me like she wanted me to sit with her, but I thought to myself, *Well, I'm not sure if she wants me to sit with her or not. I mean, that's a one-seater chair, not a two-seater.* I went over toward the couch to sit down, but suddenly Lauren scooted toward one side of the big chair and patted her hand on the empty spot right beside her. I guess she did want me to sit by her after all.

I went over to the chair and tried to sit in the spot next to her, but that sort of felt like an awkward way to sit, so I just lifted her in my arms and sat her down on my lap. She didn't seem to mind. She thought it was kind of funny, to tell you the truth.

Once she was on my lap, she stared into my eyes with her deep, beautiful, brown ones. I couldn't help myself. I thought, *Wow, what a pretty girl. She actually wants me. I can't believe it. Traveling must bring a hell of a lot of luck or something because this type of thing never happens.*

I looked down at her lips and saw a faint rosy color to them that just kickstarted my switch to getting turned on instantly. As I studied that bright smile of hers, she pressed her lips up against mine and kissed me. Her lips tasted as sweet as candy. All of a sudden, I was consumed in the warmest of feelings because it just felt so good to be touched by somebody. People never really touch me.

We sat there in that chair, kissing away and talking for hours. She mentioned taking a trip to Myrtle Beach in about a week and wanted me to come if I'd still be around the coast by then. Truth is, I didn't know where I'd be. I was just going with the wind in a way, so I told her we'd just have to see.

When the clock hit around four in the morning, it was time for Lauren to head back toward her ride, so we left the happy bald guy at his apartment. I'm not even sure if he knew what the hell was even going on anyway. I mean, when I went to say my farewells to him, I couldn't even see his eyes anymore. He sort of looked like he was meditating or something, and his eyes were all slanty and super red. So I just found a blanket and threw it over him. The poor guy looked so tired, and I thought it'd be a shame if he went and got himself too cold. After Lauren and I told everybody else goodbye, we went back down the elevator to head back toward her car.

I'm not gonna lie; on the way back to Lauren's car, I tried to convince her to go back to my room with me. I don't care for one-night stands, but after all that kissing, I was just burning to have her. I told her, "Hey, I have a penthouse apartment not too far from here. You wanna stay with me tonight?"

Lauren put on a big smile and blushed a little, and said, "Really, a penthouse?—I don't know—I don't usually go home on the first night with guys like that. You can walk me back to my car, though."

She put her hand in mine after she said that. It's a bummer when that happens, but it makes me feel happy when it does. I admire the type of girl that won't just lie down with anyone.

When we finally got to her car, Lauren started having one hell of a time getting it unlocked, and I thought to myself with a grin, *Looks like you might not have a choice but to stay with me.* I looked up toward the moon and mouthed the words "thank you" while she wasn't looking. Lauren got super frustrated. I asked her, "Oh no, what's the problem? Your buttons aren't working on that thing? Well the offer still stands. You can just stay with me if you want."

Lauren kept scrambling around with her keys, trying to get her car unlocked. There wasn't anywhere for her to unlock it with the key. She eventually gave up and sighed, "Really, I would, but honestly, I still live with my ex. He'll be so pissed off if I don't come home tonight, and I really don't want to deal with all of his questions."

Well don't then, I thought to myself. I took one of her hands and held it in both of mine. She probably still had a boyfriend. I figured as much, but I didn't really care. Well, honestly, I did care, but it wasn't me Lauren was dealing with— it was Dorian Gray. He was in control at that point, and honestly, there's nothing I can do when that guy takes over. He's a madman, and there's no hope of stopping him once he gets himself going—so really, I didn't have a choice; it was all out of my hands.

Lauren looked up into my eyes as my hands held hers, and she said, "Well, I guess I can at least walk you back to your room."

When we arrived in front of my building, I said, "Well, this is where I'm staying tonight. You sure you don't want to come up?"

Lauren looked up at me and her eyes danced within mine. I was caught in a trance and maybe she was too. It sure looked like it. She started saying, "I would, but I—"

I didn't want to hear anymore. I pulled her into my embrace and brushed the side of her dark hair back as I guided my lips back toward hers. Hers met mine before I even got there.

There we were, under the pale moonlight locked together in another place outside of ourselves. Her lips were so soft and tender, but I wanted to explore her more. I grabbed her waist and pushed it closer into mine as I moved away from her lips and started to kiss her passionately upon the neck. Lauren tilted her head toward the side and brushed more of her hair back as rumbles of pleasure started to escape from her. I lifted her off the ground into my arms and started to kiss across her collar bone. When she wrapped her legs around my waist, I felt like I was going to come undone like a volcano, but I didn't because it wasn't about me; it was about her. She pulled away for a moment and grabbed the sides of my face with both of her hands and stared intently into my eyes. I got lost in the moment, lost in those eyes of hers, but then she guided me right back to her when she pressed her lips up against mine once more.

It made me feel good to make her feel good—I'm a pleaser after all. I thought for sure she'd go back to my room with me, but after the spell of passion rapturing us both—she still wouldn't do it.

I told her, "You know what? Just head out on the road with me tomorrow. I'll take you out of this town, and we'll head out on an adventure of a lifetime. What do you say?"

Lauren smiled and giggled a little and said, "I really want to, but my ex is about to pick me up by my car. Plus I have work. I can't just run away and leave my job behind. I really had fun with you tonight, though. Are you going to make it to Myrtle Beach next weekend?"

I knew there was no way I was going to. I'd already booked spots all the way up through Maine. As much as I wanted to see her again at Myrtle Beach, deep down in my heart, that wasn't where I was being carried. I wasn't sure where my heart was leading me or what would happen next. All I knew was the road ahead would be a long one wherever it would lead. I told Lauren, "I don't know—I'll make it if I can, but I'm a road warrior, you know? I gotta keep on going. Who knows? Maybe I'll see ya around someday."

I kissed her farewell once again. When her ex started to call her, she damn near ran away. It hurt a little to see her go, but I had things to see and places to be. After check out the next day, I was off to Roanoke, Virginia.

CHAPTER VIII: BLACK MAGIC WOMAN

The next day, I was back on the road with the peddle down to eighty-five blasting that old song "Magic Carpet Ride" as I darted toward my next destination, the great Roanoke Valley in Virginia. I was super nervous about where I'd be staying this go-around. This time I'd be staying in some lady's house I didn't even know. I figured it would add a little flair to the trip by throwing myself entirely into the unknown, to where the best case scenario, I'd make a new friend and the worst-case scenario I would end up like Paul Shelton, tied to a bed, with some crazy chick trying to force feed me fuckin' yams. The lady's name was Matilda, and she seemed to have pretty good reviews on Airbnb, so I figured I'd give it a shot. I constantly reminded myself while I was on the road, *Yes, the worst could happen, but it usually doesn't.* The air was still fresh from the night before, though, and I was still thinking about it.

I couldn't believe how lucky of a guy I was to be given the time of day by someone as beautiful as Lauren. It all seemed so magical to me, like it was a moment sent from up above to say, *Great things really can happen when you least expect it. Every day and night brings the potential of a gift with it. You just have to know where to look.* Only where I looked then didn't seem like a gift at all.

When I pulled up in front of Matilda's house, my anxiety was so high I could almost hear the music from Alfred Hitchcock's shower scene in the movie *Psycho* playing through the air. I tried to take a few deep breaths as I sat out in front of Matilda's old-looking two-story home. After I turned the truck off and grabbed my bags, I thought, *Why do I do this shit to myself? This is going to turn into a nightmare.* I managed to lift my shaking hand anyway. I grabbed ahold of the iron knocker on the wooden front door and started to knock. She didn't come to the door immediately, so I stood there and got well into my colorful and casual salesman character while I waited. And waited. Then the door opened.

A woman looking to be in her late thirties or early forties with blonde hair pulled back in a bun came to the door. Her blue eyes looked surprised when she saw I was the guy who would be staying with her. The look she gave flattered me enough to settle myself down a little. Matilda said, "Oh, hey there. Are you Hawke from Airbnb? Come on in."

Immediately I noticed the house was an older style home with creaking wooden floors, and there was a fireplace in the living room with what looked like a massage table in front of it. There were also all kinds of crystals lying around everywhere, and I started to wonder, *What the fuck is up with all of this?*

She showed me around her home and to where my room would be. The massage table, the crystals, all of it kind of had my alarms going off a little bit, so I just had to find out if this lady was a psycho or not. I asked her, "So what do you do?"

Matilda was apprehensive at first, but then she said, "Well, I'm a healer. When people come to me, I lay my hands on them and help pull out all of their depressions and anxieties."

I thought to myself, *That explains the crystals then.* Honestly, I'm not a close-minded person. I believe anything is possible, really, but I could tell she was afraid of being judged. I replied, "Oh, ok—yeah—I think stuff like that's possible. Anything's possible, really. I think most people just don't want to step outside of the box and see what is, though."

I think it made her feel good I didn't see her as some sort of crazy weirdo running around planting crystals on people and everything. She seemed like the quiet type who always keeps to herself, and I could empathize with that in a way; plus, she wasn't bad looking at all, and if it came down to it during my stay, I'd accept some healing from her. What's the worst that could happen? After checking in at Matilda's house, I decided to explore the mysterious Roanoke valley.

When I made my ascent up another mountain, I noticed the feeling I had caught from the forests of Roanoke was a lot different than the one I had in the Smokys or Blue Ridge. Most people think of every tree and every forest being the same or having the same feel to it, but that just isn't true. The Smokys had more of an eerie feeling to it, but Roanoke felt so much different.

Those forests had an eerie feel too, don't get me wrong, but out there in Roanoke, it felt like the wind carried something forgotten or lost throughout the depths of time, and those shards of the past seemed to hold the legends of all who came before. In a strange sense, I felt surrounded by people while I was out there, but as I looked around, nobody could be seen. Everything seemed to be so in sync, and in its natural order, and what felt so special about it to me was I felt like I was a part of that natural order, like I really did belong. I walked through those mountains with winds of love blowing into my heart; it was the love of the world.

With each step up that mountain, I held no fear in my heart. The thing about climbing mountains is even if you're on a trail, all it takes is one slip, and your either going to roll down the most giant hill of your life, or you're going to drop a few thousand feet to your death, but out there, I knew I was ok and everything was fine. When I finally reached the top, I took in the most beautiful view you could imagine up there. I looked out across the whole Roanoke valley with its little towns sprinkled across the bright greens and yellows of the fields, with the bluest sky above holding on to its swirling clouds. I sat up there and started thinking to myself, *it's only been a week into this trip, and I'm beginning to feel completely brand new on the inside*, and I cherished that feeling so much within myself.

While I sat up there, it didn't feel like I was just looking across that grand valley below; it felt more like I was viewing a picture of the whole world. Of course, I was only gazing upon the Roanoke valley with the rest of the world lying far past the horizon, but there in that place, I felt like I could conceive a part of the true nature of beauty.

All the birds, trees, down to the bees, none if it just appeared on its own. All of the things out in that valley came from two things uniting and producing one another. Now I don't know if the birds, bees, and the trees feel love like we do, but if they did, wouldn't that mean the world is built upon love? That all of those beautiful things abounding in front of me were all sustained through love? I think happiness is love, and sure you can feel happy with yourself for a time, but when Adam was in Eden, he had the whole world and God to himself, but none of it meant a thing because he didn't have anyone to share it with. It's like the world as a whole is divided for love's sake so that beauty can be born anew through love's unification. Love is all that matters. The rest of it is just garbage.

I sat there on that mountaintop thinking about love for a while, and then I started to wonder to myself, *Do I love me?* I've become accustomed to picking myself apart my whole life, so I haven't loved myself in the past. I'd tell myself: *You're never going to get what you're looking for because what you're looking for isn't meant for you. You're too weak for this world, and you don't even belong here to begin with.*

I didn't feel like I'd ever really fit in or belonged anywhere, except for with my dad, but there on that mountaintop, I said to myself, "I do belong here. Not any one place is my home, but this whole world is. I might be different, and that's ok, but I was made this way all so my heart could hold onto this special gift that I have inside of me. I just don't want to keep it all to myself. It would be selfish if I did, and yes, I do love me."

It's just hard in this world to walk around with an unbridled heart because so many people throw it right back at your feet, and when you pick it back up, you're just standing there holding it, wondering, *Is this worth anything to anybody? Am I worth anything?* On that day, I said yes, I am, and it felt so incredible for me walking back down that mountain after finally being able to say all that to myself.

The breakthrough I had atop the mountain made me feel better about myself, but I was still very wary about staying at Matilda's house. Strange people have always been my favorite, but I couldn't deny sometimes strange people do really crazy shit, and when I walked back into Matilda's house, it was damn near pitch-black through the whole home except for the little light on in my room.

    I walked as light as I could across the creaking wooden floor. I could barely feel myself breathing as I went along. I started to panic a little, and I thought to myself, *It's too quiet in here.* The closer I edged towards the opening of my room, the faster I turned my head from left to right in the surrounding darkness. Once I was only a few steps away from the dim light of my room, I damn near leaped and done a roll right in there. I thought, *Well, I hope that didn't wake Matilda up. I guess I'm still afraid of the dark a little after all—but I've been hiking all day, and I'd rather risk whatever horrors might be waiting out there in the shadows than crawl into that bed without taking a shower.* In the words of Randy Jackson, "That's a no for me, dawg."

    The only thing was I couldn't remember where Matilda said the shower was. I had to get to some soap and water though. There was no other way. I'd just have to try each door down the hall and hope I didn't open the wrong one.

    Before I made my way back into the hall, I realized I had completely neglected to use the handy dandy flashlight everyone has on their phone. Like a kid with a night light, jammies in hand, I crept back out into the hall, this time more equipped than I was before, and I was ready for anything—well, except for if I accidentally opened the door to Matilda's room. I told myself, *I don't think that would be good at all. No. Indeed, it would not.* I opened the first door in the hall to a closet full of clothes, *You got lucky. Let's see about the next one.*

    The next door led to a thick white sheet that was nailed across the top of the doorway. I thought, *well, that's kind of odd. Why would there be a sheet nailed to the doorway?* I could faintly make out a flight of stairs behind the sheet that appeared to wrap its way around a wall towards the upstairs. I closed the door back as quick as I could, telling myself, *I don't have any desire to know whats up there. I hope she didn't say that's where the shower was.*

When I started to walk further down the hall, I came to a turn working its way from the kitchen toward two doors. One was on the right, and the other was on the left. The one on the right had a TV on in it, so I wasn't going in there because that had to be Matilda's room. So the door on the left had to be where the shower was. With a turn of the knob, I finally found the shower. I laughed at myself in relief, thinking to myself, *Well, you're the one who decided to stay with a stranger. So, of course, it's going to be a little awkward.* I flipped the light on in the bathroom and turned to lock the door, only there wasn't a lock, and the door wouldn't shut all the way. I thought, *Really—what the fuck?*

By this time, I just said screw it and started to strip down. I didn't care. I thought to myself, *Well, if she happens to walk in while I'm entirely stripped and in the shower—whatever because I'm getting in there anyway.* To my luck, I took my shower in peace without a phantom hand reaching through the curtain to scrub my back, and I felt a whole lot better afterward. It had been a long day up in those hills, and it was time to get some rest for the next day's adventure. After I finally layed down, I passed out, but not for long.

I awoke around sunrise the next day to a lot of thumping around going on in the room above me. Not just regular thumping, but it sounded like somebody was rolling around and sprinting up there or something. I stared up at the ceiling and mouthed the words, "What the fuck is that?"

It didn't sound like someone exercising or having sex either—I mean, I know exactly how that sounds; I've done both. This was something different. I thought to myself, *What if that is the last guest that stayed here? Just tied up in the room above trying to escape, and I'm next?* The more I thought, the more worried I became, especially when I heard someone sprinting down the stairs.

I closed my eyes and halted my breath immediately. It was like pure instinct. Somehow I knew intuitively the door to my room would open and it did. I just lay there pretending to be asleep as my mind started racing. It felt like someone stood in the doorway watching me while I "slept." *Is she really standing in the doorway? What's about to happen? Is she standing there naked? Does she have a knife? What am I going to do? Just play possum and hope that she doesn't hop on top of me, I guess.* Whoever it was closed the door like they were creeping. Strange to say the least. I opened my eyelids like half a millimeter to see if the watcher was in the room still. I moved my eyes from left to right, but I didn't see anybody. Once I was sure the coast was clear, I let myself take a deep breath. It felt so good. Thank the stars; I survived whatever the hell that was.

I started to think, *What in the world just happened? Was I just being watched, or did she need to get something out of the room real quick?* I chose to go with the latter because, after all, I still had to stay there because I had another night booked. I started to think, *But what was with all of that rumbling up there? And did I hear chanting too?* Then it clicked. The crystals, the healing practice with energy, *Was she a person that practiced magic?*

Honestly I didn't really care if she was. I respect all belief systems, and I've studied a little of each, but it was sunrise, and most who practice the old arts begin their morning with a ritual to balance the powers or effect something they will to change through the virgin rays of the new sun. It's been done that way for ages after all.

I wasn't sure what had been going on upstairs, but I had to find out what this lady was about. What was the type of healing she practiced? It was a mystery I couldn't pass up.

I devised a plan in my head to walk out of my room and ask her if I could fill up my water bottle in her sink to get the conversation started. When I walked down the hallway, I could hear Matilda typing in the kitchen. As my footsteps started to move closer to her, she suddenly stopped. She looked a little surprised and even more anxious until I asked her with a bright smile, "Do you mind if I fill this water bottle up at your sink? I'm about to go hiking again, and I didn't want to stop anywhere."

Matilda exhaled profoundly and said, "Yeah—sure—there's purified water in the refrigerator if you'd like to use that."

I went on to thank her and filled my water bottle up. When I walked back into the kitchen, I asked Matilda, "So you do healing work, right?"

Matilda's bright blue eyes widened and she said, "Why, yes. Do you need anything?"

I replied as casually as possible, "Yeah—I mean—I have a pretty open mind. Do you think you could try it on me?"

Matilda replied, "Sure, tell me what's been going on."

I hadn't told anybody about the problems I'd been going through because I didn't want to bother people with it, but I told her anyway. "Well, I've had a lot of issues with depression and anxiety most of my life. On top of that, I haven't got to see my kids in around four months. They're in a really bad place right now, and I've tried everything I could through the system to save them, but nobody seems to want to help me."

Matilda replied with a sorrowful look, "That's terrible, Hawke; you seem like a great guy. I'm surprised that you have anxiety problems. I mean, you look like the prom king that all the girls would fight over."

That made me feel really good. I never went to my high school prom, which was always a big regret of mine. I dropped out and ran away from the state of Ohio to Kentucky before it ever came. I had an old score to settle tearing me apart for years. Even if I would've stuck around, I wouldn't have been able to find a date anyway. Nobody ever gave me a chance back then. I'd always get laughed at if I tried to get a girl's number. One of them even said one time, "This is a joke right? I'd never date you. You're too fat for anybody ever to love you."

Only it wasn't a joke for me. I did want to get to know her, and I wanted her to get to know me. After a while, I started to starve myself. I figured it had to be the weight, right? It had to be because I was fat. Finding someone to love me was more important than food to me, and back then, I just figured that chick was right. If I stayed fat, nobody would ever find it in their heart to love me.

While I sat there thinking over the old heartbreaks of a high school virgin, Matilda pulled out her pendulum so that the spirits could aid in her attempt to heal me.

She laid out a diagram filled with numbers and another chart that had yes on one end of a circle and no on the other. She closed her eyes and started breathing deeply, like she tried to get into some sort of trance. Matilda's eyes popped open suddenly, and as she raised the pendulum, a shift in the air changed; kind of like it wasn't just her and me in the room anymore.

The air felt heavy—like it would if you were at a concert or something—only what we were surrounded by didn't feel like people, at least not anymore. Matilda called through the unknown, and things seemed to come. I couldn't see them, though. Maybe it was all just in my head, but whatever they were—they seemed to be entities of a different nature. Whatever it or they were in that room—they felt ancient. Matilda hummed a little and asked, "The most recent anxieties that plague Hawke, in what age did they occur?"

The pendulum swung toward twenty-five. Matilda jotted the number on a piece of paper. Then she started to gather information on what ages different events occurred. Most of my recent anxieties sprung from while I was in my twenties, which wasn't a surprise to me at all.

During that time, I was with my ex and it did make a lot of sense I still had a lot troubling me from back then. It was the first real relationship I'd ever had, and I struggled so much to make it work the first few years. Those years were full of building. It was all work and no play because I had a family to provide for, and I wanted to make the mother of my children as satisfied and as happy as I could, financially anyway. Still, nothing was ever good enough for her. In a way, she tried her heart out too in the first few years, but whatever she did was never really good enough for me either. She wanted affection from me I couldn't give because my heart had never fallen for her as badly as I wanted it to. That's how I know you can't pick who you fall in love with because if I could've chose anyone to fall in love with, it would've been her. I just stayed in it with her for so long to do right by my kids, but if hearts don't truly meet, everything is bound to fall apart, and that's what happened. Only the heart recognizes your true love. That's why it's so important to follow it.

I believe Matilda wanted to get to the root of my deepest issues. She asked, "When did Hawke's grief truly start?"

The pendulum swung to six. That would've been when I was six years old, which is when I lost my father, but the pendulum didn't tell me anything I didn't already know.

Once she felt like she had enough information, Matilda put the pendulum down. She believed I was way out of alignment with my energies. She told me, "I haven't encountered this much blockage of energy before. It's like—Hawke, it's like a part of your soul is missing. Your energy is extremely potent; even with things being the way they are. If what is outside of you ever reconnects itself—well, I can't even be sure what would happen. All I can say is the word great. You'd just be great."

She aided me with a wand of hers to balance my energies. She told me it wouldn't reconnect the lost part of my soul, but the balancing would give me a temporary peace.

While she ran the wand from the top of my head toward my spine's base, I have to admit, I started to feel supercharged, like I gained energy as a battery does. My vision became more vivid, and my senses even started to heighten as Matilda did her work on me. It wasn't a bad experience at all, and if something malicious were present, I would've felt it. I believe beings of a higher nature were there on that day. Call them gods, goddesses, or angels—whatever. They're all a part of the same thing anyway. They came there for me. There wasn't anything terrible in the atmosphere at all.

After Matilda was done with her healing work, I asked her, "So what do you think about magic anyway? Is it real? Do the spirits do it? Or does the person do it?"

Matilda looked away at her table for a minute and then back to me and said, "Of course magic is real. It's all around us. The whole world is magic. It's what shapes one moment to the next."

She looked me further in the eyes and said, "There are spirits out there, but they're just aids or energy you can use. They're ready and willing to help, but the spirits you attract depend on what's in your heart and the content of your mind. It wasn't a spirit moving the pendulum. I moved it. Not consciously, but when you reach a certain state, the path to the unconscious becomes clearer."

I sat there at her table, just wholly taken in by what she was saying. "What do you mean by the unconscious?"

Matilda smiled and laughed a little. Not in a creepy way or anything. I just think she was happy to share what she knew. She went on, saying, "The unconscious is what connects us all. It's the ocean and well of wisdom. Have you ever heard of Odin's Well? That's what the old ones were talking about. When I asked the pendulum questions, the unconscious spoke through the reflexes in my wrist. We all have access to everything already; it's all in the mind. Everything around us is all in the mind."

I knew to a degree what she talked about. Sometimes things just come out of me when I say certain things. It's more like a burst really that isn't even born consciously. It just comes, and it came when I said, "Absolutely. I think your right. The whole world is pretty much built through the mind. All thoughts, all ideas, if they're given enough energy through a person's will they can become a part of reality. All of what's around us came from an idea. The world was built from mind. It's sort of like the airplane. Think about how impossible that had to seem, but the Wright brothers did it because they put all the energy they could into the dream they had. It's all mind. Everything was crafted by it."

Matilda had such a proud-looking smile on her face as she looked at me before she spoke again, "And if everything around us is mind, and magic surrounds it all, that means the world is magic. It's only through the will of the mind that things come to be."

When it was time for me to go, I told Matilda how much I valued our conversation, and I appreciated how she had helped me. I bid my farewell when I said, "It was really great talking to you. I feel like I learned so much, but it's time for me to get back up in the hills. I'm sort of like a wanderer in the wilderness, you know?" I continued with a sly smile, "I'm damn near like the old mountaineer at this point."

When I walked out of the door and got in my truck, I felt foolish for how strange I thought she was at first. Sometimes people only act strange if they're treated like it by others. I could tell she faced a lot of rejection from people due to her beliefs, and that's probably what made her so reserved and secluded. I don't know; it just really goes to show if someone might come off as strange or scary to you, maybe you should just take some time to figure out what they're really about. A lot of the time, the strangest people turn out to be the most wonderful.

After I got done hiking for the day, I went to Mill Mountain to watch the sun go down. While I stood there watching the evening rays pull away from the valley below, I saw a couple standing there watching the sunset. They both looked so relaxed in each other's arms, like they couldn't get any happier or content with one another. I tried not to stare too long, but when I looked away, I felt so happy for them. I thought, *Good for you guys, you really did find it, didn't you?*

The healing work Matilda had done for me earlier did have an effect, but I still felt that black hole inside of me. I've always wanted to be that guy holding a true love in my arms watching the sunset most of my life. I sat there by myself wondering, like I had time and time again, why it hadn't happened yet. That all-too-familiar voice came to me like it always does and said, *It will. I promise it will. Believe in the journey.*

Maybe I'm mentally ill, but I love it when that presence comes around. Whenever it does, my loneliness disappears for a little while, but when it goes, it all comes back. The sunset wasn't the most beautiful thing I had seen on that mountain top. It was those two people in each other's arms.

Back at Matilda's, as I lay in bed, I started thinking about Brooke again. I thought of her every day since we last talked, but that night, I just felt overwhelmed from the silence. She was the only person I had to text who would appreciate the journey I was on. She encouraged me to take the whole thing after all, so I just had to text her. I said: *I know it's late, but I can't sleep tonight thinking about this trip. I'm really going to do it. From the Atlantic to the Pacific and the journey is going to end in 29 Palms, where my father used to live.*

You have the time; I would!! Do it!! You've already seen how much you've learned just this early on in your trip, just imagine how much you'll learn by the end.

It filled my heart with so much joy from the encouragement she gave. *That's exactly what I was thinking last night. You always say the most encouraging things. As I walk upon the footsteps of legends, I feel like I'm creating my own personal legend. I'm not going to the top tourist spots, just the places that appear in my mind. Just going where my heart takes me.*

That's what I want to do in Europe. I want to get close to the culture and find spots only the locals know about. I just want to roam and explore new. I need new. I'm tired of my everyday life being the same routine.

I knew exactly what she meant, and my trip had been full of new things. *I know exactly what you mean. You run into new destinations that you never thought of going to when you go on a journey like this. Make sure you document your experiences when you go on yours. I've had amazing things happen everywhere I've went, even in Charlotte. I don't know how I'm going to be able to go back to the regular routine after all of this. I don't think I'm going to be able to, honestly.*

It's hard to go back to a slow reality when you notice how much is out there and what it has to offer. That's why I want to convert a van and travel the US that way. I think it would be so amazing. I hate living the same day every day.

It always made me feel so good I had someone to talk to sharing the same dreams as me. *I don't think we are supposed to live* like that. It's like a poison to the soul really. What's the point of life if you don't have adventure and acquire new experiences throughout it? Your soul doesn't grow at a standstill; it only withers away.

You lied to me.

Shocked and wondering what the hell she was talking about, I replied, *What do you mean? I don't have any idea what you're talking about.*

You promised to send pictures for every place you went along your journey.

She didn't reply to what I sent her before, so I didn't feel right texting her anymore. I wasn't sure if you really wanted me to. I didn't want to feel like I was bothering you or anything.

I told you I wanted you to. Even when I don't respond, I still see the pictures. I just get sidetracked and forget about replying the majority of the time.

It made me feel great to know she really did like my pictures. Maybe I just overthought things too much. *If you say so—lol. The pictures that I've sent you I didn't post on anything and nobody else has seen them. Want to know why?*

I'm being honest. If I didn't want you texting me, I'd block or send you to spam, lol, and why?

I just approached her with my reasons from the heart. *It might sound lame, but those pictures I chose to send you were what I found most beautiful with my own eyes in that area. You're the only person I wanted to share that with.*

She didn't respond after that, not yet anyway, which was what I expected in a way. I meant what I said all the way, though. I think it's best to express what's in your heart and just say it rather than living with the regret of not saying it at all, however things might go. Sure, I was afraid of her throwing it right back at me or going cold because it was an emotional text, but I just couldn't hold it back. I wanted her to get a feel for how I felt about her. Honestly, I didn't just send her those pictures because they were the most beautiful things I saw. It was really because each of those beautiful sights reminded me of her. I couldn't help it even if I tried.

    The next day I woke up early, around 5 a.m., and made my way toward Temple Hills, Maryland, which wasn't too far from Washington, D.C. At the time, the news kept going on and on, day and night, about the riots going on in the capital over George Floyd's death. I wasn't sure what was ahead of me, but I didn't have any other choice than to ride into the eye of the storm itself.

CHAPTER IX: DANGER ZONE

    I was on a highway to the *Danger Zone*; the only thing is, I didn't realize I was. You see, I'm an amateur when it comes to maps, and I only booked a spot in Maryland because it seemed like a good enough place for me to stop on my way to see my grandpa. I went with the private room gig all over again because, at this point, it just seemed like the fun thing to do. Sure, when I first pulled up at Matilda's, I was damn near petrified, but I ended up making a new friend by the end of my stay, and in my heart, I hoped this place would turn out just the same. When I saw the signs for Washington D.C., though, I started to get nervous.

    I swore to myself, *If you stay in Temple Hills, you should be fine*, but having the adventurous spirit I have, that just wasn't an option.

29 Palms

When I pulled up to the little home I'd be staying at in Temple Hills, it wasn't as scary as pulling up to Matilda's house in Roanoke, honestly. I'd be staying with strangers again, but this time it would be with a girl around my age that had a couple of kids the same age as mine, so I wasn't half as worried as before. Everything that came before on my journey had made me a lot more comfortable with just being around other people in general.

By this time, it felt like everybody was family in a way. Before, I only felt safe around my own family and what I knew. Anybody outside of that circle just about scared the shit out of me. So there I was, parked in front of my next stop, looking out at a little one-story white house with rose bushes in the front, ready to meet my next hosts.

When I walked up to the house, I felt pretty anxious on the inside about meeting this girl named Jane posting a private room for rent on Airbnb because from her profile picture, she looked pretty hot. I might as well be honest; that's the biggest factor that led me to booking a room there. I'm most definitely a guy that wouldn't mind staying with an attractive young female, so it kind of felt like a bonus, and who knows what could happen? I'm not saying I wanted to get laid or anything, but hey, if it happened, it happened. I wouldn't have put up a fight.

When I got to the door, I leaned up against the left side of the doorframe, trying to look all sexy when Jane opened the door to her fine little home. I rang the bell with mischief on my mind, but when the door opened, my sexy little pose turned into an upright, respectable one. You see, it wasn't Jane who opened the door. It was her dad. With the fakest smile ever, I said, "Hey there, sir. I'm the guy who rented out the private room that you listed for rent on Airbnb."

He wore a surgeon mask like everybody else in the country at the time. I guess to protect himself from the Covid, and I thought to myself, *Here we go again with the mask shit. This is starting to get annoying.* Jane's father replied, "Oh yeah, hi, the name's Bob; come right on in." With my red duffel bag in hand, I followed Bob into the house to check into my room.

Bob said, "Well, there's the room. My daughter, Jane, forgot to tell me that she rented the room out again, but she'll be back later. She rents an apartment out through Airbnb down there in D.C. as well, and she's handling that over there right now, but you'll get to meet her later on."

I replied, "Oh ok, thanks, man; that sounds good. Hey, I have to ask, is D.C. as crazy as the news is saying right now? When I booked your room, I didn't realize it was that close to D.C. I'm terrible with maps, man."

Bob's expressionless face replied, "Oh, the riots going on down there in D.C.? Yeah, I wouldn't recommend going down there at all, but there aren't any riots going on around here in Temple Hills. It's still pretty safe around here for the most part."

I felt relieved after Bob told me that, but downtown D.C. was only ten minutes away, and from what the news said, D.C. sounded like it was damn near a warzone. So I sat there in my room and tried to think of the best way to handle the situation I was in.

I thought, *Yeah, I definitely don't need to go down there to the White House. I might end up getting my ass kicked if I do, but—Maryland is kind of boring. I can tell that just from trying to find places to visit here on Google so—D.C. sounds like the place for me. Screw it; I'm going down there tomorrow to see all the madness for myself. If I don't make it out of there, I just don't. It is what it is.*

I pretty much had my mind made up after that. There was a storm brewing in the country, and I would've regretted it later on if I would've passed up the chance to be on the front lines of history—right there in the eye of the storm.

The next day, I woke up thinking, *Am I really going to go down there today?* I was pretty anxious and afraid for myself as I climbed into the Frontier to set out on what seemed like a suicide mission. When I drove toward D.C., I couldn't believe I was headed into the thick of it all, but hey, I couldn't pass up setting my eyes on all those cool-looking monuments, and if things got nasty, I'd do my best to hold my own. I didn't know what to expect.

Would there be people running around smashing monuments up and karate kicking cops in the face and whatnot? Would I see a cop backhanding the shit out of people like, "You're going to respect my authority. This is my town, pal!"

Would they be naked while they did all that? I didn't really know. I just hoped a cop didn't think I was a protester or something and end up getting my dick knocked in the dirt over taking some pictures of old honest Abe chilling out in his chair. I didn't really care, though. Whatever I ran into down there on those streets, I'd be ready for it.

When I arrived in downtown D.C., it was pure hell trying to find a parking spot somewhere, but while I drove through what the news described as hell on Earth, I noticed it didn't look like that way at all. It was actually a beautiful day out. Nobody smashed anything up, no tear gas, just a few old ladies walking their dogs going on a late afternoon stroll, like there was nothing to worry about at all. I thought to myself, *Well, things may look ok from the driver's seat, but on my feet, it may be a completely different story.* Then, bang—there was a parking spot. It was time to do a little investigating on foot.

I made my way to the Washington Monument first because it always seemed to have a mythical vibe reminding me of Egypt. Egypt has always fascinated me since I was a little kid, and I made a promise within myself that if I ever became a world traveler,

Egypt would be my number one destination. Still, I'd have to save the best for last if it came down to it.

Pictures don't do the Washington Monument any justice at all. In person, it feels like you're just a tiny little ant in the presence of a colossus of architectural magnificence. What was even more incredible about the monuments was how perfectly aligned they were.

I knew the Masonic forefathers of our country very carefully designed the layout of D.C. to exhibit and incorporate a lot of symbolism from ancient civilizations. While I stood by the Washington Monument, I got a sense of what D.C. was.

It was a city marking the beginning of a new world but was a giant ode to the older one. It was like those old architects of the square and compass wanted to honor all of what came before through the mighty Greek and Egyptian designs stretching their way across the city. People say the roads and monuments of D.C. align perfectly to form a pentagram and it's all satanic symbolism, but I don't believe all that.

How can you call a symbol evil anyway? I mean, did the symbol grow legs and rob somebody's grandma or what? How can a symbol be evil? Because somebody evil used it? Or because people says it is? Think about it. What if a mass shooter had a Care Bear sticker on his gun? Would that make Care Bears evil? Of course not, they're the most lovable little guys ever. The pentagram wasn't considered evil when Christians used it to represent the five wounds of Christ. I don't know. I guess I just don't let what everybody else thinks define the world for me. I put my own meaning to things and paint the world through my own understanding.

Along the way to the Lincoln Memorial, I started to wonder where all the chaos was the media kept spouting off about. There wasn't any trouble, and I hadn't even seen a protester yet. Instead, I saw women jogging, friends taking walks and telling jokes; it all seemed so—normal. I wondered, *Is the media blowing the protests out of proportion to get everybody in panic mode?*

I think that's exactly what the media did. Why do they like to scare the shit out of everybody all the time? Who knows. Maybe the plan was, as it usually goes, to get the public worked up in enough panic to distract them from something bigger going on.

When people are in fear and panic, they willingly give up whatever kind of rights they have just to get things back to "normal," and that's just how it works every time. They become stricter on something, or they just take a right away completely. People fall for it every time.

Things were getting down to the "nitty-gritty" the closer I edged toward Lafayette Square, where the protest was happening. I came upon a sea of graffiti, defaced statues, and busted out shop windows men were already boarding up. The graffiti was the most abundant out of all the damage. The famous catchphrases Fuck 12, dick eaters, and Black Lives Matter were displayed everywhere the eye could see. My favorite ones were the graffiti art that said things like "one love" and "unite to fight." It seemed like the folks who sprayed those on the walls were trying to promote unity rather than hate, even though they sort of vandalized their way through downtown D.C. The further I walked, the more people I saw, and the closer I got to the crowd, the more I felt like I had to take a piss.

I didn't have to piss out of fear or anything, honestly. By this time, I felt perfectly fine being in D.C., even when I walked right up in the middle of everyone outside of Lafayette Square. There was a good majority of protesters out there, and besides the shouting, they seemed like a pretty peaceful bunch. They were even listening to gospel music out there singing about peace and love, which surprised me because I expected to hear some heavy metal or something. I didn't want to interrupt anybody with their signs and all, but I had to piss really bad, and everywhere was closed because of the Covid and the riots. Finally, I decided to walk up to this one guy who bounced around screaming, "Fuck the establishment!" and "Trump needs to be gender-neutral!" I didn't know how that had anything to do with George Floyd, but I couldn't help it anymore. I had to ask, "Hey, man! Wait! WAIT!"

The guy eventually stopped bouncing up and down, and said, "What, man?!"

It was embarrassing, but I couldn't help it, "Do you have any idea where I can take a piss around here? I mean, everything is closed, and most places won't even let you in."

Mister Screaming me-me shot back fast with, "Are you fucking serious, man?! There's an alley right over there, dude. Just go piss over there!"

Oh yeah—the alley—why didn't I think of that? I looked over to the alley the pink-haired man pointed at and rushed through the crowd immediately. With a sigh, I let it all out, and as soon as I did, I heard a cop siren go off nearby. So I scrambled to get everything packed away, and I exited the alley as quick as I could, about to run away, but the cop went right by. Thank god, I was in the clear.

I stood at the entry to the alleyway and started to study the crowd amassed in front of the fence thrown up around Lafayette Square to keep the protesters away. It was indeed a wonderful sight to behold regardless of the circumstances of why everyone was there and what they were protesting against. It was such a colorful and diverse sea of people from different races coming together for a common cause. For once, everyone was on the same page, and there wasn't any white or black issue, but it was everyone's issue. Everyone had come together on that day to fight against police brutality and to get justice for what happened to

George Floyd. It wasn't a mean-looking crowd but a happy one. It made it hard for me to believe these were the same people who broke into stores and spray-painted "dick eaters" all across town. It was hard to believe because it wasn't them who did the wrecking at all. It was another group.

 I stood there for a while and talked with a pretty chick protester, or at least I think she was pretty. She wore a mask, and sometimes those masks will get you fooled; before you know it, she's pulling the mask down and bang. Bugs Bunny's yellow teeth are in your face—but anyways. The perhaps ugly or maybe pretty protester told me they hadn't been the ones vandalizing everything.

 At first, I was kind of skeptical, but the ugly/pretty protester said there would be a group of white guys wearing bandanas across their faces that would come out of nowhere at night and vandalize everything. It was like they were hired by somebody to make a peaceful protest look bad. If that's the case, it wouldn't be the first time, and what made me believe what the girl told me was the countenance everybody had toward one another in the crowd. It was all peace and love out there.

 While I stood there talking with the protesters, I all of a sudden remembered my parking meter probably went out close to an hour ago. So I ran back to where my truck was, just hoping it hadn't been towed. Thank god maps kept its location locked in. Without even realizing it, I'd parked damn near right by the White House without even knowing it. I thought to myself, *Well damn, I literally walked the whole downtown area because I'm terrible with maps, and here I was parked right by the damn White House the entire time. I guess I really am dumb.*

 I hopped back in my truck and sped past the secret service agents stomping around everywhere. I didn't have too much else to do for the day because, besides the protests, there was nothing you could really do in D.C. with all of the restrictions everywhere. Being the capital of freedom, there really wasn't any. You had to wear a mask everywhere, and having a beer and a smoke out on a patio somewhere was just out of the question. So I decided to drive to the Potomac River's Great Falls to get me a view of nature and, of course, get some more pictures for Brooke.

Once I reached the road leading to the Great Falls, it was completely barricaded off. I got out of my truck and asked a passerby, who was a Joe Dirt lookalike, why the road was closed. He replied with a southern twang a little too strong for the New England states, "Goddamn corona bullshit, that's why it's closed. Ya can still walk down the road though. Ya just can't drive down it, I guess."

I thought, *Wow, that makes perfect sense; let people walk all along the road in the open air to protect them from the virus. I mean, if they were in their vehicle driving to the park, they'd most definitely be more at risk.* I replied, more annoyed than ever, "Wow, I'm getting so sick of this shit. The restrictions get worse the further I go up the coast."

Joe Dirt replied with a joke I've only heard around a thousand times, "Man, I'm just ready for corona to just be a light beer again, y' know?"

With the fakest laugh ever, I replied, "Yeah, man, I know, right? Well, I guess I better get to it then. Nice talking to ya."

I left Joe Dirt in the dust and started to make the four-mile hike toward the Great Falls of the Potomac River.

Once I reached the falls, they were absolutely breathtaking, like so many other amazing spectacles I had laid my eyes upon. The clear as crystal water stampeded like a pack of lightning steeds across the gray and dark boulders of the river. The trees' backdrop acted as a beautiful bright-green filter blanketing the surrounding Earth with its red and yellow flowers sprouting from the damp soil as it all hung across the landscape under the bright blue afternoon sky. I stood there alone, watching that ancient force run its course as it had for hundreds of years before, and I started hearing that all-too-familiar voice say, *It's better to go with the stream than against it. Sure, you may hit a few rocks along the way, but who knows? It may just carry you right where you've always wanted to go.* It really reminded me of something my father might've said, and I could feel my heart fill up with all of the joy and beauty of that natural wonder I beheld in front of me.

I texted Brooke what the all-too-familiar voice told me out there, but I didn't say, *Hey, I often get this feeling that something or someone is following me around, and they say these really poetic things sometimes; want to hear what they said?* No, I figured that would just make me look even crazier, so I just tried to be poetic in my own terms with it and sent a few pictures too. Brooke texted back, **Those rapids are sick!! I bet kayaking down that river would be a fantastic rush of adrenaline!!**

Her reply took me off guard, but then I remembered she was a maniac who loved putting herself in dangerous situations, like diving off towers or out of airplanes and whatnot. That stuff just isn't for me; I replied, *Lol, you're one hell of a daredevil.*

I would love to take on those rapids, lol; it excites me just looking at the pictures!

I'm open to kayaking, I thought, *but every time I try to be a daredevil, I always come close to losing a limb or busting my head open, but I'd take the risk to impress her.* *You make me want to go kayaking, lol; I've never done anything like that.*

Gosh you've gotta live and live boldly!!!! Where is that?

I have to admit I'd never seen anybody get that excited about rapids, so I replied, *It's the Potomac River Great Falls in Maryland, and I know, right, lol; I think I'm getting there.*

Good! That's my life motto.

I didn't text her back after that because, even though I would've loved spending the rest of my day talking to her, I had to pull in the reins a little bit. I started to wake up thinking about her every day. I didn't want to, but when you have this unknowable force inside of you just magnetizing you toward someone, it's like trying to fight a wind blowing one hundred miles an hour right at you. I kept telling myself; *You can't be getting caught up, man. She's made it clear time and time again that she just wants to be friends.* I couldn't help hoping she'd realize I was different, though. Genuine and unique people are a rare thing, after all.

After making the four-mile hike back up the road to my truck, I headed back to Jane's house for the day because after walking all through downtown D.C. and hiking at the falls, I was burnt out.

When I got back to Jane's, she was there that time to open the door, and she appeared to be as surprised as Matilda was when she saw me. It's always made me feel so good inside when people look at me like that. It makes me feel like a real star. It reminds me I'm not just some other ghost out here. I looked at Jane with a big smile and said, "Hey there, I'm Hawke; you're Jane, right?"

She was shorter than I'd expected, and she had pretty dark hair. It did look like she was swamped from all the remodeling work they were doing. Jane replied, "Yeah—nice to finally meet you; come on in."

I struck up a conversation about traveling with Jane after I walked inside. The whole motive behind it was to impress her by me being this travelin' man on the road and whatnot, rebel without a cause shooting across the country, but little did I know she was in the Navy for eleven years and had damn near been all over the world. I wasn't as big of a traveler as I thought.

She eventually had to go back to her remodeling work and everything, though. I mean, I offered to help even though I don't know my ass from a hole in the ground when it comes to tools. She said she didn't need any, though. She said I could still hang out and talk, but I didn't really want to. Truth is, I just wanted to be by myself all of a sudden, so I told her I was going to get a shower and I'd probably be down later on.

On the way back to my room through the kitchen, I saw Jane's little boy watching some YouTube on his tablet, and it reminded me a lot of my oldest little boy, Robbie. He started showing me all of his favorite cartoons he liked to watch, and I asked him, "Hey, do you like Sonic? My little boy loves Sonic; he's his favorite."

The boy replied pretty uninterested and said, "Uhhhh, no—I mean, I guess he's ok. I liked the movie, though."

I started to smile a little bit at that. I started thinking about how wonderful it is when kids get drawn to different things, and how they grow to become so passionate about what they love. It's always a pleasant thing to behold when you get a kid to talk about what they're interested in. You can tell it really means a lot to them that a "grown-up" is actually listening to them. The further they get into what they want to say, the more they light up. I missed being around that. I really missed talking with my son, Robbie.

Eventually, the boy shooed me off after getting tired of me asking him questions about all this stuff he watched. He sounded irritated when he said, "Ok, you can go now."

I laughed a little at that, thinking, *Ok then, little dude; I'll get out of your hair.* Afterward, I took a shower and went to my room. I needed to be alone.

That was probably the worst thing I could've done, though. While I lay in bed, I kept thinking about my kids. I wondered, *Are they ok? How are they doing? Did they forget about me? Do they think I forgot about them?*

My mind just wouldn't stop running to the worst places. I thought about how life was before I had my kids and how empty it all felt. I couldn't find a purpose anywhere, and I felt like a complete nobody—just another high school dropout who would smoke his whole paycheck up going on a road to nowhere. When I had my kids, I had a purpose. One of the most wonderful moments of my life was the first time I laid eyes on Robbie.

The day was February 7, 2014, and on that day, I had the honor of holding my first son in my arms. He just looked so little and happy to be in his daddy's arms. I just kept thinking, *Is this what love and happiness really feel like?* I figured if it was, there wasn't anything out there that could beat it.

In that moment, I held a little person that was a part of me and, better yet, a part of my own father. That's who I named my first son after. Robert Thomas Smith seemed like the only name I could give my son because, after all, it was a way for me to fulfill a promise I made to my dad when I was just six years old. I can remember it all like it was yesterday.

I sat by my father's hospital bed on that day, holding one of his big hands in one of my little ones. In that hospital room, there wasn't any conversation in the air between us—just the sound of the heartbeat machine and his ventilator going off.

While I sat there holding his hand, I knew he would have to leave me for heaven. The same place he used to tell me about that he saw in his dreams. He used to say heaven was a place like no other, and it was like a city of gold in the sky. I used to think back then that if heaven was a city of gold, then that must've been where all the treasure comes from. Of course, I thought more along the lines of gold coins stowed away in a pirate's chest, but I think I had the right idea.

I pictured him going on a quest through the clouds in old-fashioned, King Arthur style, with golden armor and all the works, and when he reached heaven, he would finally get his wings so he could fly. I felt happy for him rather than sad, but I was afraid he'd forget about me after he got up there. So I put all of the toys and comics I had with me on his bed and said, "Daddy, I want you to take these to heaven with you so you don't forget about me because I promise that I'm never going to forget about you. You'll come back anyways. You're going to come back for me, right, Daddy? I'm always going to love you. Are you always going to love me? Always and forever, right?"

I felt like he could hear me, but he couldn't answer me. He couldn't say he loved me back anymore.

I knew who put my dad in that hospital bed because I was there with him when it all happened. We all knew why he was there, and it was all Christina's fault. I couldn't understand how she could've done something like that to my dad. She was always so nice to me, and she played with me more than anybody else. I really did love her just as much as I loved my dad. In my mind, I thought, *Does this mean that I have to hate Christina now? Everyone else does.*

Christina was still allowed at the hospital during the investigation, which made everyone even more upset because nobody could figure out why she wasn't behind bars. My grandma didn't look the same way as I was used to seeing her. It was like her whole face changed, and she couldn't stop crying. It made it even worse for her when Christina was around.

Eventually, grandma couldn't take it anymore. When she walked up to Christina at the hospital, she said something I won't ever forget because the way she said it—it didn't even sound like her. It's not really what she said, but how she said it, and I think it stuck with Christina for the rest of her life. Grandma looked her in the eyes and told her, "You're never going to find anyone that's going to love you as much as he did."

I fulfilled the promise I made to my father the day my son was born by naming him after his grandfather, and while I held that little boy for the first time in my arms, I almost dropped to tears at how everything seemed like it had begun to come full circle. I had a son, and my story actually had a meaning. I held someone in my arms I could love no matter what. Things weren't going to turn out the same way they did with my father and me. No, this story would be different.

I'd get to watch that little boy in my arms grow up, through his crazy childhood antics, to his high school days, all the way into adulthood. I'd teach him how to tie a tie and give him tips on what to say to girls, even though I don't even know what to say half the time. I held a baby full of an abundance of happy possibilities for the future to be better than the past was. My son's story would be so much better than mine, at least that's what I told myself, but there I was in D.C., powerless and with no rights as a father to give my children what I've always wanted. Even if I was back in Saraland, Alabama, my children would've still been a million miles away.

CHAPTER X: GOING UP THE COUNTRY

    I woke up early the next day, bound for a small town near Boston, Massachusetts, and I'd be staying with a few folks again; only this time I knew them pretty well. I couldn't wait to see my Grandpa Tom, who's my dad's father, and his wife, Betsy. They'd always been a lot of fun to be around. Grandpa and I would always have so much to talk about. From aliens to god to how much grandpa hated liberals, we'd talk about it all. Betsy, on the other hand, always seemed like a pretty energetic and free-spirited type of person I always wanted to get to know better than what I did. I couldn't pass up the chance to go to see my grandpa's house for the first time on my way to Maine, and I knew he'd be just as excited to see me as I was him, but the drive through the New

England states was going to be a long one, and I had a few stops to make in between.

I headed toward Rehoboth Beach in Delaware first to catch a glimpse of the morning sun as it began to hover and rise over the Atlantic. The sun's rays seemed to turn into liquid flame as it cast its reflection upon the blazing blue waters. My mind automatically went straight to Brooke when I saw it. I thought to myself, *Just stop it. Maybe you should focus on this sunrise and just get your mind off of her. This moment will never happen again, you know. Sure there's always another sunrise to see, but what you're feeling in your heart varies from moment to moment. That's what makes each moment unique.*

Well, I thought about Brooke while I watched that sunrise no matter how much I didn't want to, so I took a picture of it and sent her a corny text that said, *Well, it's kind of pretty, but it's not as beautiful as you are.* I didn't care. I hoped she would text back, but if I'm feeling something and I need to vocalize it in some kind of way, then I'm going to. How the person takes it is on them.

I sat there on the beach for a while and allowed the wind to stroke my thoughts and blow them toward wherever they wanted to go. My mind went back toward a picture of my father taken back in the late eighties of him standing on a beach in California with a big smile on his face.

    I thought, *I know he isn't here anymore, but what if, somehow, on the other side of this ocean, he's waiting for me with that smile on his face just like in the picture? I'm on one side, and he's on the other side. Maybe at this moment we're both looking out across a bridge between worlds.* I sat there on that beach feeling all the love I have for my father pour through my heart. After some time, as the seagulls squawked overhead, I climbed back into the Frontier and continued the drive onward to New York.

    I had no intention of stopping in New York City at all along the way to my grandpa's. The city itself, as I passed through, looked super foggy and barren, like an episode of the *Walking Dead* or something. I couldn't even get a good view of Lady Liberty, that's how obscured my view was. There's a funny thing about the Statue of Liberty, though, that a lot of people don't know. The entire colossus is a rendition of Hekate, the Greek Goddess of Magic.

Lady Liberty leads the modern-day traveler into the new world, just as Hekate in the days of old. Only back then, she didn't lead the traveler, or even better yet, magus, into a new world, but more like an eternal otherworld entirely.

Nevertheless, I tried to post the best video I could of the city on Snap, but it looked like shit and kind of scary, to be honest. Brooke slid up on the video I posted and said, *Look at you go*, with a little heart emoji. Brooke hardly ever slid up on the videos I'd post, and it made me happy in my heart because I felt noticed, you know? Nobody ever slides up on anything I post. Not that I give a shit—I mean fuck 'em, but it felt good to be noticed by her. She was the only person I cared to talk to anyway. As bad as I wanted to stop thinking about her, I was, and by that point of the drive, I didn't even try to fight it anymore.

Brooke asked me, **You mean you're going to just go through New York City and not even stop?**

I had to laugh a little bit at that. I thought to myself, *Well, New York is probably the worst place you could go in the entire world right now with this virus going around and everything—so yeah, that's not exactly on my list.* I told her I'd just devote a whole trip to New York later on, for a week perhaps, so I could get a full sense of what the city was about. I figured it would be great if she'd go with me.

Brooke had already been there once before in her own travels, so she'd know where to start. I, on the other hand, would be lost entirely, but the thought of doing something like that with her made me feel even better on the inside. Then my mind returned to the three-and-a-half-hour drive I still had ahead of me, which was a lot more grueling to think about than Brooke. Grandpa Tom's house was just past the horizon, though, and I was nearly halfway there.

All these years, I thought my grandpa lived in Boston, but the truth is he hates Boston. I guess he'd always get caught up in a fit of road rage every time he entered the city. He told me once, "If you're ever going through Boston, you have to be aggressive. People are real assholes there."

After dealing with the never-ending road, there I found myself in North Grafton, a small town amongst many others that could easily get lost in the shuffle. What made it stand out to me was the place appeared to be full of flowers of purple, red, gold, and white lying across all the fences and through everybody's yards. You could tell from the way each house looked the person living there felt passionate about their home, and I got the same sense from Grandpa's house when I got there.

Even though I stayed with family, I still felt nervous when I rang the doorbell. It's not that I was afraid to see my grandpa and Betsy; it just felt shocking I was actually there, and on top of that, I hadn't seen them in a while. So I stood at the door, wondering what I'd talk about and what I would say, but then it dawned on me. *Hey, you've had one hell of an adventure so far, so don't even worry about it. You have plenty to talk about. Everything's going to be okay.* I knocked a couple of times on the door, and as soon as I did, I could hear grandpa's dogs barking, and Betsy yell, "Well, what are you waiting on? Come on in!"

I hugged Betsy, and she seemed pretty excited that I'd finally made it. I was, too because the drive there really sucked, especially when I went through New York. Betsy made herself a mudslide drink real quick, and we walked outside for a smoke on the patio. I was ready for one even though I'd pretty much smoked the Frontier up. What was Enterprise going to do? Sue me? I didn't care.

I wasn't used to seeing Betsy with a drink because whenever I'd visit with her and grandpa in Ohio, they would always stay with my Aunt Teresa. She didn't really approve of alcohol too much, so we all respected that—well, sort of. I mean, to tell you the truth, I'd just have my beers before I got there, but that was beside the point. At grandpa's house, I could already tell this visit would be a lot different because we could all be comfortable and more at ease with being ourselves.

Before I knew it, I saw what could've been an older version of myself walking in the door. He was a lot more structured with his routines and way more into politics than I could ever hope to be. He's a tall, skinny guy sporting the eyeglasses of a brilliant scientist with light blonde hair that's never seemed to go gray. Maybe it's from natural genetics or hair dye; who knows? But there my grandpa was, brushing past his little dogs Skyler and Roscoe with his arms spread out, saying, "Hey, you finally made it! How the heck are ya?"

We gave each other a big hug, and I said, "I'm doing a lot better now after getting off the road. That traffic in New York was the worst."

Grandpa Tom replied with a confused look, "You didn't take the way I gave you? You wouldn't have had to go through all of the traffic if you would've gone that way." He shook his head in remembrance and said, "I had to drive back and forth through New York a few years ago, and they wanted me to move there at one point, but screw that. New York drivers are just way too much to deal with. It's really ridiculous."

I could tell the thought of New York bothered him just as much as the thought of driving through Boston did, which I thought was funny in a way because I get aggravated by a lot of the same things he does. Driving through cities doesn't bother me that much, though.

We all sat around and caught up with one another for a little while, which felt so wonderful to me because I spent what felt like an eternity without having any family around. It was lovely to have a conversation with people I actually knew.

Grandpa eventually showed me around his house, and it was full of things he'd collected over the years. The basement seemed to be grandpa's workshop. Down there, he had all kinds of tools and projects he liked to tinker around with. That's always been a thing of his. He's the type of person who could probably build a desktop computer from scratch, and he prefers to fix what he has by his own means rather than pay somebody to do it, which might be the reason why he almost blew himself up.

At dinner, grandpa started telling me a story about what happened to him while he drove along the interstate a few days before after Betsy brought it up. Grandpa said, "Well, I switched into this lane, and before I knew it, this ladder flies out of the bed of this truck in front of me right across the lane. I couldn't switch lanes fast enough, so I started to brace myself for impact and ran right over the damn thing. When I made it home, I checked to see if anything was leaking and there was a leak from the gas tank. So I chewed up some gum and stuck it over the hole—it was about a quarter-sized hole—"

Then Betsy interrupted, laughing, "When I walked outside and saw what he was doing, I told him, 'Tom you can't do that; you're going to blow yourself up!'"

Grandpa smiled at Betsy and continued, "Well, that would patch it up good enough to get me around for a few days. I put duct tape across it to hold it all into place."

Betsy continued Grandpa's story with a big grin on her face, "But then it ended up breaking down right in front of the house when he was coming back from work—"

29 Palms

Grandpa chimed in next, "I just threw my hands up and said screw it, I'm fucking done with this thing." He finished off the story with a laugh and a wave of his hand. We all managed to finish dinner without spitting up our food from cracking up. After catching up that evening, we all went to bed to get ready for the next day's adventures.

Once we all woke up, I promised Grandpa I'd get him some pictures developed of the boys since he didn't have any. While I printed off all the pictures I could, I kept looking at how their little smiles differed from each picture and how they had grown up so much over the years. I thought, *When is the day finally going to come when I get to see those little smiles of theirs again? Are they even happy at all right now? They were when they were with me, or I at least tried to make them feel that way.*

29 Palms

I could feel my mind tumbling toward the dark places again, so I put their pictures away in the photo envelope. It was hard for me to do, but looking at my kids' pictures didn't make me feel happy anymore. I couldn't do anything for them, and I wanted to enjoy the day so I could make another great story to bring back to them when they'd finally run into my arms again.

Grandpa loved the pictures, of course. We didn't discuss what went on with the boys too much because we already had a pretty lengthy talk on the phone about it before, and it upset him as much as it did me—to a degree anyway. I'm sure we both had the same idea in mind for the day; to not focus on the negatives but to focus on having a fun day together, and that's just what we did. Grandpa asked me, "Well, there's not too much to do around here. So what do you want to do?"

I wasn't even sure. I thought he had a plan, so I just told him, "I don't know—ummm—we can check out the Revolutionary War sites if you want." It was settled after that. We headed out toward Lexington.

Parking meters are probably one of the most annoying inventions ever patented on planet Earth, and I think Grandpa and I both felt that way when we were trying to figure out the parking meter we stopped at in Lexington. Grandpa said, "I don't trust putting my card in that thing." He looked at Betsy and asked her, "You sure this is the right meter for this spot?"

I wondered the same thing because there was a meter on each side of the spot. I thought to myself, *Looks like a gamble to me—right or left—towed or not towed—*

Betsy replied, "Yeah, I mean, I think it is. We'll just pay for it and see."

Grandpa had a look of uncertainty stretch across his face after Betsy said that. At least it was my truck or a truck I rented anyway. I wasn't really too worried about it. So I figured, *Oh well, if it gets towed, it gets towed. We'll figure it out.* I wasn't sure if Grandpa was more worried about my truck getting towed or getting stranded in a place where rainbow flags were hanging up everywhere. I asked him, "Man, I've seen a lot of rainbow flags here in Massachusetts. What's up with all of that?"

Grandpa replied, somewhat annoyed by the prospect of it all, "The frickin' liberals are taking over everything. I mean, they're even hanging on churches now."

I didn't mind the rainbow flags. I've just never seen them hanging up everywhere like they'd been in Massachusetts. I liked messing with him about it, though. I went on to say, "Yeah, that's crazy. Looks like you're in the danger zone, buddy. Better not stand too close to the bushes around here; you might just disappear."

Grandpa shot a serious "yeah right" look at me and didn't even respond to my joke. We continued our walk toward the trolley station looking damn near wholly abandoned.

When grandpa read the sign, I could tell he was confused. He turned to Betsy and said, "It's closed due to the Covid. I guess we're walking today. This Covid business is really getting ridiculous."

I couldn't agree more. I told him, "It seems like it gets worse the further I go up the coast. You can't go anywhere without dressing like a surgeon everywhere you go. I don't even think it really even helps, honestly."

Grandpa replied, "It's like any other virus; some people get it, and other people don't. I'm not even supposed to be working right now because of my age, but I'm going in anyway, and I haven't caught a thing yet. I'm as healthy as a horse."

I asked, "Do you think we can even get it? I mean, I've made my way up the coast, and I haven't caught anything yet—fingers crossed. I think a lot of it boils down to how strong your immune system is and probably even genetics, but who knows? I'm just ready for everything to go back to normal."

Grandpa replied, "It's all being used for propaganda. After the election, we won't hear a thing about it anymore."

I never thought about it that way. At the end of the day, there aren't too many of us that are scientists out there, but there does come a time when you have to ask yourself why does the news highlight specific stories and leave even bigger ones behind the curtain? Why are people that have died from a heart attack being labeled as dying from Covid? This country is controlled by propaganda that injects fear into the public, which leads to more control. None of us know what's going on, but we should never accept things as they are. Always ask questions.

Walking through Lexington didn't feel as magical as I thought it would be. The town itself seemed fairly modernized, and most of the old battlefield was paved over with roads, which seemed like a big waste to me. I can understand things need to grow to prosper, but when it comes to important historical sites, I think it's best just to leave them alone. The old tavern those old patriots shot from still stood in the middle of town, though.

After Lexington, we had to visit Concord, where the battle starting the revolution back in the day took place. It was the type of ground seeming to whisper back with each step you took. Not to get all metaphysical or anything, but it felt like some of the energy around during the battle was still there. I don't know; maybe it was just me. Every area has a different feel to it, though. Sort of like if you were to take a map and each area has a coordinate to it, right? Well, each coordinate or different place sort of has a different frequency to it— like a radio, and each place is a different station or something, you know?

I could tell grandpa was in deep thought about the place too. He gets really quiet when he starts thinking a lot. I wondered if he picked up on the same type of things I was. It was a battlefield where many people died, but it had a beautiful, old-world feel to it that seemed to rush within you as the wind blew. The old brick house on the hill seemed to be calling to me, though. It looked so beautiful perched up there like that.

Once we reached the house on the hill, I could tell Betsy and Grandpa were sort of exhausted by the walk because there wasn't any shade out there, and the buzzards were crowing overhead—like they were waiting for one of us to collapse or something, so after they decided to take a break in the shade, I headed toward the wildflower garden wrapping its way around the house.

It's not difficult for me to admit I love flowers. I like poems and stuff like that too. I'm not with all that fake masculinity bullshit everyone else is on. If I like something, I like it. I'm not going to pretend I don't just so I can look more like a man. That just seems so stupid to me. I'm not an actor, and I like what I like. I'd rather be me than try to fit into a mold. If God wanted clones, he would've made us all the same.

I don't know, though. I've always found it excellent you can look at a whole rose bush, full of flowers, and each flower looks similar, but none of them are the same. Some have different curves with more petals than others, and of course, if you were lucky enough, you might just find a star in the bunch. One exquisite flower that shines as bright as a real star. It's like finding a treasure in a natural work of art that isn't afraid to stand out on its own.

Of course, as I intoxicated myself among the different colors and scents of that wild garden, I had to take some pictures for Brooke. I couldn't forget about the promise I made her, and I couldn't think of a person I wanted to share all of that beauty with more than her. So I sent her the best flower pictures I'd taken and texted, *It's a city of flowers. It's really going to kill me to go back to Alabama when all of this is over.*

I love the white. I know it is; there's hardly anything special about this town. I wouldn't come back either. I don't know how I'm going to spend six months in Europe and actually want to come back here, lol.

I really couldn't imagine going back to Alabama at this point. *I somehow had a feeling that you would like those, lol; I've been getting lottery tickets along the way, so hopefully, I hit for some money or find some rich lady to take care of me so I don't have to come back, lol.*

I sent another text after sending her a lot more flower pictures. I couldn't help it. *I'm not going to blow you up today, lol; I just keep on running into things to take pictures of.*

That would be so nice, lol. I love the pictures; don't feel bad.

I had to joke back, but I couldn't help sprinkling a little hint in there. *Maybe you'll just hit big out in Vegas; who knows? I'd really be after you then, lol.*

Well, I'm not going to be gambling too much, but maybe the penny slots will give me a nice birthday present, lol.

When we started talking about Vegas, I was dead set on heading out west anyway, and I began to play around with this fantasy in my head of meeting up with her in Vegas, but I wasn't sure when she'd be there. If it were destined to be a magical moment, then destiny would lead the way to the right time. I didn't give any sense of the dream I had for her at this point. I texted, *Lol, what's the first thing you would do with the money if you did?*

Travel??? Is that even a question, lol.

It was honestly an earnest question I should've already known the answer to, but as I started to become wrapped up in the fantasy I built in my head, I decided to still keep it cool in my corny little way. *Lol, shocked. I'm addicted to traveling now because of you, lol. I feel like we've had this conversation before, for some reason, lol.*

No, I don't think we ever have, lol; we have talked about winning money when I go to Vegas though, lol. I just solely believe life isn't meant to be lived in the same place for 70+ years, doing the same thing every day on a routine. It makes me sick to think about me working five days a week with only two days off for the rest of my life. Wasting SO much time when I could be seeing the world. I might not have many material things to my name, but I have memories, stories, and experiences to tell for the rest of my life. Now that is far better than what any material thing could ever bring me. I wish we all could just be happy and enjoy life to the fullest because we never know when we can be taken from it. Gosh, I just don't know how to word it. I have this fire in my soul that lights up when I think of all the places I could go and how many cultures I can experience.

I started to think I know exactly how that fire feels because I'm beginning to kindle a fire like that in my heart for you, but I pulled back the reins as best as I could. *You really do have a special kind of fire inside of you. It's like I can feel it when I'm around you and even when I'm talking with you. It's something phenomenal that's really unique and magnetic. I know now that the world can be traveled with ease, it just all depends on what you want to dump your money into. Materials that don't mean a thing or use all of what you have toward adding as many colors that you can to your soul through experience and exploration.*

Exactly. My family doesn't understand it, especially my brother, but I'd rather spend my money on a trip instead of bills. Idk, I hate having to give my money to a corrupted government. I'm glad I was able to influence your life. I feel like God made me someone that is supposed to make an impact in everyone's life that I encounter. I'm supposed to be memorable. Time does get in the way; that's why you

just gotta go out there and feed your soul with what makes you happy. What will fully fulfill you.

I thought to myself, Wow, everything she says just speaks directly to my heart. Her words just hit places that have never been touched before. She really is my muse for this journey.

I replied, You're the most lovely person I know and I really mean that. This journey is really starting to make me feel enflamed with passion. I'm starting to see a line of direction to open up a world of possibilities. I'm going to use this journey as a framework to tell my story. I got something inside of me that I want to give. I'm going to call the book 29 Palms. If I can really put my heart and soul into this book, it will give me the means to see the entire world.

That means a lot to me. Well, I hope you do put your heart and soul into everything you do!! I think you could make it a beautiful book. Your whole life is a book really. Embrace every chapter.

We shared so many of the same dreams, and in my heart, I knew she was the only one that could understand how the journey made me feel.

I responded, It's like living out a real-life adventure story; it really is. There's real magic out here in everything. Through the forest with its trees to every corner that the birds fly, it's really there; you can just feel it out there. You just have to find a way to break out of the system that you were forced to accept. We don't live in reality anymore, but a design. You just have to find a way to break out of the mold.

We didn't talk the rest of the day after that, which didn't bother me much at all. Sure, I could've sat under that tree in the wildflower garden and texted Brooke all day until the stars were above me, but with the words she sent to me that day—well, that was enough beauty to fill up my heart for the rest of the week. She always made me feel so full on the inside with her words. I'd think and wonder to myself, Wow, she really took time out of her day for me, *the uninteresting guy that nobody ever really wants to talk to. She made time for me.*

When I started to find my bearings again, I remembered, *Hey, I have to find Grandpa and Betsy; they're probably looking for me.* When I found them, they were still hanging out on the bench under the wild oak I left them under. Apparently, they had already made their rounds in the garden and were ready to go back to the car for lunch. So we headed back to the little parking lot in front of Concord.

I have to admit having this picnic with Grandpa and Betsy was probably the first picnic I think I've ever had. While we were eating, Grandpa asked me, "So does it pass the sandwich test?"

I looked back at him, pretty bewildered, thinking, *What sandwich test? What do you mean?* Betsy then said, "Tom makes the best sandwiches, and he has this little test for them."

Grandpa went on to say, "It only passes the sandwich test if the juices start running all over your hands and the sandwich starts getting everywhere. When it does that, it passes the sandwich test."

I grinned and laughed a little at that while I thought, *Well, I hope it doesn't pass the sandwich test because I hate it when food gets all over me, but it is a pretty good sandwich I have to admit, so it passes my own personal test, I guess.* After we got done with lunch, Betsy and Grandpa wanted to take me to an old insane asylum that had a clock tower standing guard over the whole facility, so that's where we went next.

On our way to the old asylum, Betsy and I started to have a conversation about some of the abandoned places you can run across that tend to be haunted, and to my surprise, she loved doing stuff like that as much as I did. Betsy said, "Tom won't go into any abandoned places with me; it's just not really his thing."

Grandpa didn't reply to what she said, but I knew why he didn't. I don't think he believes in ghosts too much. He leans more on the belief ghosts are demons masquerading around as people who have passed on before. From the little amount we know of the paranormal, I think that's a pretty valid possibility, but not all spirits are evil. Some are just lonely wanderers caught in a place between two worlds, always searching but never finding. It's the saddest story of them all if you think about it.

Speaking of searching, while I drove toward the asylum, a wild turkey ran out in the middle of the road like it was looking for something. Betsy said, "Wow! Look at that, another turkey! That's so weird. We never see turkeys around here," she went on laughing and said to me, "not until you showed up anyways. Isn't that right, Tom?"

Grandpa replied, "No, we never do. I've been seeing all kinds of wildlife along the road that I'm not used to seeing at all. It's kind of strange."

Betsy laughed and said, "What did you do, Hawke? Bring the whole forest with you from the mountains?"

The fact is I was just as surprised as they were—sort of. I've always had an affinity for animals. They all seem to love me for some reason, especially dogs. They just lose their shit when I'm around. I grinned a little and replied, "Who knows? Maybe I did."

When we reached the old clock tower, it did have a creepy vibe ebbing away from it as the wind blew. Grandpa walked up behind me and pointed toward the old asylum, and said, "Well, there's the old nut house right there. Of course, they don't like you calling it a nut house anymore because it offends people—so now I guess it's a called a *wellness center.*"

It was so funny to me because it came out of nowhere, and I didn't expect him to say that at all. He's good at catching you off guard like that sometimes. "Yeah, everything offends everybody now. It's like walking around in a world full of eggshells, only half of the time you don't even know where the eggshells even are."

Then I continued with one of the crazy scenarios I always imagine up in my head, "Wouldn't it be crazy if the alarms starting going off over there, and some dude came running out trying to wrestle his way out of a straightjacket? Then what if he forced us to drive him from here to Mexico to make his escape? That'd be nuts, wouldn't it?"

Grandpa replied, "Yeah, I don't think that would make a good way to end the day."

I started busting out laughing. "No, but it'd be a hell of a story to tell."

After the trip to the asylum, we decided to go back to Grandpa's house for the day, and later on that evening, like I knew we would, Grandpa and I ended up getting into one of our in-depth talks about how mysterious the world is. We started off talking about the subject of aliens like we had many times before, and Grandpa said, "I think that they're demons because every encounter or abduction story that you ever hear is never a good one. You don't hear a story that goes, 'Hey, we went to this planet that had this Martian there with three titties, and then we went cruising along in space just having a good old time.' It's never a good experience."

He got me with that one. I thought, *So a Martian with three titties would be a good time for you, huh? Looks like we need to party together sometime then.* I tried my best not to crack up because he was serious, but I considered what he said. I mean we really don't know what they are or if they're even real. I replied, "Yeah, I know what you mean. Encounter stories hardly ever turn out to be a good story, but what if they just look at us the same way we look at animals?"

Grandpa replied with his arms crossed and said, "It could be that way. I just wonder—if they're so friendly, why are they so secretive about what they do? It just sounds demonic to me."

I didn't want to bring up the theory they could be more evolved versions of ourselves who found a way to come back through time to change some terrible outcome to come in the future. I sort of built my own idea about it from listening to a couple things Joe Rogan said on his podcast.

Of course we talked about the bible too, like we always do, but I held back a lot of what I thought. I didn't think he would accept my theories if they weren't grounded in scripture, but eventually, I had to ask him, "Have you ever wondered if the bible's been edited? I mean, it's a book that's passed through a lot of hands over the centuries; what are the odds that it hasn't ever been tampered with?"

Grandpa replied, "Well, we have what we have. I'd rather live my life believing it and it turns out not to be the way than not going by scripture, and it ends up all being true because if you don't follow what scripture says and you end up being wrong, well, then you're fucked."

I understood his logic and the point of view he came from, but I'd rather follow something because it speaks to my heart, and I feel an abundance of love from it. There are many different beliefs out there that all have something beautiful and wonderful to each, and if it brings others happiness and fulfillment, I think that's great. I've just never been able to follow a specific book. It's not because I disagree with them; it's just more because I don't trust other people. I find it hard to believe religious texts have never been tampered with by the "powers that be" in an attempt to set a standard of control among the public. A lot of inspiration can be found from what's been written throughout the ages, but the true book is the one we are all living in right now—the natural order of the universe.

After a little while, Grandpa and I were both pretty tired; after all, we'd been running all day long. Since we swapped knowledge on a good number of ancient complexes, I told him about the old Mystery Hill site about an hour away in New Hampshire. He never heard of it, and I told him, "Man, we gotta go there."

I couldn't pass up the chance to visit America's most ancient site, and Grandpa seemed like the perfect person to go see it with. After he went to sleep, my mind started to run even further as it always does late at night. I looked up at the stars on Grandpa's patio, with a nice smoke, and thought more about our talk.

For some reason, when I look out across nature with all of its vibrant colors and out across the dark indigo night sky, I can see the relativity in it all and how one thing connects to another. It's almost like this relativity is the same for everywhere, and everything has its twin or correspondence. The gears of the world turn through the probability and polarity of opposites. It's like the world, the universe itself, is one giant, everlasting book that can be read if you learn to open yourself up to what it has to teach you. I've just always thought a book written by man could easily be edited, but the laws of nature are set in stone. It's that simple.

We each have our path to follow, and that's why it's essential to follow what's in your heart the most. That's where your destiny is written. You might come across things you didn't expect and are up in the air about, but let your heart translate it for you. How does this unexpected thing make you feel when you think of it? If you feel moved toward it, then go for it; don't worry about what others think or what might happen because, in my experience, things never go as planned. Often when a plan seems to be going off course, it's because you were following the wrong path to begin with. With all that's around us and how relative the universe is, we can't simply read it with our intellect, but the heart is the true eye beholding what is written across the stars. As long as it doesn't hurt anybody else, just go for it. Don't let your fear decide everything for you. Passion is the compass to the true will of your destiny. After all that thinking, I eventually settled my mind long enough to get some sleep, and it was pretty hard. I'm an insomniac to tell you the truth.

CHAPTER XI: DRAGGIN' THE LINE

The next morning, Grandpa and I headed straight for Mystery Hill. Betsy had to work, so she couldn't join us, which sucked because I had a lot of fun getting to know her better the day before. Even though it was dark and cloudy, it didn't do a thing to damper Grandpa and my's excitement on seeing this mysterious place. Unfortunately, my excitement didn't give me the same "pick me up" energy caffeine did, so I had to make a stop at a gas station. All of the parking spots were filled up, though, so I figured I'd just park in front of the pump. Grandpa asked me, "Didn't you get gas last night before we went home?"

I sort of knew what was coming. I replied, "Yeah, but I need to get me some caffeine; it's just something I guess I've gotten way too used to."

Grandpa looked worried, like we were breaking the law or something. I mean, I'm pretty much an outlaw, so I didn't care, but he said, "Hawke, you can't park at the pump if you're not getting gas. You can't do that. Just park in that spot over there."

It was a dire thing to do; he was right. I parked in a spot to make him feel better. After chugging as much caffeine as I could handle, I put the pedal to the floor and headed off toward Mystery Hill. I don't think Grandpa knew what he had gotten himself into.

When we pulled into Mystery Hill, it didn't look like much at first. We checked out the place's museum right away. While we were in there, Grandpa went around to each plaque like he was a detective or something. I just breezed through pretty quickly because I was ready to get to the nitty-gritty of it all and see the observatory. I figured I'd just let Grandpa read all the signs and get any info I needed from him later on.

Grandpa told me he didn't learn much in there, though. They had no idea who built it. I once heard a theory it was built by the Celtic people who crossed over to America a long time ago because of the old runes found carved around the place, but even more legends say it wasn't built by people at all, but giants. Once we reached the actual complex, both of us knew right away whatever put those stones in place wasn't a regular human being. There was no way it could've been.

The central complex appeared to be circular initially, but part of the site was ruined by old rock miners back in the day supposedly. The center circle was surrounded by an even larger circle with four lines running from it through four completely cleared paths in the surrounding forest, each to mark the solstices and equinoxes occurring throughout each year. It was used by an ancient group of magi who revered the sun and nature to the most profound degree I could tell. With each solstice or equinox, a sacrifice had to be made, and this would've been done at the center of it all—the sacrificial table. You could tell it was used for sacrifices because it had grooves on the edges so that the blood could run off it and sanctify the ground. I didn't like the pictures I saw in my mind when I went into the tunnel underneath that thing, but there definitely was something about the place.

It felt full of an ancient force just unimaginable to describe. The air was super thick and heavy, but I didn't feel drained from being there. I was being charged. It wasn't a negative or a positive energy; it felt like a place where dark and light sat down together to finally come to an agreement or something. I could tell Grandpa had something on his mind by the disturbed look he had on his face while we walked through the site. He didn't say anything at all. He felt that something too; I just knew he did. So I asked him, "Does this place feel strange to you?"

Grandpa stopped for a minute and stared at the ground. Then he looked to me and said, "I'm not exactly sure how to put it. It's an extraordinary place, that's for sure. It doesn't feel evil to me, but it doesn't feel good either. I don't know."

I can probably count on one hand how many times I've heard him say I don't know. The place affected him in a big way. Grandpa went on to say, "Just look at all these massive stones. I can't believe they think a few farmers did this just messing around. Archaeologists don't know shit."

I couldn't agree with him more, but I wanted to get to the bottom of what we both felt. I replied, "I don't know what to say about this place either. I was wondering if it was just me or if you were picking up on something really strange too."

Grandpa replied with the same serious look he always has when he's trying to figure something out, "I don't think I've ever felt anything like this before. There doesn't seem to be a category for it."

He was right; there wasn't. "It feels like something between good and evil."

"That's exactly how it feels."

Where I wanted to go next was as clear as ever to me, but I knew Grandpa didn't want to go there at all. He kept suggesting all of these different parks and monuments completely away from Boston, and I knew he did it so he wouldn't have to go there. I couldn't help it. I had to break it to him. "I want to go to Boston today. I mean, I can't say I visited Massachusetts and didn't go to Boston, you know what I mean?"

Grandpa put his hand on his chin like he was already starting to picture an episode of some road rage. I don't know why. I mean, I'm a good driver. I've only run over a median and popped all the tires on my truck once. It's not like it happens all the time. We were going to be fine. He'd see.

Grandpa seemed to accept we were going to Boston after he settled himself down a little bit. He said, "Ok, we can go to Boston then. I'm not sure what all is open with all of the Covid crap going on, but we can see. Now when we get there, you have to be aggressive. If you need to get over, get over because there's a lot of jerks that live there."

I figured since he knew so much about driving in Boston, he might as well be the driver, so I said, "Well, you probably know the area a lot better than me, so I'm just going to go ahead and pull over so you can take the wheel."

Grandpa replied, "Nope, I'm going to let you do all of the driving today. I brought my map books with me in case we have any problems finding our way around. So I'll need to read the maps anyway if we get into any trouble."

Oh no, not the maps. Why maps? I have a GPS for a reason, man. I replied, "I have a GPS on my phone, Grandpa; if we get lost, I'll just use that."

Grandpa replied with complete confidence in his map reading abilities, "I don't use those things. You can't trust them. Nothing works better than a map, in my opinion. You can get lost by using your GPS, but I have my maps, so that's not going to happen."

There was no way he was giving up on his maps, but I figured with an expert in map navigation at my side and the grand old GPS on my lap, we didn't have anything to worry about. Even with all of that, we still got ourselves into a mess later on.

When I laid my eyes on the city of Boston for the first time, I came face to face with the usual skyscrapers accompanying any of the major cities in the US. Still, this picturesque town had a dark dramatic backdrop to it on this particular day from all the shadow-like clouds hovering around.

The city had people in it of course, but it wasn't as alive as I imagined it to be. It looked like the city was dying. It was like the pandemic sucked the life out of American culture everywhere. Everyone looked worried, and nobody seemed happy. Maybe people were delighted, and I just didn't know it because they were all wearing masks, but it sure didn't feel like it, and of course, I know what your thinking—yes, we bent the knee Game of Thrones style and wore our masks too.

I had no idea where to start in Boston, so I asked Grandpa where the most historical places were. Grandpa said, "I'm not sure where to start either. We can go to the Boston Commons first if you want. There'll be a lot of picture opportunities for you there."

Then his face dropped a little, and I could already tell what he thought when he said, "It's going to be hell finding a parking spot there, though."

I figured, well, if there isn't a parking spot, I'd just have to make one then. After all, I drove a rental, and if it got towed, I'd just call Enterprise on the phone and act stupid about it. Maybe even get a better ride; who knows? We didn't have too much of a problem finding a parking spot, though, and I could tell Grandpa was relieved with how lucky we were. He said, "The Covid must have given us some luck today because usually everything is packed everywhere. Today isn't as bad as it usually is."

The walk around Boston Commons was absolutely great, even with the dark foreboding background the sky held above us. The darkness didn't take away from the lavish liveliness of the sprouting bright and dark green hues seeming to shoot from the ground right up through the trees. Grandpa started directing me on how to take better pictures, and I'll admit I needed all the help I could get. Pictures were always his kind of thing. On his annual visits to Ohio when I was a kid, you knew for sure you were going to get two things, a bear hug from Grandpa, and you'd most definitely be getting your picture taken. My cousin Jordan always hated being in pictures, but Hannah and I were always good sports for it.

While I tried to take a picture from the regular way I held my phone, Grandpa chimed in and said, "You know you can get a lot more of the skyline if you hold the camera horizontally." I felt like an idiot for never thinking of it.

Once Grandpa and I made our rounds around the Boston Commons, we hopped back in the truck to cruise around the city until we got to the site of where the Boston Tea Party occurred. While we were driving along, I almost turned down a one-way street. Grandpa started screaming, "No! No!, Hawke, that's a one way!"

He eventually calmed himself down, though, and said, "There are a lot of frickin' one-way streets that you have to watch out for around here. It almost seems like they designed this city to confuse people. I don't see why all of the one-ways are really that necessary, but they're there."

Although I almost got us into a pileup on a one-way street, I still had to hold back from cracking up. Not because a wreck would've been funny, but anytime Grandpa loses his cool a little bit, it's always hilarious. Most of the time, he's a pretty calm and collected guy—just going about piecing the world together and trying to figure it all out, but once that calmness breaks, it's one hell of a show because you never know what he's going to say.

When we continued onward toward the tea party site, Grandpa pointed to a car turning toward our end of the street and said, "Look, Hawke! Look at that guy driving by himself with a mask on!"

He looked at the guy with the most confused look, like he was trying to figure it all out. Grandpa continued, "I don't get it. Is he trying to—what is he doing? Is he trying to protect himself—from himself? Well, ok then—trying to protect yourself from yourself. That doesn't make any sense."

I just couldn't hold it in anymore. I held it for so long from comments he'd been dropping all day, but that last one just brought it all out to the point I had tears in my eyes. He just rambled on as I lost it, "Well, it doesn't make any sense. If the guy is wearing a mask to protect himself from himself, that would mean he already has the virus anyway. If no one is in the vehicle, who else would he be protecting himself from?"

I was losing it at the wheel. I think I almost pulled down another one way. I tried everything I could to pull myself together. I replied, "I don't know, man. It really doesn't make any sense at all.

He was lookin' all business casual and everything. I don't know what's wrong with people." I eventually pulled myself together so we could get to where the Boston Tea Party happened without getting in a wreck.

I already passed the site up earlier because I couldn't find any parking spots, but I had to get a picture of the ships, even though the shop was closed because of the 'vid. So I popped a u-turn real quick that shook Grandpa up a little bit and parked my truck in a bus lane. As I jerked my seat belt off, Grandpa started to enter panic mode again and said, "Hawke, this is a bus lane! You can't park here. What if a bus pulls—"

Before Grandpa could finish, I was already gone. I bolted out of the truck towards the ships. I guess it was wrong of me to leave him there in complete panic mode like that, but I had to get a picture. I didn't really have a choice.

I snapped a quick pic, and made sure that I followed Grandpa's advice by shooting them horizontally this time around. Afterward, I dashed back to the truck and hopped back into the driver seat. Apparently, Grandpa had calmed himself down. He said, "Ok, illegal parking. We got away with that one. Do you want to see the *U.S.S. Continental* now?"

That's exactly where we went next. No wrecks from pulling down any one ways, and we managed to find a *legal* spot to park in on this go around. When Grandpa and I walked toward the *U.S.S Continental*, my view was fixed more on the whole city of Boston rather than the ship we came to see. From that harbor lookout, I could feel what seemed like the breath and energy of the whole city falling upon me. It wasn't from the people per se, just the atmosphere. It seemed to be a testament to how far we've come since the times of old Boston.

We've made it a long way through technological achievements for sure, but I wondered as I stood there, have we come that far as people individually? Have the values we hold toward one another improved or gotten worse? It was apparent to me from my personal experiences we as people don't care about the other guy at all anymore, for the most part, but did people back then value each other? They didn't have much of a choice because to accomplish anything, it always took a team. Now all you need is a computer. The world is more connected now than it's ever been, but in our hearts, we couldn't be separated more. I wasn't alone on that day, though. This had been the best time I'd ever had with my grandpa, and I know he enjoyed it just as much as I did.

After snapping a few pictures of the Boston skyline, we hit the gas toward trouble when we tried to find our way out of Boston. If we had followed the way the GPS took us, we would've never gotten lost, but Grandpa kept insisting we were going the wrong way. He said, "Look, I don't know what the fuck that thing is telling you, but the signs are pointing the other way toward 93; we have to be going the wrong way."

He continued, "Just go by the signs, trust me; that GPS doesn't know where to go."

I thought to myself, *Well, ok, but I have a feeling this is going to lead to disaster.* By following the signs, we started going directly back into the city. In a fit of frustration, Grandpa said, "Ok, I don't know what the fuck is going on with the signs. I guess you should just go by that thing."

After he paused for a minute in an attempt to figure out where we were, I started pleading to myself in my head, *Dear god, please don't pull out the map books, man; we'll never get out of here if that happens.* Grandpa started getting even more frustrated than he was before and said, "You think if the sign is pointing that way, then you go that way; it doesn't make any fucking sense."

I wanted to ask him so bad if he wanted to drive, but I didn't. I had to focus. I couldn't risk losing it at the wheel again. By following the GPS as we should've in the beginning, we finally got back to 93 and headed back toward Grandpa's house just in time for Betsy to get home from work.

Back at Grandpa's, we all tried to figure out where we wanted to go next. I knew Grandpa wouldn't go, but I asked, "What about Salem? I've always wanted to check that out."

Betsy seemed down for it. She said, "Oh, I love Salem! Tom won't ever go with me to see it. It's too *witchy* of an area for him."

I looked at Grandpa and said, "Come on, you'll be fine, man. Let's just go do it."

Grandpa replied, "Ah no—no, I don't want to go to Salem. What about Chief Joseph's? We haven't taken Hawke there yet, Betsy." Grandpa looked back at me and said, "You'll like Chief Joseph's a lot; he always has all kinds of different things on display there." It was settled. Off to Chief Joseph's garden we went.

Along the way to Chief Joseph's, Betsy and Grandpa filled me in on where we were headed because I had no idea what type of place it was. They told me it was a place not too many people knew about and it was a garden an old rich Indian guy set up for people to simply enjoy. Apparently, the place was chalk full of oddities. We started back with all the 'vid talk, though, before I pulled up to Chief Joseph's and got ready to park.

While I got out of the truck, I said, "Yeah, I mean I get the whole mask thing, but if you're not wearing one, you risk the chance of offending people now more than ever. It's like people always need something to pick on or complain about."

When Grandpa opened his door to get out, he said, "You know why you always have to worry about offending someone everywhere you go?"

I asked why and as Grandpa slammed the door to my truck, he said, "Because everyone's a bunch of bitches."

It was something I never expected to come out of his mouth, and I started to think, *I'm not sure why he just slammed the door on my truck like that, but he said all that with some force, with some real meaning. I can get on board with that. Alright, I like it. Let's head on up to this garden.*

Chief Joseph's garden was a hidden spectacle that could be found not too far from Grafton. While we walked along the path, you could spot so many statues of dogs, bears, rabbits, wizards, angels; almost anything from a fable or legend could be found in that little garden. The paths were strewn with colorful, chipped pieces of glass making the pathways crisscrossing across the garden look like magical trails leading you toward another surprise. I just saw it as wonderful somebody created that special place for people to come and take a walk in. If I lived in the Grafton area, I'd probably go there at least once a week just to see what new oddity the chief decided to lay out. Once we all got our fill of that little magical garden, we headed back to the house to play some dominoes.

I didn't want to play dominoes because I never played the game before, but Grandpa got me when he said, "If you ever go to jail, Hawke, you should already know how to play dominoes. I heard that they play it a lot in there."

I thought to myself, *Well, there are a few people back home I'm pretty upset with right now, and if I do end up in jail, I'd like to at least fit in, so what could it hurt?*

It was a mistake as soon as I picked up my first domino, but it was a fun mistake. I didn't stand a chance against Grandpa because I could tell dominos was his game. I'd lay a domino down, and he'd be ready to rack up more points, and of course, he had to rub it in by saying, "Hey, you're a real nice guy. A really good guy, thanks."

Again and again, he would score on whatever I'd throw down. And again and again, he'd say things like, "Wow, thanks pal. Got you again."

It was really funny to me the way he talked shit because it was a side of my grandpa I'd never seen before.

It was like all the years that went by, as soon as I'd get to see him, he would always have to leave. I wish we could've had a lot more quality time together as I had grown up, but the visits we did have are times I'll cherish forever. That visit during my trip to his house was the best visit of them all though. It was going to be hard to say goodbye in the morning when I'd hit the road again toward Bangor, Maine. The next day, I told him I'd be back again to visit, and next time, I'd have my little boys with me. He knew as well as I did I wasn't going to give up on getting my kids back, and I'd do whatever it took to make sure they were safe again. I promised him I'd be back, and it's a promise I intend to keep.

CHAPTER XII: NIGHTCALL

When I pulled into Bangor, Maine it was just something different. This was the town that Derry was based on from Steven King's novel about the killer clown, *IT*. The whole world was finally starting to catch on to how good of a book it was. Everybody came a little late to that party, though. I'd been reading Stephen King's books forever by that point, but it was the old *IT* TV movie from the nineties that got me into his books.

I kept picturing Pennywise, the dancing clown, while I crossed an old, crackled bridge running over a creek; Pennywise wasn't there, but my fears still were. Those kids from that movie felt like my friends when I was a little boy. Even though I was scared out of my wits watching it, in a way, I wasn't terrified, not how I usually was, because I wasn't just a loser all by myself anymore, but I was a part of the Loser's Club. I knew from the start of the film I was one of them.

What was so special to me about watching movies with other kids in them was I could make myself feel like I was a part of that group, like the Loser's Club on the screen. I didn't have to worry about anybody making fun of me or feeling like I didn't belong. I could follow the whole story through and through as one of them, even if I wasn't in the movie. I was just the invisible kid on the screen in my head. Sort of like a ghost, but I wasn't the mean clown Pennywise stalking them around. I was just another little boy like they were and in my mind, me rooting them on helped them win in the end, and it made me feel good because it made me feel like I was apart of something after all.

When I had to deal with my own monsters that stalked around in the dark at night, the TV wasn't on anymore, and the Loser's Club wasn't there. It was just me down in the basement, lying in my bed, peering through the darkness that had a faint glow to it from the little moonlit windows resting atop the crest of the underground walls. I didn't want to keep my eyes open, but anytime I'd close them, it felt like something or *someone* was down there—approaching with light, grinding footsteps across the sandstone floor.

It had to have been the old woman down there with me in the dark again. She was mean and menacing, and she would speak with a sharp, shrill voice in words I couldn't understand. I couldn't move when her sharp whispering started as it did before. My legs were numb, I couldn't even run, but I knew she was getting closer. I'd see her pale face again with that grinning smile peel its way through the shadows; I just knew it. I told myself *move, move, move your legs—you have to*. I couldn't. No matter what I would try to do, I was stuck. It wasn't until the toolbox hit the wall on the other side of the basement I found myself running up the steps in the blink of an eye, screaming as I had before. My stepdad would never believe me, but my mom eventually did.

I didn't want to tell her at first, though. That was when I was in the room upstairs. I shared that room with my little brother, Pavin. Everything was fine for a while. I didn't see a thing, but after my dad died is when I started to see *them*. At first, it wasn't *them* at all, just *him*. It was a little, dark-haired boy around my age at the time, who would show up in my room late at night. He didn't want to play with me, though, at least I don't think. He couldn't play with me even if he wanted to because his neck was caught in a rope hanging from the ceiling, right in front of the doorway. All he had was his underwear on, and his pale skin glowed from the street lights shining through the window of the other room behind him. His neck was too twisted, and the rope was too tight for him to get out of. He never even struggled. He just hung there with his eyes wide open. There was no escape for me, no matter how scared I was, and I didn't want to yell because I didn't want my stepdad to get mad at me again. After a while, I couldn't take it anymore. I had to tell my mom even if I didn't think she would believe me. Somebody had to help me.

On one car ride home late in the evening, my mom drove me back home from my aunt's farm, and I grew real quiet the whole ride because I knew all of what would be waiting for me back home. When I was out at my aunt's farm with my cousins Hannah and Jordan, we would have so much fun out there I would forget about all of the troubles at home. My aunt's farm was my new safe place after I lost my dad, and I always felt so drug down when I had to leave. Hannah and Jordan were my best friends, my only real friends, and I had to leave, but to make it even worse, I went back to that house where the boy was, and he wasn't my friend at all. My mom kept looking over at the blank stare I held while she drove, and she asked the same question she asked all the time after everything had happened with my dad; she said, "What's wrong, Hawke? Are you ok?"

I didn't reply right away. I was still afraid she wouldn't believe me, but that all-too-familiar voice seemed to say, *What are you more fearful of Hawke? Telling your mom about how afraid you are at night or that boy?* I had to tell her. I began slowly by saying, "Mom—do you believe in ghosts?"

Mom seemed surprised at first, and then she got a more serious look and said, "Well yeah—I mean, I guess. Why?"

I started to feel better about opening up to her after she said she believed. I replied, "There's a boy in my room at night."

Mom started probing me for more information on what exactly I talked about, eager to know more, and she asked, "What boy? There's another kid in the room with you and Pavin?"

I knew I had to spill the whole can of beans this time instead of just a few, and as I looked out of the passenger side window toward all the trees, I said, "Yeah—but he's not in there to play—he just hangs there staring at me all night long, and he never goes away."

Mom wasn't sure what to make out of it all at first, but she figured whatever went on, switching rooms would probably help me out the most. She still left my brother in there, which was sort of fucked, to be honest, but I wasn't too lucky either. The only available room was in the basement, which is where everything seemed to get worse. Years after we moved out of that house, Mom finally told me she knew what I saw in that house was real because a neighbor had told her a few months after we'd moved in a young boy had hung himself in one of the back rooms. I'm not sure if she told the neighbors I'd seen him; maybe it was best to keep that part of it all secret, but I didn't need my mom to tell me it all happened. I knew what I saw was real, and I'll probably never know why the boy did what he did, but I have a gut feeling it had something to do with the hag in the basement.

The horrors I'd experienced in that little house on Stewart Street back in Zanesville, Ohio, seemed to play in my head like a movie as I entered Bangor. It was like the town's atmosphere seemed to awaken those old, dead, and buried terrors I hadn't thought of in so long. I'm sure it didn't have anything to do with Bangor itself; it probably had more to do with the fact this was the old hometown of Stephen King, the master of horror some call him, even though he doesn't consider himself a horror writer at all.

It was hard for me not to associate what King had written in his novels with the town because, in many of his books, all of the horrors occur in a little town located in Maine. To my surprise, my anxiety wasn't as high as it had been before, and I felt a lot more relaxed after visiting with my Grandpa. Even if I'd just relived some of my own more terrifying moments mentally, I knew I wouldn't have to worry about any of the *things* I had seen as a kid. After all, it had been nearly ten years since the last time I saw one of—*them*. The last one I saw—that thing seemed to take its last shot at me when it came for me. I was only eighteen years old when the man with the hat appeared in my rearview on that dark highway. He, or it, whatever it was, almost killed me, but it didn't.

I finally reached my next Airbnb, though. It was a beautiful, blue, Victorian-style home—just my type of house. When I walked inside, a sigh of relief seemed to flow out of me. Finally, some much-needed space to myself.

I hadn't realized how much I needed it until I started to walk across the wooden floors and my footsteps echoed across the empty halls. It was a four-bedroom house, and there I was with it all to myself. As much as I wanted to relax and have a little quiet time, I itched to get more of a feel for the town. So I found a restaurant in Bangor's downtown area, and after driving all day, I wanted to go for a walk and stretch my legs a little. I could get a better feel of the atmosphere that way, plus Stephen King's house would be right along the way. When I walked toward the front door though, I caught something out of the corner of my eye in the window to the left making all of my mental sirens go off at once. My heart started to speed up and pound so hard within my chest as I slowly walked toward the window to get a better look.

This red-headed girl hung some clothes out to dry along some clotheslines in her backyard, and I started to think to myself, *Who the fuck still hangs clothes out to air dry like that anymore? How very odd*—but it wasn't the clothes pins snapping across the line driving me crazy; it was the girl.

She had these short light-blue jean shorts on, exposing some of the smoothest legs I'd ever seen, rounding their way up to her hips. Her long red hair bounced across her black tank top too. The wind blew a little, and she reached her hand back to brush her hair out of her face. As she turned, I caught a glimpse of a rosy cheek that had tiny little freckles dancing across it. Suddenly, she snapped completely toward me. My reflexes pulled me away from the window to the wall immediately right before she saw me. *Or did she see me?* I wasn't quite sure, but either way, I wasn't ready to talk to her yet. I didn't have all of what was required to do a successful button test.

Now, if you're wondering what the button test is, the first requirement is a button-down shirt—it is a must, and it is carried out like this. First, if you spot a chick from the window and manage to get her attention, you hold up a bottle of Malibu (not my first choice, but girls love it), and you undo your first button at the top. Now, if she continues to watch, go to the second button, but if she storms inside or away from the window, lock your doors and hunker on down somewhere because her husband might be loading up a shotgun and headed your way. If you get past the second button, however, and her look begins to grow more sinister in a sexy way, like she's ready to attack you, button-down, but keep your pants on, this is not a full-blown striptease. Next, you point to the bottle of Malibu, then her, and end it all with mouthing the words, *me and you*. It works every time or not a time at all because I've never actually done a button test before, but it sure did feel like a good idea to carry out in the future.

After I heard rosy red go back inside, I headed outside because I was almost sure she caught me creeping, and I didn't want to be confronted about it as soon as I popped out of the door. While I strolled down the street, I had images of the old *IT* miniseries running through my head again. I could see Bill Denbrough riding his trusty bike Silver down the road, and I could hear Mike Hanlon's voice in my head saying, *There's something wrong here in Derry*. I couldn't believe I was there where that wild story was inspired, and just a few blocks away was Stephen King's house.

I don't think he was home, but I wondered if he was as I stood at the iron gates of his home. It had a real gothic look to it with its deep blood-red color. Honestly, I'm not sure if you would call it Gothic or Victorian or maybe both; who knows, I'm not an architect, but with the two-story balcony seeming to connect both of the right and left towers, it was something that stood out as unique across the Bangor landscape.

While I stood there, a lady passed by me with a look spelling out, *Fuckin' tourist*, all across her face. People can be so mean. What a bitch.

The surrealism of the moment sunk in as I stood there a while longer, thinking to myself, *Wow, the guy that lives there is a real creator. He doesn't just write books, but he creates worlds and people within those worlds that sometimes feel more real than I do. He gives people a place to escape to through his words, and even though his tales* are full of horror, it's easier to face that than the true terrors of the real world. He's a master writer, and the more I think about his writing, the more inadequate my own feels, but I'll keep on trying to give it a go.

I continued my walk toward downtown after staring at King's house for probably a little too long. After all, I didn't want to get caught creeping again.

Along the way, I saw this wonderful pair of lovers that seemed like a match made in heaven, but they were arguing. Really bad. This chick sounded like she didn't smoke but ate cigarettes chased after her man after he slammed a screen door in her face. She said, "Fuck you, Tony! Go back to your old fuckin' whore, you rotten motherfucker! If you ever come back to my house, Tony—I swear, Tony! I'll bite your goddamn dick off!"

My peaceful evening stroll was halted immediately. I just stood there completely flabbergasted. *What the fuck was going on?*

I'm guessing his name was Tony—well, Tony was scrambling trying to get his car to start, and this chick was still coming for him, but somewhere she'd gotten a two by four, and this is when shit really started to get ugly.

As Tony continued to struggle to get his car to start, he yelled at the chick, "Now goddammit, Alice! You better get away from me with that stick of yours! I'm not fuckin' with you! I will skull drag your fuckin' ass!"

Alice charged toward Tony with her board and said, "Don't worry, ya lazy bastard! I ain't gonna hit you yet. I'm gonna hit that baby of yours that you're sittin' in first."

This chick swung that board like Babe Ruth and busted out this guy's headlight and screamed, "Try goin' back to your whore in this now, Tony! Ya rat bastard!"

All of a sudden, Tony jumped out of the driver's seat like a wild raccoon or something and yelled, "You're gonna get it now, bitch!"

But as soon as he charged her, she clipped Tony right across the head. Tony fell to the ground, and Alice swung the board on him again. I thought, *Goddamn, Tony's getting his ass whooped right now, and I'm not trying to be next.* I turned around the other way and bolted, but while Alice and Tony were still in hearing distance, I could've sworn I heard Alice say, "Now get your fuckin' ass up and get me a pack of Marlboros! I need me a fuckin' cigarette."

I was so glad I didn't get caught up in the middle of all that. It was so crazy and unexpected. It reminded me a lot of my own hometown Zanesville back in Ohio. Stuff like that would happen all the time. It didn't matter where you were; something crazy happened just about every day, especially in the South end of town. That's where my mom's side of the family lived, and I used to spend a lot of time at Grandma and Grandpa's house after school. Me and my grandpa Gene St. Clair would come across something every day we sat on the porch.

This one time, when I was around nine or something, I sat there reading one of my books, and Grandpa listened to some Al Green on his radio, and all of a sudden, the mood changed real quick. We both heard a, *Pop! Pop! Pop!* It was definitely gunshots, but it wasn't too close by, so we weren't really too worried about it; we were trying to see what was going on. A few minutes later, this dude with the biggest afro I've ever seen came running down the street like a deer, and then the police sirens started closing in. The cops boxed this guy in right at the corner by my grandparent's house. The police got out and pointed their guns at the guy and screamed, "Get on the ground right fuckin' now, dirtbag!"

The guy got on the ground alright—he was surrounded; he didn't have a choice. Later on, Grandpa and I found out the guy robbed one of the stores right up the street and tried to make off with like two hundred dollars, but that's just how it was. It was something every day. I could tell Bangor was a lot like Zanesville.

Once I got to Downtown Bangor, I figured I'd chill outside of this restaurant called Blaze for a little while—have a few drinks, sneak a smoke in, you know, if they told me I couldn't.

I approached the hostess and said, "Why hello, a table for one, please."

I couldn't tell if she smiled or not because she had a mask on, but she had really pretty green eyes. She replied, "Just you? Well, ok, here's your—wait a minute, are those your real eyes?"

She caught on. Of course, I wear contacts. I can't see a thing without them, but if I'm going to wear them, I'm going to wear them right. I just like wearing different colors. I wanted to play around a little bit, though. So I decided to pull out my extremely gentleman-like character that I call Kristoff. I replied, "Why, of course, they are, my dear. Your eyes are quite the dazzling color as well."

Her laugh was a little muffled behind her mask. I think she knew I was playing around, but she was a good sport about it. She replied, "Why, thank you. Aren't you quite the polite gentleman. Would you like me to show you toward your table, sir?"

I moved my hand up to twirl a mustache I didn't have and said, "Why indeed, madam; lead the way."

Once she led me to my table, she said, "Well, here you are, mister—what's your name?"

I had hoped she'd ask because I was ready to answer. I told her, "Alexander—Kristoff Alexander, to be more precise. I believe the name suits me quite well, and what would your name be, ma'am?"

It got her laughing, so I guess I did my job pretty well. She said, "Well, I am wearing a nametag, you know; my name's Sarah."

She laughed again and said, "You don't really talk that way, do you? I don't think that's your real name either."

She had me. I couldn't keep up the charade any longer. I replied, "No, I don't; you got me. I'm really just fucking around because I'm bored. I thought I had you there for a minute, though. My name's Hawke—you know, like the bird. I'm a travelin' man. Sort of traveling the whole country right now."

I couldn't tell if she was surprised or not. You know, because of the mask and all. She came back with, "Oh wow, that's amazing. How long are you going to be in Bangor?"

I replied, "Just for tonight and tomorrow night. Then I'm going to be headed my way out west toward the Ozarks. Are there any parties or anything going on around here tonight?"

Sarah replied, "No, not that I know of—but I have to get back out front. It was nice talking to you, though. Here's my Snap if you want to get ahold of me later while you're still in town."

It surprised me she offered her Snap first, but then I realized something. I wasn't that nervous at all while I talked to her. For most of my life, it's been so hard for me to communicate with other people and find common ground, but it seemed like I was getting better at it. I wondered; *Maybe I've only made myself believe that I wasn't a good talker this whole time.* I noticed the words came more effortlessly for me when I just went with the flow and didn't give a shit what came out of my mouth. Maybe that's been the key all along.

When the waitress came to take my order, I was more than ready for a drink. I told her, "You got any drinks that'd be big enough for me to dive into? It's been a pretty long day."

29 Palms

Once my drink finally came, the feel of the air began to take me over. I was swept up in the sight of the setting sun dimming its radiance beneath the clouds and past all the old-styled buildings strewn all around me. It sort of reminded me of the early nineteen hundreds from the way the buildings looked. There were old fire escapes etching their way across the old brick tapestry, and I'm not sure if there was an old-fashioned trolley there or not, but it sure felt like there should've been. I had one drink after another while I sat there, but for some reason, the cheerful mood I was in started to run away. That's the thing with alcohol; it's sort of like rolling the dice and opening up Pandora's Box; not sure what you might find or what might come out, but I started thinking about home a lot.

Not Alabama. No, Alabama could never be home to me, but Zanesville—yeah, that was home, or at least it seemed like it at one point. The town itself is pretty rundown and shitty, to tell you the truth, but that's where most of the people I love the most are. They say home is where the heart is, but I've never been sure where to let it rest.

There was a time before, when I felt like I really knew where home was without a shadow of a doubt, but that was all taken from me. Zanesville was home, but in a way, it's the place that broke my heart. I've thought so many times over the years, *What if my father would've never gone back to Zanesville? What if he would've just stayed in 29 Palms? Would it all have still happened? Or would it all have been different?* I didn't know. There's no way for me ever to know if things would've been different, if that night would've never happened at all.

CHAPTER XIII: ALWAYS & FOREVER

    I was so excited for my dad to pick me up that night. I rushed to get my favorite toys to take along with me even if Dad planned to surprise me with some new ones like he sometimes did. I'd get in the car, and he'd say, "How are you doing, buddy? I have a surprise waiting for you back home."

    I'd ask him with a burst of excitement, "What is it, Daddy?! Is it another small soldier?! Is it a Gorgonite?!"

    Dad and I had gone to the movies together, as we always had, to see the movie *Small Soldiers*, and it was my favorite movie at the time. My number one goal was to collect all of them, and even though my dad didn't have a lot of money to spare, he'd try to surprise me with a new one as often as he could.

That evening when he picked me up, he didn't look as happy and cheerful as he usually did. He had a stressed and torn look about him. It was a look I've seen over and over again in the mirror. I didn't know what it meant then, but I sure understand it now. He was in so much pain, I could just tell, and he did everything he could to hold himself together.

I knew what that look meant. When he had that type of look, it meant Christina wasn't at home again. That made me sad too. Even though I loved my dad with all of my heart and couldn't wait to see him, there were a lot of times I was more excited to see Christina than I was him. Everything seemed so much better when she was around.

When Christina was at home, Dad would be happy and smiling again, and he would be more in the mood to play with me when she was around. When she was there, we would have so much fun together. Sometimes, Dad would sit cross-legged on the floor right by her, and I'd get to sit in her lap while we played video games together. If I started to win, she would tickle me so I'd mess up, and then she'd let out that huge laugh of hers and say, "I got you!"

The three of us would have wrestling matches in my dad's room, and I'd launch into his arms with the strongest kick I could come up with, only for him to catch me before it landed, and send me launching back every time. Christina would get ahold of me then. I'd laugh and wrestle back with her at first, but I loved it more when she'd hold me, so I wouldn't fight her for too long.

She'd always make my dad and me laugh all the time. She made me happy, and she made him happy. Most of the time, when we'd watch movies together, I'd always sit closer to Christina so she could stroke my hair and give me those surprise kisses of hers. Still, sometimes Dad would lay with her on the couch and hold her real tight with a look of real love and warmth pouring across his face, and just like that, all those sad looks of his would go away. It seemed like everything changed after my baby sister was born, though.

All the other kids would always talk about the little brothers and sisters they had at school, but I didn't have a little brother or sister to play with back at home, so I devised a plan. I went to my mom and Norm and asked them for a little brother, and then I went to my dad and Christina and asked them for a little sister. Not too long after, mom and Norm gave me my little brother Pavin and Dad and Christina gave me my little sister Josci. It was just like magic, and I felt like wishes really could come true. I loved them both, but they weren't old enough to play yet, and all they ever wanted to do was cry. Everybody kept telling me, "Well, Hawke, you have to give them time to grow so they can run around and play like you do. They're still babies."

I couldn't wait for them to get older so we could go on adventures together, but after Josci was born, Christina wasn't home as much as she used to be, and most of the time, it was just Dad and Josci at home when I'd get to visit. I knew Christina wouldn't be there this time either, but I really hoped in my heart she'd come back home so I'd get to see her again.

It was freezing on that January night, and I had to bundle up in one of my big coats to stay warm, even though it would start to get hot in Dad's car from the heater. Christmas really wasn't that long ago, and snow was everywhere. Dad's house was in this big white building where a bunch of other people lived that had doors you could walk in where their homes were too, but Dad's home had a number one on it, and I figured that was because we had the best house in the building.

Dad got Josci out first and took her inside, then he helped me out of the car so I wouldn't slip on any ice as we walked inside. After we both took our coats off, I rushed for the PlayStation because I didn't have one at my mom's house and Dad had a game called *Crash Bandicoot* where you played as this big goofy-looking fox, and you had to jump over all kinds of stuff and in some boxes peaches came out of them. I planned on getting as many peaches as possible because I figured the more you could get, the closer you came to winning.

Dad kept dialing numbers on his cell phone and putting it up to his ear. He sold cell phones for a living, and he told me that in the future, everyone would have one, and they would become so much better than what they were. He wouldn't even need the phone in his car anymore. I liked that car phone a lot, though. It reminded me of the secret agent movies Dad and I would watch all the time that had Arnold Schwarzenegger in them.

Dad had finally gotten ahold of whoever he had been trying to call on the phone, and he looked relieved but panicked all at the same time, and he asked with a sad, trembling voice, "Where are you?"

It looked like he was going to cry after he'd asked, and I knew it had to be Christina he talked with on the phone. I started back to playing *Crash Bandicoot* again, but I kept missing the jumps, and the little fox would just die over and over again, and each time that happened, I'd start banging the controller on the floor as I screamed. While he was on the phone, Dad said to me, "Hey! Hey! Hey! Don't do that! Do you want to watch a movie or something?"

Lion King was my other favorite movie, besides *Small Soldiers*, so I turned the PlayStation off and slid *Lion King* into the VCR.

Dad kept pacing back and forth across the living room as he talked on the phone. I saw him stop to remove his glasses, and he placed his hand on his forehead with tears in his eyes and said, "Why don't you want to come home? We can work all of this out. I know that we can." Then he paused for a minute and just stared off into somewhere else it seemed like. Then he said, "You know I love you, right? I don't understand why you won't come home. Just please come home. I love you. You know that, right?"

I didn't like to look at my dad when he was sad like that because it made me sad too, and Josci started screaming as Dad went on and on on the phone. He picked her up with his free hand as he held the phone to his ear and rocked her in his arms to stop her from crying. After a while, Dad said, "Ok, you're almost here?" He shook his head and said, "No, I haven't checked the mail yet. Ok, I'll see you in a minute."

He hung up the phone and placed Josci back in her pack-n-play. I can remember him in that moment so vividly; his hands pulling that leather jacket of his tight around his shoulders and tying his boots up really quick. He stared at the door for a minute, almost like he thought about something, but then his face turned to me. It's hard to describe the expression he had on his face. It almost looked like he was on the verge of crying, but he had hope resting in his eyes too. I could see it. He said to me, "Look after your little sister, Hawke. I'll be right back."

With a rush, he turned the doorknob and went outside. I had this weird feeling come over me after he left; there was just something in the air that night. It was as if when he walked away, I felt outside of myself. I don't know why or where that feeling came from, but it felt like a longing; that's the first time I felt the abyss. I wanted to go outside with him so I could see Christina too, but he told me to stay inside and look after Josci, so that's what I had to do.

It seemed like Dad was gone too long to be back as fast as he said he would be, but then I heard the screaming outside. It wasn't two people shouting at one another, but it was the type of horrifying screams that go through your flesh and tear at the bone, rattling everything inside of you with terror until that's the only thing you can feel anymore. It was crippling—those screams crippled me.

Josci started screaming too. I shuffled my way across the carpet toward her and just sat by her pack-n-play with my toys. I didn't know what to do, but Chip Hazard and Archer would protect us.

Dad told me to protect her, but I didn't know how, and I didn't know what was going on. I wondered if my dad was ok, and I wondered where he was. I didn't know who it was letting out those awful screams outside. The *Lion King* just ended, but I was too afraid to put another movie in. The song "Can You Feel the Love Tonight" by Elton John played along with the credits as the screams started coming closer and closer to the door. Then the door swung open, and Christina's friend scrambled for the phone to call 911. I jumped up and said, "Where's my daddy?"

Christina's friend, Tina, looked at me with a twisted look of panic on her face and held out her shaking palm toward me. She pulled her hand back toward her mouth to muffle the words she couldn't say as tears of panic poured out of her eyes. She scared me, and I didn't want to look at her. I just wanted to find my dad. I ran for the door to pull it open to get to him as Tina screamed, "No! No! Don't go out there!"

All I can remember next about that night was staring at the TV's blue screen, and then my stepdad Norm rushing in and scooping me up into his arms. He held his mouth up to my ear and said, "Come on, buddy, everything's going to be ok. I'm going to get you out of here. Alright?"

I was so glad to see him. I put my head on his shoulder and collapsed into his arms. It was hard for me to make out all the words I wanted to say. It was like I was broken. I just kept saying, "Are you—Are you—you're here. You're here. You're here to save me."

Norm didn't answer, but as he carried me outside, I saw the ambulance's flashing lights and the police cars everywhere. I didn't see my dad anywhere.

On our way toward the car, I saw mom talking to one of the policemen, waving her hands around with tears all over her face. She had a look of horror when she saw me in Norm's arms. Norm said to Mom, "I'm taking Hawke with me to Rob's mom's house. Somebody has to tell her; she has to know."

We drove out to Grandma's house, and I can't remember too much along the way, only pulling up in Grandma's driveway, and then Norm driving me to the hospital.

When we got to the Good Samaritan Hospital in Zanesville, too much happened way too fast for my little mind to comprehend. I went into a room that looked darker than it could've been in my memory, with this older woman who looked like a doctor. She led me to a chair and sat down in front of me, and said, "Are you doing ok, little guy?"

I didn't know what to say—all I could do was nod. She started telling me I was about to see my dad, and I could feel a rush of excitement well up inside of me, but then she said, "He's not going to be able to talk to you, though. He's not doing too well right now, but we're doing everything we can to make him better, ok?"

When I finally got to make my way to see him, I saw everybody there along the way. Grandma, Aunt Teresa, all of the family was there, and somebody had said Grandpa Tom was on his way too. When we got back to where my father was, someone pulled back the curtain.

29 Palms

He lay there with a white sheet pulled up to about the middle of his chest with this oxygen mask over his face. I can remember hearing him breathe through it as the heartbeat machine's beeping sound continuously went off in a rhythmic pattern. His breath was shallow. He was there, but not like he used to be.

I walked up to him to grab his hand to let him know I was with him. Even though we couldn't laugh and talk with one another like we used to, it still felt great to feel that warmness coming off his hand. I stood there, hoping by some miracle he'd turn his head toward me and open his eyes to smile at me again, but he didn't. I never got to see that smile of his again. The closest I'd ever get to it would be from pictures, like that one of him in 29 Palms.

He was only thirty-one years old when he passed away. Everything seemed to be like a daze for a while, even at the funeral. Christina was there to open the door for us as we approached the church to enter the service. His funeral was an open casket one, and I can remember standing there staring at him, lying there in his Marine dress blues with his head shaved. He didn't have his "high and tight" haircut anymore. I didn't even want to look at him. He didn't look like my father anymore, even though I knew he was.

During the graveside service at the cemetery, I had to sit next to Christina in the front row facing my father's casket. They wouldn't allow my mom to sit up there in the front row with me, which I couldn't understand at all at the time. At the hospital, as my mother stood over my father crying, she threw her arms across him and screamed, "If you wake up, I'll take you back, Rob! I'll take you back, I promise!" I felt like mom deserved to sit up there in the front row. After all, she was his first love.

Everybody told me it was Christina's fault my father was gone, and I knew that as I sat there. Everyone said she'd ran him over multiple times with her car out in the apartment parking lot. He'd gone out there to talk to her, to try to get her to stay with him, but she didn't want him anymore. Did she plan to kill him? Only she knows that. Accident or not, the result is still the same.

After Christina and I sat there together watching my father's Marine brothers fold up the American flag, they walked over and handed that flag right to me. Christina burst out into tears because Marine tradition states a fallen brother's flag is supposed to go to the wife, but in this case, it went to me, my father's son. I felt a flicker of happiness well up within me as I sat there holding that flag in my hands. I knew my dad was special, whether he was a Marine or not, but when they handed that flag to me, it made me feel special too.

Nothing was ever the same after that. All of my father's family made me a promise at the hospital they would be there for me, but few of them kept the promise. I could only spend time with Grandpa Tom when he'd make his annual trips to Ohio. My Aunt Teresa and Uncle Matt had tried to be there as much as they could be, but they were wrestling with a lot of their own grief at the time. After all, they both lost their big brother that had always been there for them.

I spent as much time as I could with my dad's mom, my Grandma Reese, though. It was through her I got to know who my father was and what he was really about. I'd spend all day with her on the porch listening to her tell me stories about him. There was one that always stuck with me that we still talk about to this day. It was about a dream of his he told her about. He wanted to build a log cabin on a hill to the back of her property where he could get a good view of the sunset. Sunsets always bring out what's running the most in my heart. Maybe that's why he loved them too?

Josci was allowed to be included in our lives for the first four years of her life. Christina lost custody of her after she was sentenced to six months in jail for what she did. Josci ended up in the care of Christina's mother, who ended up making it hell on Earth for my grandma every time she would go to pick up Josci for visits. She told my grandmother once, "I just want to let you know that my daughter meant to kill your son. I just thought you should know that." It was on Thanksgiving of all days, but grandma still got Josci.

    That was another reason why I loved going out to Grandma's. I'd get to see my little sister out there. I'd get to play with her in Grandma's yard just like I'd always wanted to. We were two little kids playing together like nothing had ever happened. I knew she couldn't remember any of it, but I did. She was there with me in the room with all of the screams. The last thing my dad told me was to look after her and to protect her, but eventually, she was taken out of our lives too. It would be another eight years before I'd get to see her again, and by that time, she was twelve years old. Only she didn't live with her grandmother anymore. She lived with Christina.

CHAPTER XIV: I CAN'T FIGHT THIS FEELING

After my eighth beer, I figured enough time had passed. I couldn't stop thinking about Brooke in that empty house while I lay on the couch flipping through the channels trying to find something good to watch. I didn't plan on drinking at all that night, but with the mixed drinks I had in downtown Bangor, along with the to-go drinks I double fisted on my walk back to the house, I figured why not attack the case of beer the host had left for me in the fridge. What's the worst that could happen? Me getting in my feelings was the worst that could happen, and I did. So I carried on to drunk text Brooke in my alcohol-infused vulnerability. I shot a text through the ether that said, *Can you make me a promise?* It didn't take Brooke long to reply at all.

What am I promising to?

The truth is, I started thinking about death. At this point, I didn't really want to die anymore. I began to fear it. I knew Brooke was one of the few people I could be my true self with. I replied, *I was just thinking a lot I guess, but if my boys ever come to you when they are older asking questions, tell them all the truth you can about me. I act for everybody else, but I've let you see a fraction of who I really am. I'd rather them know me than the characters I play.*

Well, if that ever happens, I promise. You show them your real self every time you're with them, though. They know your heart!

She was right. I knew she was the best person to text when I needed someone to talk to. Her words had a curing effect. I started opening up to her about why this promise was important to me. *I hope they get the chance too; I really do. I guess I just worry about something happening to me and people not really knowing who I am. It scares me a lot. The person that knows me the best took the most from me, so I'd never want them to go there to find anything out. They will know who you are because I talk about you in my writings.*

Well, maybe one day you'll tell me about the one that broke you. Maybe they will, who knows what the future holds. You have writings? I think it would be nice to have someone that looks up to me or has that kind of trust in me.

Little did she know, it wasn't a woman I'd been romantic with I talked about. It was Christina who was on my mind when I said that. I wasn't ready to tell Brooke about what happened with my father. I never talk about it with anyone, so I decided to go into my own writings instead. *I know I really think a lot of you, if that means anything, and yes, I journal quite a lot. I don't keep why I'm broken secret for any kind of reason. I just don't want anyone to think I'm throwing a pity party for myself.*

What do you write about when you write me in?

I started to panic a little at that text. Could I really show her what I've written about her? *It's kind of heavy, and I don't want to scare you away.*

I don't think you will. I know you're a passionate person. I promise, no judgment.

She obviously really wanted to see what I wrote. *I just took a screenshot of the most recent ,so I'll send it. It's just a part of my journal and there is a lot more.* The entry said:

What I loved the most about Concord was the wildflower garden. I took so many pictures for Brooke there, and I held on to what I'd said about sending her pictures everywhere that I went. When I woke up before we went to Lexington, I immediately went out into Grandpa's backyard and took a picture of these beautiful purple flowers that grew on one of his trees in the back yard. As I was sending her the pictures I took of the wildflowers, I wasn't sure if she really liked them or not. It might be my own doubt getting to me, but I'm just afraid of being rejected again. It's like this whole trip she's been on my mind so much, and when I reach the end of this journey, I really do hope she finds it in her heart to give me a chance. She's the most beautiful person inside and out that I could ever hope for, and in my heart I know I'll never be able to do better than her. I just wish I didn't feel this way and I could just blow her off, but I cant. She's just unforgettable.

Brooke replied minutes later with a heart emoji and said, **Thank you for being so vulnerable.**

Surprised because I wasn't expecting to ever hear from her again, I replied, *Why do you say that?*

Because no guy would ever share something like that.

No, there isn't any guy out there that would, but I did. I decided to jump right in and tell her how I felt—to a degree anyway. *I just worry a lot. My brother tries to tell me how to talk to people, but I'd rather just be myself. If that's not good enough, I'd rather not. I really* meant what I said, though. I think a lot of you, and out of this whole trip, you've been on my mind the most. I see so many beautiful things throughout each day, but none of them top you. It's like the most beautiful things I see I know you would love it, and I wish you were here with me. That's why I send pictures, but I refrain from doing so sometimes because I don't want to get my hopes up too much.

You shouldn't have to change yourself to attract someone. The right people will like you for who you are. I am very flattered. Honestly, I really am. I'm just not ready for that part of my life yet. And I'm not just saying it to you; I'm not talking to anyone in a sense of a relationship, and I don't plan to. I don't see the connection between you sending me pictures and getting your hopes up? I appreciate the pictures and wanted you to send them as much as you wanted just so I could see what you're seeing. I'm so happy that I could help you find yourself, and I wouldn't want anything less for you. I'm just trying to be you're #1 supporter in this travel journey.

She told me that time and time again before. Like every other time, she would say that I started thinking, *Why isn't she ready? Your one of the first images that come to my mind every morning and you're in my dreams when I sleep. Why does it have to be this way?* But I couldn't say that to her. I couldn't go that far. If she wasn't ready to be with me, that was fine because, in my heart, I knew whenever the day came where she was ready, well—that would probably be the best day of my life.

Brooke was the only person I wanted to share my journey with, and I loved having her support. I really did, so I replied, *The way my mind works, sometimes I start to think that there's something wrong with me and that's why I can't seem to find what I'm looking for. Plus with the wisdom that you have, I forget what age you are sometimes. You think like a person even older than me, so sometimes it's easy to overlook, but I appreciate your support a lot; I really do. Your kind of support is like none other. When you encounter something phenomenal* like you, something so rare, it's often hard to find a way to interpret, but I'll continue to share things with you along the way. It's made the journey not seem so lonely.

It's okay! I understand. There's nothing wrong with you at all. You're just a very passionate person, and that's very rare these days. It's not a flaw at all. Always hold on to who you really are, no matter how heartless people can be. Always remain true to yourself. Like I told you before, sometimes when you look too hard, that's what prevents it from coming to you. You've got to embrace every page, every chapter of your life journey. Not just the "good" parts.

Every one of her words spoke directly to my heart. You always know the right things to say; that's one of the reasons I admire you so much. This journey is really teaching me a lot. I just hate the thought of it ending because I don't really have anything to come back to in Mobile. I'll just have to see what else I learn along the way. Maybe the road ahead will give me just what I need; I don't know.

You're just really overthinking it to an unhealthy point. I guess I just don't have that desire to always be looking. Sure, I notice when a guy is attractive, but I don't really have that desire to think "oh, maybe he's the one." I actually want to be alone, lol, but I also understand your age and being at the point of wanting to settle down with someone. I know Mobile literally has nothing to offer, so that doesn't help much, but you are right, maybe you'll find where you belong on this journey. You've really gotta focus on yourself during this solo trip, though. No more "if only I had someone to share it with"; more of, "look what I can accomplish by myself. I have such an amazing life." When you're on your next hike to the top of a mountain I want you to take a deep breath when you get to the top and just look out into the landscape with a smile. Really take in the beauty. No pictures, no distractions. Just you and nature's beauty. Just be with yourself in that moment. Feel the peace run through your body. And tell yourself

out loud, "I'm going to be okay." But you've gotta really believe it as you say it. Keep repeating it until you believe it.

Her words sang a song of inspiration through my heart. Your words are so breathtaking; I'm not even sure what to say. I feel like you can read my mind sometimes, and I really do overthink things too much. I guess that's one of my biggest downfalls. I'm going to try and do just what you said so I can see if it will really help. It seems like it works perfect for you. You have the most beautiful heart I've ever encountered in a person. You have helped me out so much when it comes to how I look at things you really have.

It helps me 100% every time. Even saying it in the mirror helps my peace of mind when things get hard. Thank you for all the words of adoration, I appreciate it a lot. It makes me happy to help people.

I put my phone down on the coffee table after reading that text with a blushing smile on my face and a song singing in my heart. I started thinking: *Brooke inspires me so much even when she shoots me down. She might not be ready for a relationship, but I'd rather be her friend than not have her in my life at all. Her words really do sing a song in my heart.* With that thought, I drifted off into my dreams and prepared myself to make Brooke's words of encouragement a reality.

Acadia National Park in Maine was and still is one of the most beautiful places you can visit on planet Earth; through the bright green of the rolling hills and the jutting mountains rolling across ancient streams, it's a true reflection of beauty as one mountain looks upon another across the reflective waters of Jordan Pond. I looked into that pond and saw my face among the backdrop of a brightly lit sky in those crystalline waters. I'd been atop Cadillac Mountain earlier that day, and even though Brooke told me to take in all of the beauty atop a mountain, Jordan Pond seemed like a more suitable place to carry out the song of inspiration she had planted in my heart.

I sat on the edge of the pond and took in the view to obtain the perfect image of it all within my mind as I closed my eyes to internalize all that beauty within myself. I could feel it all flowing within as the wind blew and the birds sang. In my mind, I watched the waters ripple as the elegance of all that was around me poured into my heart. I could feel it. It felt like I was a part of everything around me. I started to think about all the times I felt like I didn't have a place in this world, and that all-too-familiar voice came to me and said, *You do have a place here, Hawke. You just have to believe it in your heart. You've never been alone as much as you think, you know? I never went anywhere.*

I opened my eyes to look back across that pond, and I said, "I do. I do have a place here, and I really do belong." That all-to-familiar voice came back and said, *This whole time, you've been searching for your place in the world, but there isn't any one place that's your home. This whole place is. The whole world is your home.* That feeling never lasts forever. I felt it in my heart on that day, though.

I had that song playing in my heart all the way back to Bangor, but while I drove along, though, I saw something I hadn't seen the day before, a beautiful classic car. I slowed down to get a better look at it. It was a dark blue '69 Chevy Caprice, with hideaway lights, that appeared to be for sale. I sped up and thought to myself, *Damn, I've always wanted a car just like that, but whoever is selling it probably wants twenty-five grand or more for that thing.* Then the rather active all-too-familiar voice said, *Hawke if you don't go back and look at that car, you're going to regret it for the rest of your life. Doesn't it remind you a lot of the Torino?*

My dad had an old 1969 Ford Torino he had left to me. It was being kept at my grandma's house back in Ohio, still waiting to be restored. *But this car,* I thought, *this car looks like it's already restored.* I pulled a U-turn immediately and went back to look at that old '69.

As soon as I pulled into the lot, I hopped out of my truck and bolted toward that '69 Chevy like I spotted a million dollars. I scrambled around and around the car. It had a graphic on the trunk looking like the Kraken from the stories of old; only it had the skull of death above its tentacle arms. The interior looked just as great as the outside did, but I couldn't spot a for-sale sign. I yelled, "Well, where the fuck is the sign at?!"

Then I saw it on the driver's side window I had passed I don't know how many times. The sign said, *seventy-five hundred or best offer*, with a phone number under it. I was in so much shock over the asking price that I felt like Medusa herself had turned me to stone. When I came to, I dialed the number immediately. The phone rang once, then again, then again. As sweat started to trickle down my forehead, I started thinking, *Come on, come on, pick up the phone. Pick up the fuckin' phone, man.* Then all of a sudden, there was an answer in an old Boston accent, "Yello."

I replied immediately, "Yeah—uh—hi, there—umm— I was calling about the '69 Chevy that you have for sale. Does it run and everything?"

The Boston accent replied through the phone, "Oh yeah, she runs alright. It's got a new battery, a new fuel pump; I put a three-fifty engine in there when I got it, so that's almost brand new. Oh yeah, she's a real cruza."

My heart was damn near pulsating through my chest at that point, but I still wanted to haggle a little bit on the price. Grandpa Gene taught me how to bargain with folks when we'd go about town together when I was little. So I shot back, "Ok—ok, that sounds really good. Will you take six grand for it?"

Mr. Boston accent replied with an unsatisfactory tone, "No, absolutely not. Sixty-five hundred is the lowest that I'll go."

I was damn near doing cartwheels around the car, "Ok, you got a deal. You want me to bring a check or—how do you prefer me to pay you?"

Mr. Boston accent replied, "Cash. Bring me sixty-five hundred cash tomorrow, and the car is yours. The name's Jimmy, by the way."

I jumped up in the air and screamed, "Ok, alright!! Sounds great, man!! My name's Hawke. See you tomorrow, Jimmy!"

After the phone call ended, I stood there staring at that car in complete disbelief. How in the hell did I get so lucky just to be driving along, whistling away down the road, and run smack dab into what appeared to be a damn near fully restored '69 Chevy Caprice—in Stephen King's hometown of all places! Was this really happening? And then reality started to set in. I knew I had the sixty-five hundred in the bank to get the car, but what if this guy just planned to kick my ass and take the money? Was this deal too good to be true? I thought, *Fuck it, if I get robbed, I get robbed, but I'm going to do everything I can to head out west in this car tomorrow.*

CHAPTER XV: RACING IN THE STREET

    I felt guilty after I handed over the keys to the Frontier to the attendant at the Enterprise. That little blue truck had taken me so far. Even though it was just a rental car, we started the journey together. We had been through so much and came so far. It's kind of funny feeling like you made a friend out of a vehicle, but I didn't care; that's just how I felt about the Frontier. I thought to myself, *Well, friend, I guess this is where we part ways. We've come a long way together, but who knows, maybe another fellow will come along and take you out for another spin around the country. I sure hoped somebody would.*

    I couldn't believe I managed to get the cash out to buy the '69. Despite Jimmy telling me to bring cash for the car, I couldn't think of a way to withdraw sixty-five hundred in cold hard greenbacks because my bank was a southern one, and the closest branch was nearly over a thousand miles away. I couldn't withdraw that much from an ATM; Wal-Mart wouldn't produce a money order that held the lump sum of dough I needed either. The lady at the counter said, "Ok, let me get this straight. You mean to tell me that you want to put over six thousand dollars on a money order?"

Of course, I did. I mean, it's not like I lied. I told her, "Well—uh—yeah, pretty much. Sixty-five hundred to be exact. I'm tryin' to get this car, you know? And I really can't leave town without it."

The customer service lady looked concerned when she replied, "You're trying to buy a car? From a dealership or just a person?"

I wasn't sure why she wanted to know, but she was an old lady, you know? So I had to be polite when I replied, "Yeah, and I'm just gettin' it off some guy who's selling it on the side of the road. He seems cool enough to me, I guess, and the car is one hell of a ride. I just gotta have it, really."

The customer service lady looked so bewildered and shocked. She didn't say anything at first; there was just an awkward silence between us for a while. I didn't know whether to pull out my phone and check the book or what, but eventually, after our staring contest was over, she said, "You really need to be careful doing that. You really seem like a good kid, and I wish I could help you, but we don't do money orders for that much. I'm sorry."

I was so distraught walking out of Wal-Mart. I told myself, *I can't leave without that car. If I have to rob a bank, I guess that's what I'll have to do. Can't be too hard to do since everyone's into wearing masks now anyway.*

I didn't want to go to jail, though, so that was out. Then I started thinking, *Well, you could always sell yourself for sex*—but that thought left my mind as quickly as it came. I never really liked the idea of becoming a male prostitute; it's always seemed very distasteful. Then the perfect idea came; *Hey, why don't you just try to go to a bank around here and see if they will withdraw the money from your card?*

The plan was set, and I drove off toward the nearest bank. Along the way, I thought even more to myself, *Wow, I was really about to sell myself for sex so that I could get a car? Maybe I do have a few problems I need to work through.*

I called the First Key Bank right down the road to see if they'd withdraw my funds for me so I could finally calm my nerves with some cash in my hands. When the bank answered, they said, "First Key Bank, how may I help you?"

I answered, "Yeah, hi man, what's up?—um—could you help me out with something?"

The teller was kind of hesitant. He said, "Yeah—sure. What do you need help with today?"

I had so much adrenaline pumping through my system I probably sounded like some madman who'd been on a speed binge for days. I couldn't help it. I really wanted that car. I tried the best I could to sound more professional when I replied, "Well, sir, you see— I am facing the deal of a lifetime at the present moment, but unfortunately, I have found myself in quite the predicament. I have money, but most of my investments are locked up in a branch that is over one thousand miles away. Timing is imperative. Is there any way that you could help me withdraw six thousand and five hundred dollars off just my debit card?"

There was a long pause and then a deep breath from the teller. He finally replied, "Wow, sounds like you've gotten yourself into a—well—quite a situation. Sure we can try to give it a shot. You can't come in, though, because of our Covid regulations. So you'll have to pull up to the drive-thru, and we'll get it all figured out."

I was relieved beyond what anybody could ever imagine, but once I was at the drive-thru speaker, the teller said, "Well, sir, I've tried your card twice, and it declined. You can try to call your bank, but I can only try it one more time."

My mind started to ramble, as I thought, *I told the bank to raise my limit to at least eight thousand, and here we go again. They're fucking me all over again just like they did in Savannah.* I was as polite as I possibly could be with Sharon at the bank. After she gave the green light that everything was good, I just had to make sure. I asked her, "Ok, everything is straight now? Are you sure?"

Sharon laughed on the phone and said, "Yep, you should be all set. So you're buying a car, and you're in Maine—what are you doing up there anyway?"

I couldn't help laughing at that. After all, I just decided to hop in my car basically out of nowhere, and a weekend in Savannah turned into an odyssey across the whole country. Bursting with excitement and trying not to laugh, I told her on the phone, "Well, I guess I decided to go ahead and travel the whole country. I'm going all the way out west after this."

Sharon replied shocked, "Really? Wow, that's amazing. Well, you have fun out there, Hawke, and be careful."

I laughed into the phone, "Well, thanks, I'll try not to get into too much trouble. Later on."

It was now or never. The moment of truth was upon me. I clicked the button for the man in the speaker to appear and said, "Ok, it's a go. Let's do this."

After he agreed to give my card another go, I could feel pure adrenaline galloping like a herd of steads all through me, and I started to think, *If this card doesn't work this time, then it's bang, bang.*

Guess I'll have to rob a bank after all. The man in the speaker came through again and said, "I'm sending the cash out. Have a great day, Mr. Smith."

When I snatched the cash and started counting it, I felt thankful that the transaction was through a speaker versus being in the bank because I probably would've hopped over the counter like a lunatic and screamed, "Group hug, everybody! Come on, don't be shy! Everybody love everybody! Especially you over there—yeah, you the blonde! I'm about to get a '69 Chevy!"

There wasn't a red light that could stop me. I was so excited. While I sped down the road, this guy honked his horn at me and screamed, "Hey, asshole! What the fuck is your problem?! Huh?!"

I didn't care. I honestly didn't even see the light turn red, plus he was in his truck, so why did he even care? I just waved and smiled. It was time to get my dream car.

After I handed in the keys to my excellent traveling companion, the beloved Nissan Frontier, an Uber picked me up and took me to Jimmy's, where the car of my dreams waited.

Along the way, I started thinking, *If this guy knew I had sixty-five hundred cash on me, he would probably smack the shit out of me and just kick me out of his car,* but I assured myself; *He doesn't know, though. I haven't even said anything about buying a car.* I bid the Uber driver a friendly farewell and stood there as he drove off, with nothing but a red duffel bag in one hand and a backpack in the other. Here was the real moment of truth.

I couldn't find Jimmy at first. I even called him ahead of time to tell him I was on my way, but apparently, he spotted me running around his building like a speed demon. Suddenly, out of nowhere, an older guy who reminded me a lot of Whitey Bulger from the movie *Black Mass* came out to meet me. Jimmy walked toward me with a grin on his face, and a hand reached out to shake mine and said, "Hi ya there, pal. You Hawke?"

Even though I started to get nervous over the fact the guy looked like he came out of the movie *Goodfellas*, I still tried to keep my cool. Whatever happened would happen. I replied, "Yeah! Hey there, Jimmy; nice to meet you. Well, I got the cash if you're ready for me to get that '69 off your hands. I wanna look it all over first, though."

I thought, *Well that was a dumb response. I told him I already have the cash, and I was damn near ready to leave in the car before I even looked under the hood. Well, this guy looks like an old mafia guy, so he's probably going to shoot me in the head next and just take the money. The trip ends on Cold Case Files then. It was a nice run while it lasted, I guess,* but Jimmy replied with a grin on his face, "Ok, come on over here. I'll pop the hood for ya."

It looked great under the hood, even though I'm a complete idiot when it comes to anything mechanical; everything looked to be fine to me, though. After checking out what was under the hood, I followed Jimmy toward where the trunk was. He popped it open and said, "See right there, pal. It's gotta big trunk. I'd say you could fit about four or five bodies back there if you really wanted to."

Yep, Cold Case Files here we go. Jimmy closed the trunk with a laugh and handed me the keys after signing the car over to me.

When I climbed into that '69 Chevy for the first time, I gripped the wheel and was just in complete shock. *Was this really happening?* I probably looked like a little kid at Christmas when I looked at Jimmy standing there at the driver's side window.

Jimmy said, "So where are ya headed off to first? You driving her home?"

All the possibilities just kept running through my head. I couldn't believe it. I replied, "Nope I'm far from heading home. I'm going to make my way out to California. At least that's the plan anyway. Think it'll make it?"

Jimmy looked apprehensive. I could tell he didn't think it was a good idea. He said, "Well, the plates aren't good on it anymore. I just put 'em on there so there'd be something back there. You'd do best to get it registered along the way." He looked out toward the road for a minute and said, "All the way out to California, huh? What's all the way out there for ya?"

I just shrugged my shoulders and said, "I don't really know to be honest. I mean—my dad used to live out there, and I've always wanted to see where he used to live, I guess."

Jimmy replied, "Where's about in California?"

I told him, "29 Palms. You know, where the Marines usually station at? My dad used to be a Marine back in the eighties, and that's where he used to be stationed at."

Jimmy paused for a minute, like he understood the rest of it without even asking. He grinned again and said, "Used to be? Once a Marine, always a Marine. There ain't any used to be."

Jimmy looked out toward the road again. He appeared to be thinking about something. I just wasn't sure what, but then he looked back to me and said, "Now remember, you're gonna have to get another starta down the road. I already called Mike down there at the auto shop; he'll take good care of ya." Jimmy continued, "She's a cruza now. She might not make it as far as your plannin' on going, but she'll take ya far."

With that, I gave Jimmy a big thanks for the deal and started to drive off. I saw Jimmy's grin disappear in the rearview mirror, and it was replaced with a look that said, *I sure hope that kid doesn't kill himself in that car.*

I knew I'd be ok in my heart, and if he would've been close enough to hear, I would've told him the same. I started thinking about the trunk comment he made again, though. The trunk liner was damn near completely stripped out. I started thinking as I drove off, *What the hell was that guy doing with this car? Maybe the old liner in the trunk had the blood of—what did he say, four or five bodies? Hmmm, maybe it was an old mob car.* If so, that'll just add to the story I guess.

On top of that, after Mike had tuned the car up and put everything in order, I tried to get the thing registered, but they were giving me problems about it because I was an out of towner. So basically, I said, *fuck it.* This journey was like destiny it seemed like, and it had gone pretty good so far. Whatever happened would just happen. I shrugged my shoulders a little and rode out toward the Bangor sunset, driving illegal as hell. It was time for the '69 and I to make our way out west.

CHAPTER XVI: BREAK ON THROUGH

Heading out West felt like a dream come true. I kept thinking about how ecstatic Brooke had been when I first started the trip and how she said, "Just wait until you get into Tennessee; you'll fall in love with that state. Or even if you go out West!"

I never thought about going out west at all before she said something about it. It's like her words acted like a match to my own consciousness, lighting up yet another idea of inspiration I could set my heart upon. I started to become aware of the possibility the story of my journey could inspire my kids to take one just like it someday.

A brand new family tradition could be written in stone through my actions and passed down to them. Maybe, at some point after they both grew up, I could send one of the boys out in the old '69 Chevy I had just bought, and the other would set out in my dad's '69 Ford Torino. I'd tell them, "It's important that you each take the trip alone so that you get to see the world for yourself by yourself. You'll get a hell of a lot more out of it if you do it that way. Don't go to the biggest towns or the best attractions, but wherever your heart leads you. After the forty-two-day mark, meet up in a place where you've both always wanted to go and share your travel stories with one another. Tell each other about the lessons you've learned along the way. I promise it'll be worth it if you do it just like that."

I was living my own dream and making a dream for them, and even if I have more kids later on in life, I'll do just the same with them. I was living in a real-life adventure story and building a legacy all at the same time.

When my hands were on the wheel of the '69, I felt like I reached back in time. There was just something different about that car, like I could feel a real soul and personality running through every inch of it as the wind blew back and forth between the windows. Déjà vu kept crashing in on me by being in that car, like I'd done it all before. They say Déjà vu usually occurs when various different quantum realms line up and they're crossing over into one another. Supposedly, it's a sign you're on the right path, but who knows?

I was just going with my heart and it carried me a lot further than I could've ever imagined. I had damn near a twenty-three-hour drive ahead of me from Bangor to the Ozarks in Missouri. To tell you the truth, I knew damn well I couldn't make a twenty-three-hour drive without stopping, so I figured, *why not check out Niagara Falls?*

Grandpa Tom gave me the idea to stop there back in Massachusetts when he said, "You can't drive past Niagara Falls without seeing it. Everything about it is mind-boggling. It's like when you're standing there, watching all that water crashing down, you wonder to yourself, where is all that water coming from because there just never seems to be an end to it at all. You'll have to just see it for yourself, Hawke; you'll regret it if you don't."

Niagara Falls didn't even cross my mind, to be honest, and I felt stupid for not thinking of it on my own. The falls were located on the edge of New York State, that much I did know, which was pretty much on the edge of the biggest hotbed in the world for Covid, but like any other time— I wasn't that worried about it. I thought, *Well, I haven't caught the plague yet, so I might as well keep pushing forward no matter what the cost is. I'm doing this thing one way or another.* Plus, the falls were the perfect halfway point between the Ozarks and Bangor. So I just kept on driving.

I got so many honks and thumbs up on the road since I'd hopped behind the wheel. It was almost like people were finally beginning to accept me, which made me feel so good inside. This one chick even blew me a kiss and everything. She looked like she could've been a movie star or something; she was so pretty. It made me think, *Is this all that it took for people to notice me finally? All I needed was a nice car?* All the attention I got put me even more outside of reality because I'd never experienced anything like it before. I didn't feel like a ghost so much anymore.

Speaking of outside of reality, it didn't feel like I was alone in that car either. There was some sort of familiar presence in the car, and it filled the air with love. It felt like I traveled down the road in a piece of cloud nine augmented even further by the old tunes coming across the car's old radio. Jim Morrison's voice echoed across time with "Break on Through to the Other Side." Jimi Hendrix's electric guitar screamed back from the grave through "Voodoo Child," and Freddie Mercury jumped back onto the stage as he sang his heart out in "Bohemian Rhapsody."

29 Palms

It was like in that car, I wasn't just listening to their music, but they all had hopped in that old '69 to go along for the ride. Maybe Jim's words put a spell in the air, and I really was breaking on through to the other side. Either way, I broke toward something at last.

The magic started to dissipate, though, and my worries started crashing back into the picture when I couldn't get the headlights of the '69 to come back on. When I pulled out of a gas station earlier, I hadn't even realized the headlights weren't working until I found myself going down a pitch-dark road without a street light in sight. On top of all that, I didn't have any idea where the hell I was.

My panicked thoughts started to race: *Shit, maybe taking a classic car on a road trip across the country wasn't a good idea after all. I mean, I don't know a thing about modern cars, let alone classic ones; what the hell am I doing?*

All I could do was plot in a course toward the nearest motel and make my stay there for the night. The closest hotel was only ten minutes away, but ten minutes turns into eternity when you're going down a dark road with your head stuck out the window. I was so nervous somebody would come out of nowhere and hit me before I could make it to the motel. Luckily, I finally made it after going through an anxiety trip through hell that led me right toward another pile of shit motel. Honestly, I didn't even really care at the time. I just hoped I didn't have to deal with any wildebeests roaring through all hours of the night like I did back in Savannah.

When I got out of the '69, I saw this real dirty lookin' chick standing under a street lamp. She looked like a bruised-up meth head really, and of course, she saw me. She cupped her hand together and bounced it toward her mouth. I gave her a dirty look, to be honest. All I could think was, *What's that all about? Is she trying to say she's hungry? If I don't have any food for me, why would she think I have some for her?* It was just ridiculous. All I had the energy to do was shake my head and shoo her off. I didn't have time for all that. I was just ready to get checked in.

It might've been a shitty motel, but the bed felt so wonderful when I plopped down into it. I could feel the pressure in my back release right away, and for a moment it felt like I was forever falling into an abyss carrying me past the world, and before I knew it, I was within a dream.

In the dream, I sat behind the wheel of the '69, and like I had all day, it didn't feel like I was alone in there. All around me there was nothing, no trees, not even the road, just the pale moonlight shining down above me. I still couldn't fight the feeling of the presence or the familiarity of it, but there was still nothing in sight to my right or left.

Then, I felt someone place their hand on my shoulder from the backseat. I looked in the rearview mirror, and there was my father, wearing the same leather jacket and glasses I last saw him in. I was shocked in the dream at first, and I felt the tears more than the words I wanted to say. From the backseat of the '69, my father said to me with a smile, "You sure are making your own way, aren't you?"

For some reason, I didn't flip around to look at him; I just kept staring at him in the rearview mirror. In dreams, you usually don't react the same way you would in reality. I would've done so much more if I would've seen him in real life. The dream just ran its natural course when I replied, "Yeah, Dad, I really am. I can't believe I'm actually doing it."

My father gripped my shoulder tighter as he smiled and said, "What made you think you couldn't? You've always had this story in your heart, and now you're living it. What's in your heart is always there. It just doesn't show up right away."

I just kept staring at him in the rearview mirror. I don't know why I didn't reach for his hand. I replied, "But what if what you hope for the most shows up, and you just can't have it? Like you're forever chasing that star within the wind that's just within grasp but couldn't be further away? What about the other things? What about the things in my heart that have already gone away?"

My father kept his hand steady on my shoulder with a smile and said, "What is coming is what you deserve. Your heart has already paid the price for it. It's all already here no matter if it's now or later or even if it's come before." He patted my shoulder in assurance and continued with a laugh, "Just have faith in yourself. That'll carry you further than what you think, and where you're trying to go, well, you'll get there just fine."

I stared back at that smiling face of his and said, "I don't know, Dad, but I hope you're right. All I really know right now is that it all has to be for something. All of it, everything that's happened, it all has to mean something in the end."

I leaned back on the seat of the '69 as he folded his arms and said, " Trust me, son, it'll all work out fine. Just enjoy the ride."

I awoke the next day with a dream on my mind and hope in my heart. When I finally reached the actual falls, it was a true wonder to behold. It was one of those surreal moments that burst like a nuclear bomb within my soul. It sent sparks of pure, pristine magic all throughout the misty air surrounding me and ran its way across the thundering water. It was a postcard picture of true beauty.

Grand, gigantic streams of majestic blue continuously crashed down into a pool of motherly waters giving birth to a rainbow casting itself across the Toronto landscape lying just across that unbelievable miracle of nature. The falls were a miraculous thing in themselves to behold, but what was even more unbelievable to me was the colorful cast of the multicolored hues emanating from the rainbow. It was like it gave more color and life to an already beautiful moment. It was all so breathtaking.

It filled my heart with treasures of pleasure as my eyes fixated on all they held in front of them under that clear, cloudless, blue sky, but I also felt a hurdle of tears coming to my eyes. It could've rained, and it could've poured, but everything in that moment was just perfect, almost like it had been written and etched out through pure destiny in a time unmemorable. In that moment, I couldn't deny I was in the presence of something great and grand. I thought to myself, *I'm not sure if this moment was supposed to feel perfect to me or not, but if the architect of all designed this moment to be this way for me, well, I can empathize with whatever you are as much as you can with me.*

I've always thought there was a lot more to God than what can be found in a book, but there was one thing still sticking with me; it was the thought that maybe whatever intelligent thing designing all of this—perhaps it's the loneliest thing out there. I've always felt like he, she, or it, whenever it woke up in that time so long ago, it had to have found itself in darkness, but then there was light. It's like all of it, everything out there, was created to fill an old architect's, lonely heart. It filled the world with so much beauty and wonder to place people in to enjoy, to live, and to love in. The architect made all of this and us, for us to love and to be loved. How wonderful or grander could a plan be?

I closed my eyes and let the sound of the crashing waters fill up my spirit as if I were a cup. I felt love in the moment. Right then and there, I sent that love and empathy back into the world to whatever is and what always will be. Within my mind, I said to what is, *Well, I love you. I know I can't possibly understand all that there is to you, but I feel like I can empathize with you so much. You seek a connection with as many people as you can, but most of them reject you* and pretend that you're not even there. I know that it was you that placed a heart of gold within my father and me. It was built to hold all of this unconditional love that beats within my heart as a gift that I want give to the world, but I only want to give the entirety of it all to one person; that true love that is my greatest heart's desire. Like you, I try to spread my love to as many as I can, but out of probably fear of not understanding, I always find myself abandoned. Is that how you feel too?

I felt great, but the shades of sadness began their pursuit again, reminding me of what was lost and may never be found. Even in my joy, I am forever in torment. Right before my tears started to fall over the ever-longing presence of the abyss, Brooke's words fell like a saving grace upon my shoulders. *Really take in the beauty*, she had said. *Just be with yourself at that moment. Feel the peace run through your body and tell yourself out loud, 'I'm going to be okay.' But you've gotta believe it as you say it. Keep repeating it until you believe it.* When I inhaled the misty air into my lungs, I tried my best to believe it.

I left Niagara Falls with something new in my heart that I couldn't really grasp or understand entirely at that point. All I knew was it was hard for me to walk away. As hard as I tried to be with myself in that moment, I had thoughts of Brooke beating like a melody all through my heart. I sent her a picture of the rainbow over the falls while I stood there, but the picture I held in my heart of her felt more beautiful than the falls back there ever could. She replied, **Freaking beautiful. I'm so jealous. That's one place I want to go when I build my van. I want to visit Canada too.**

Filled full of bursting passion, I wanted to say so much to her, but I had to go with the flow and keep it casual. She wasn't ready for what I wanted to say to her after all. Still, I had to at least let her know how much I believed in her. *I bet a lot of people don't think you're really going to do all that, but I believe in you, and when you really do set out to do it, it's going to be so wonderful for you. Niagara*

Falls will leave you speechless. I feel like I took apart of that place with me when I left; I really do. It almost made me cry, lol.

A lot of people don't believe that I'll actually leave for Europe next year, but I don't let their doubt stop my progress. Every day is a step closer toward my goals, to me. I've never been one to let others stop me because of their doubt. My family can tell you that. When I tell them I'm going to do something, they 100% know I'm going to do it, lol. I've always been that way. Niagara Falls looked beautiful from that picture. We didn't get to go there when I visited NYC, but it's definitely on my bucket list. I'll get there one day.

I wanted to say so much more to her on that day from what the falls had awoken inside of me, but I couldn't. *She just wants to be friends. She's not interested in me romantically like that, and if I don't throw these feelings that I have for her away, I might just end up heartbroken.* At least I have her as a friend. With Brooke, I'll take whatever I can get because having her as a friend is better than not having her in my life at all. That's one thing I never allowed myself to think about, not having her in my life. It was just too unbearable.

The Ozarks of Missouri waited for me in the winds. It seemed like a great place to spend the weekend because I was more than due to let my wild side loose and show the folks around that lake what an Ohio/Alabama boy was all about. I couldn't believe it. I was really headed out West. I thought to myself, *I'm doing it. I'm really doing this.*

I started to flip through the stations of the '69s radio until I caught a tune from the eighties called a "Space Age Love Song." That old tune felt like it brought something back along with it. Almost as if it were a presence gunning its way out of my dream from the night before. The rumble of the engine I heard running up alongside of me sounded a lot like the '69s, but it came from a completely different car. It felt so real, like I could see him right there pulling up in the lane beside me in his '69 burgundy Ford

29 Palms

Torino. In my mind's eye, I saw my father riding there alongside me, sporting some Wayfarer sunglasses with a big smile, and the all-too-familiar voice said, *No, we're doing this.*

CHAPTER XVII: KICKSTART MY HEART

"Hotel California." That old song just so happened to be playing on the '69s radio when I pulled into the parking lot of the historic Randall Hotel outside of the Lake of the Ozarks. It gave me a Bates Motel kind of vibe when I stepped out of the '69 to get all squared away with my room.

The Randall Hotel was surrounded by a small, Midwestern town kind of atmosphere, especially when a couple of fellows that could've been named Dewey and Huey shot me a, "We don't like your kind around here," kind of look from their old, beat-up pickup truck. I thought to myself, *Well, the locals seem very friendly. Maybe "Hotel California" playing on the radio when I pulled in here is a bad omen.* I sure hoped not.

When I approached the counter in the Randall's front office, I was met with an absolutely dazzling smile casting the warm expression of an admirer from a lady who looked to be just a few years older than I was. I did find her attractive, and I had trouble wrestling with a few fantasies of my own at the time, I gotta admit. She was hot, but I didn't have a problem talking to pretty girls by this point. I said, "Hey there, how are you doing today?"

The hostess replied warmly, "I'm doing great. I love your car; what year is it?"

I was kind of full of myself, I'll admit. "Oh, that car out there? Well, that's a '69 Chevy Caprice; we just drove all the way from Maine. I got it back in Stephen King's hometown."

The hostess seemed to light up like a light bulb during a power surge behind the counter, and she said, "Wow, that's amazing. You drove all the way here from Maine? What brings you here?"

I replied kind of nonchalantly with a laugh, "Nothing really—I mean, I like the show on Netflix a lot, plus, I heard there isn't a whole lot of social distancing going on around here, so it sounds like just the place for me. Any ideas of where I should start off?"

The hostess replied, "Well—the lake is where you should probably start first. There's plenty of places around there you could check out. It's Friday night, so you can find fun just about anywhere here."

I replied, "Ok then, around the lake. I got it checked—I'll try not to get myself into too much trouble."

The hostess replied with a grin, "Well, have fun tonight. I got you all set. Here are the keys to the room, and if you need anything during your stay, either my husband or me will be up here in the office."

29 Palms

With a jingle of the keys and a thought crossing my mind, *Fuck, she's got a husband*, I gave the hostess a wave and walked on over to my room to throw my bags in and get freshened up for the night. I googled for a couple of restaurants around the lake, and lo and behold, Lakehouse 13 popped up. I thought to myself, *Lakehouse 13, hmmm—sounds like a lucky place to go*, so off I went.

I pulled the '69 into the Lakehouse 13 parking lot, kicking gravel and dust everywhere to Van Halen's "Runnin' with the Devil." It was an outside lake house bar just like I imagined, so everyone out on the back patio bar saw me as I charged in with my mind set on getting full of Blue Ribbon bravery.

The bar gave off the vibe of an old lake house, if that's a giant surprise. I think it was two-stories—not sure, but it looked like the type of place where a few lads would meet and drink themselves down to Davey Jones, if you know what I mean. The deck was littered with people everywhere, and the whole setup was surrounded by a dark lake holding a dock full of big boats, little boats, and jet skis that had a few empty Bud Light cans floating around them. It all seemed crested by a rounding view of trees that had an ever-approaching glimmer cast across them from the waning dawn of the sun. Suddenly, this older bald gentleman with a beer gut jutting through his disproportionately buttoned shirt shouted, "Hey there, you!"

I looked around pretty confused and pointed toward myself and said, "Who me?"

The balding beer gut guy replied, "Yeah, you! That there old Chevy that just came pulling in—that yours, fella? What year is that?"

My ego started to get a little inflated from all of the attention, to be honest. I had begun to feel sort of like a rock star really. " Yeah, it's mine. It's a 1969 Chevy Caprice. You like it?"

Balding beer gut guy replied with a belch, "Goddamn right, I like it. That's a fine automobile right there." He shouted to the bartender, "Hey, get this fella here a beer. Ya enjoy yourself there, pal." He might've been a drunken fat guy, but I basked in his acknowledgment with a blushing smile and said, "Ok, yeah, you too! Thanks, man!"

I didn't stay at Lakehouse 13 that long, though. I loved the atmosphere, but I couldn't help feeling out of place by the sea of gray hair lying across the shores of the lake like a thirty-year high school reunion. The bartender, though, sort of looked like Matthew McConaughey from the movie *Dazed and Confused*. He seemed like a pretty cool guy who knew his way around the lake, so I asked him, "Hey, man—where's the real party happening around here?"

He knew about mischief just as much as I did; I could tell. He pushed a Blue Ribbon across the counter my way and said, "Where's the party happening? You know where Backwater Jack's is? That's the place to be, man. Either that or Dog Days, that's a good place to go too."

I replied, "Backwater Jacks? Hell yeah, then—I knew you were the guy to talk to around here."

Backwater Jack's was just how you would imagine a badass lakefront bar to be. It had a look that tried to maintain a backwoods vibe of a down-to-Earth country hangout, but it was a lot cleaner than that. There was a roundabout bar on the outside deck overlooking a stage hosting a band ripping across the dancing bikini-wearing ladies of the lake. Inspired by the Matthew McConaughey look-alike I ran into earlier, I nodded with a mischievous smile and thought, *Alright, alright, this is what I'm talking about.*

At first, I didn't feel like I had it in me to mingle with the crowd. It all seemed so overwhelming to me because here I was a stranger, a ghost in this town, just blending in with the crowd, not having a clue who I should talk to first.

I started to observe this beautiful brunette sitting on the other side of the bar with a magnificent golden skin tone lining the edge of her breasts popping out of the white tied-up blouse-like shirt she had on. Now I usually don't look directly at a chick's breasts, but they were just there, you know? I couldn't help it. Maybe it was from the beer or just the warm summer air; who knows? She looked so amazing over there, and it made me feel so sad to see her alone. I had to approach her.

I came up to her in a pretty nervous, awkward kind of way, I have to admit, when I said, "Hey there, how you doin'; wanna drink?"

Here I am, acting like the normal throwaway douche bag that you could find at any other bar; what am I doing? This isn't me. She let me down when she said, "Sorry, I have a boyfriend."

I didn't really believe it. Where was he at if she had one? If I were in a loving relationship, I wouldn't want to go out alone. I didn't really care. I was just trying to be honest when I said, "Oh, ok—well—I get it. Honestly, I've been like staring at you from the other end of the bar for like twenty minutes now. I'm pretty much a creep—I'm terribly sorry—well—I'm going to go jump in the lake now. Have a good one."

If the plane crashes, might as well let it burn. Sometimes I make an ass out of myself for my own amusement if I'm bored. The shock factor you get from people always makes it worthwhile, especially if you know you're never going to see them again. I wasn't really on my level yet, so I returned to my barstool to get another drink—just as trouble began to brew.

A shirtless local as red as a pent-up firecracker stomped his way toward a group of guys near me and shouted, "Hey you there,

Daniel, you motherfucker! You still owe Johnny some money, and don't think he forgot about it! I'll whoop your ass right now!"

I thought, *Here we go, a true scene from the show the Ozarks. Is Marty about to pop in and break everything up? Better yet, is Ruth going to show up? I wouldn't mind that. There's something sexy about that country girl, after all.*

The fellow that had been the victim of the firecracker's explosion replied pretty annoyed, "Really, Dale? Do we need to do this shit now?"

Pint-sized firecracker Dale replied as he walked off, "I got your number, motherfucker!"

I looked at the firecracker's victim with a confused look and said, "Dude—what the fuck was that all about, man?"

As soon as I said that, though, a lady with a pretty sexy voice told the group, "Don't worry about him. I know everybody here. I'll get his ass kicked out."

I turned around immediately to get a view of where that voice of authority had come from. Suddenly, my eyes fell upon a beautiful older woman with glowing blonde hair flowing down and around her chestnut brown eyes. She had soft, luscious-looking perky lips that I had to steal my eyes away from. It made me feel guilty—like a thief in the night or something. My eyes danced across her curvy figure anyway as a fire of lust started to well up inside of me. I could feel my cheeks getting hot as I listened to her seductive voice order another drink with a couple of shooters from the bartender. My mind started to race with desire as I thought about how I'd make my move. If I didn't make a move, I figured I'd probably regret it forever. I noticed the seat next to her was open, so I started to channel my best James Bond impersonation for my approach when the words fell out of my mouth, "Hey there, what are you drinking on?" *Not James Bond at all.*

When she turned her gaze upon me, her lips curled up into a smile as she looked me up and down. Her words melted me when she said, "A pain in the ass—always with a shooter."

Then she wrapped her lips seductively around this straw as her eyes pierced into mine. I thought, *I've never wanted to be a straw so much in my life.* Her next words lit me up into a lustful flame when she asked, "You want me to get you one?"

Her name was Debra, and we sat at the bar for a while joking with one another, and of course, I had to tell her about the adventures I'd had on my journey so far, but I never brought up the '69. Even though I was filled with pride for that car, I didn't want to brag about my ride to her. It would've bored her anyways, most likely, and I didn't want to come across as the regular type of guy that just had to brag about what I had to look more worthy in someone else's eyes. She looked like she had it all anyhow. She was a divorced older woman approaching fifty carrying herself like she didn't have a care in the world. I wondered if she was a part of the rich older lady parade that seemed to be about everywhere you looked in the Ozarks.

While I talked to her, I thought, *Well, if she is, fuck my job. I wouldn't mind being her pool boy. I could swing that. I'll even throw on some tight short shorts for the hell of it while she lounges out in the sun watching me scrub her Olympic-sized pool. I'd make sure her cocktail never went empty—She's sexy enough. I'd do it.*

The lady bartender watched us and kept shooting little grins toward Debra as we flirted with one another. I knew Debra found me attractive, just like I did her, but she seemed a little wary of me because of my age. Debra gave the bartender a confused look with a red-cheeked smile and asked her, "Well, what?"

The lady behind the bar was wide-eyed and grinning evermore; with a shake of her head, she said, "It ain't gonna hurt you to rob the cradle at least once."

My heart started to do jumping jacks in my chest as my eyes bulged and my mouth dropped open. I unconsciously nodded my head while thinking, *Yes, please. Rob the cradle and take advantage of me. You can use me; I don't care.*

I could tell Debra was still thinking about whether or not she wanted to take on a lover as young as I was as she tilted her head to take another gulp of her drink. Then came another type of look. She started staring at me like she was just mesmerized by me. It made me feel so wonderful because I hadn't had many people ever look at me that way—before I took the trip anyway. I loved entertaining the idea of her taking me home, but for it to happen was another thing. I felt pretty anxious at the thought of it all. You know—about what I might or might not be in for as shot after shot carried both of us through the night.

After a few more, Debra wanted to get me on Snap because she'd be at the lake all weekend just like I was. I was more relieved than let down to finally get the final clue on whether or not she wanted to take me home. If she wanted to, I wouldn't have refused, but I would've been nervous going along with it; after all, I barely knew this woman. This could easily turn into a *Basic Instinct* type of situation, and I didn't want to relive the feeling of some crazed woman sticking a screwdriver to my throat like I had before. It didn't scare me all that much, though; I had kids with the chick after all.

I walked Debra back to her car through all the spraying beer shooting its way across the deck from the crowd of shouting folks shot-gunning beers around every corner. *There definitely isn't any social distancing going on around here. I love it,* I thought.

29 Palms

When we reached the parking lot, Debra and I stood underneath a light lighting up the dock under a backdrop of stars along the lake to say our farewells. She grabbed ahold of me as my hands ran themselves down along the sides of her waist, and then she kissed me. I felt warm and cared for when she did, which was a feeling I've seldom ever felt in my life, but it just didn't feel right to me. I didn't feel that magical spark there that awakens the heart and makes the outside world a lot more appealing than the inside one. I knew who I really wanted it to be by that lake with me. I just wasn't ready to admit it to myself. Debra walked away with a flirtatious wave and said, "See you tomorrow, sweetheart."

Backwater Jacks started to clear out not too long after Debra left, and I found myself sitting alone at the bar again. I asked the lady bartender where everyone was going, and she said, "Oh, the strip is where everyone is going now. There's a big car show there tonight."

I started to think to myself, *A big car show? What are the odds of there being a car show my first night here in the Ozarks, and I just so happen to have a '69 Chevy waiting to get revved up right out there in the parking lot.*

I closed out my tab and headed for the '69 with that thought. I had no intention of entering the '69 in the car show, though. It might sound odd to keep a beautiful ride like the '69 out of the spotlight, but I've never been a person that's liked to show off for a large group of people. I'm more of the low-key type of guy, and that's just how the '69 and I rolled into the strip. As low-key as you could possibly be in a '69 Chevy anyway.

"The Boys are Back in Town" blasted through the '69s old radio as I drove down the strip's streaming neon lights on that pale moonlit night. As my head turned from left to right, searching for a parking spot, I set my eyes on country girls walking up and down the road everywhere; they were dressed up in plaid shirts tied just above their belly button rings atop some cut-off booty shorts. I saw a few of them chugging beers faster than I could ever hope to, and I thought, *If she can chug a beer that fast, she could probably kick an ass even quicker. So I better not give any of them a reason to get pissed off at me—or should I?* There's always been something attractive about an angry woman to me. I like to tease a little, you know? When I get a chick pissed off, I'll get kind of close to them, enough for them to get even madder, and I'll say, "What are you so mad about?"

Usually, they'll say, "You know why! You just don't know when to quit!"

If it's an Ohio girl, you might get smacked right away and get every bad word in the book thrown at you. Ohio girls are extremely dangerous, but if it's a regular non-psychopathic chick, I'll go in a little closer. Close enough for our lips to touch, and I'll grin a little and say, "Well, what are you going to do about it?"

Then before she can say anything else, I'll just go in for it. You just can't get a chick too mad to pull it off. Just a little is all you need, and then if it all goes well, you'll have the best sex you've ever had. There's something passionate about a woman's anger. It's like they're out to teach you a lesson or something.

The '69 and I blended in pretty well amongst all the other classic cars, which surprised me in a way and left me kind of disappointed because I didn't feel like that much of a star on the strip like I had on the road. So I figured, *Scratch out being low-key and blending in. I'm going to let out my Jordan Belfort side all over this strip. Fuck it, what's the worst that could happen?*

I just had to find a crew for the night to party with. Screw being shy and backward, I had my mind set on doing it up the right way. Lucky for me, I didn't even have to try. It didn't take long for one of those down-home country girls to say, "Hey there, hippie boy, if your man enough, how about shot gunnin' a beer?"

Or Twelve. Of course, they weren't one after another consecutively. I've done that before. That time a stream of puke shot out of me like something off *The Exorcist,* and it left everyone around me saying, "Ewwww, what the fuck? Are you ok?"

I didn't want that to happen there. That would've been just terrible. Even though I wasn't out to find a date for the night, I still didn't want to embarrass myself in front of these girls. After all, they'd adopted this blue bandanna headband wearing hippie into their party crew. I didn't want to get sick, but I still had to show off my legendary drinking skills and let them know, *Hey, your messing with one of the best tonight, and I'm not going to stop until the sun comes up. Better be ready.* I'll have to piece together the rest of the night from the few remaining fragments I have left of it because there are glimpses of parts of it, then a fade away to nothing, then a coming back. So here it goes.

We walked down the strip, or should I say everyone else walked, and I more like hopped down the street, toward this outside club that had speakers blaring up some Biggie Smalls.

This guy hollered, "You ready to fucking go!"

With a bark at the moon and a beat on my chest, I screamed, "I'm ready to fucking go! Whooo!"

I heard a girl laugh toward her friend and say, "This guy is fucking awesome." We all hammered shot after shot of I don't know what. All I know is I bought a round and probably another round and maybe even a round after that for what could've been just four people or a group of eight with me included. I'm not really sure.

The next thing I remember was brushing my hands through a bunch of mist—but no, it wasn't mist—it was just a bunch of thick white smoke in the back of this van with this red-eyed girl in a yellow shirt sitting cross-legged by me laughing on my shoulder. There were a few other people back there with me, and someone who sounded like Pee-Wee Herman, or maybe he was just gay, said, "Ya wanna hit again, big guy?"

    Through the haze, the smoke, and the darkness, I managed to say, "Who me, man? I don't know, man, I don't know."

    The rest of what I can remember is someone pulling a hit out of a gravity bong and the girl beside me laughing through my eardrums. I'm not saying it was me that took the hit. For all I know, it could've been the Pee Wee Herman guy, but right after that sound, the fade away came again.

    The next thing I remember makes me question what could've happened after I got out of the van. Still, I can clearly remember being in the bathroom of this bar with a fat dude in a Hawaiian shirt looking just like Chris Farley. He was going erratic, shaking his head around everywhere while he said, "I just really respect what you're doing, man. That shit is fucking awesome!"

    He let out a laugh and then continued at a rapid pace, "I'm a world traveler too, you know? I've been everywhere, man. The last place I went to was Mexico, and I got the best blow from there I've ever had in my fucking life, man. Let me show ya! This is the best way to snort coke." He snorted a line off the sink faster than a person could blink, but right after that, he turned on the sink and started splashing water up his nose. This guy shook around so much his love handles were jiggling around and everything. He turned back to me in a flash with gritted teeth and said, "Wooooh! Now I'm ready! We gotta get the fuck out of here before the bouncer catches us again! Come on, man, let's go!"

    The fade away happened again after me and Chris Farley left the bar's bathroom, but it couldn't have been as long of a fade away as the one after leaving the van. The very next thing I can remember, which is vague at best, was grabbing ahold of this guy and shouting, "Give me the mic! I can sing! I got songs memorized and everything, man! We gotta turn this place up!!"

The guy, whoever he was, pushed me away and said, "Dude, keep your hands off me before I break your fuckin' nose."

Everything faded to black after that. The whole night pretty much disappeared, for the most part anyway. The next day I woke up in the early afternoon drenched in sweat from the beating hot sun, lying on the bench seat of the '69. It was parked on this old dirt road somewhere, and luckily, it started up just fine as I lit the ignition up with the flick of my wrist. I thought, *Hippie van, Chris Farley, and did I get kicked off a stage somewhere last night? What happened? How did I get here?*

My nose wasn't broken, thankfully, or anything on the car. I just hoped there weren't any warrants or deputies out there flying around looking for that blue-headband-wearing hippie guy trying to snatch a microphone and everything the night before. I shrugged my shoulders and thought, *Well, it is what it is. It's my last day in the Ozarks, so I'm just going to keep it on rollin'. Exploring some caves today sounds like a lot of fun. Maybe I'll do that.* After a shower and a supercharged nap of recovery time, I did just that.

CHAPTER XVIII: I WANNA KNOW WHAT LOVE IS

The descent into Stark Caverns gave a feeling of unexpectedness to the air. Sure there was a tour guide, along with a few other people in the group, but what was so unexpected about those dark cavernous hollows were the feelings and images it spontaneously seemed to invoke within my heart. All-around, on all sides and edges, were secret places carved out of the Earth long ago. The long, sporadic tunnels in this ancient place put me in the mind of the labyrinth existing within, not just the heart and mind, but within the universe itself.

Life itself feels like a descent into darkness. It's never a fall into a pure hollow shadow, but it's a blind stumbling around leaving you hopelessly touching and grabbing your way to find the path that will lead you out alive. Like Pinocchio, you're a puppet;

you're not real 'til you find yourself. You could always get lucky and make it out on your own, but the true lost and lucky ones find a light along the way.

On the surface, there's an infinite amount of lights out there; you can damn near find one just about anywhere, but when you find that one thing shining in the shadows, it's not just another light. To your heart, it's a glimmering star of wonder making its way to you from the other side of the labyrinth. The same star that would become a savior of the lost; hand in hand, the light and the lost would make it back to the surface under the stars where they always belonged. The lost would look to the light and say, "I love you because you have made me found," and the light would reply, "I love you because, through you, I now know myself."

The light led the lost, but without the lost, the light didn't know its own nature. Neither would've valued the founding of the stars above without one another, and through love, they became each other's guide. The lost and unkindled flames shine brighter than they could ever imagine together, rather than alone. Doing it all alone could leave you lost forever.

Going to Stark Caverns reminded me why I set out on my journey in the first place, and of course, it brought to heart the light I knew I had found through Brooke. I was a blind and stumbling man when she found me, and she awakened something new in my heart each time we spoke. The only thing was she didn't know how much of a light she was. I wanted to tell her so bad how I felt about her, but I couldn't even admit it to myself. She didn't want me as a partner; I knew that. I told myself, *No matter how much you want to talk to her, you can't. You can't allow yourself to love her because she doesn't love you.* It didn't make any sense to love her.

Back at the Randall Hotel, I tried on everything I had to find the perfect outfit for the night. I was about to be headed to the swimming pool bar, Dog Days, after all. I heard so much about it the night before I just couldn't let myself pass the place up. It was supposed to be the place to be on a Saturday night, and I had my mind set on feasting on as much variety the Ozarks had to offer. Still, I had no intentions of getting my ass nearly kicked like the night before, so I wanted to approach the night in the chillest way possible. *Just be calm and cool, man, with no expectations. Just take in each breath and savor every moment of this place that you can,* I told myself.

I didn't want to make too much noise when I pulled into Dog Days because for all I knew, the '69, and I could both be wanted from whatever happened the night before, so I really did make everything as low-key as I could this go around.

The place was packed. You could look out across the bay of the lake Dog Days sat alongside and witness a prettier sea than the lake could provide through all the blondes, the mysterious brunettes, and the occasional exotic scarlet woman that could be found all across the crowd. Every girl there was beautiful in their own unique way. Whether if it was through a seductive smile, a joy-filled laugh, it didn't matter. The waves were majestic and everyone was beautiful. Except for the dudes. I figured I didn't have any competition there, especially after I downed my first drink. *I may not have a six-pack, but at least I have a pretty face. I had someone say I looked like Brad Pitt when I walked in, so I must be standing out because of something.*

I didn't desire to seek out anybody, but somehow I ran into someone that seemed to be looking for me. With another mixed drink in hand, Debra popped from around the corner of the deck at Dog Days. Her eyes widened, and a glimmering smile spread across her face when she said, "There ya are, stranger. What are you doing here?"

I replied as casually as possible, "Hey there, ma'am! What are you doin' here?"

Debra replied with a more stern look when she pushed her eyebrows down a little at me. She was still grinning at me, though, when she said, "I was about to ask you the same. I was out on the boat with some friends all day. They started to argue a little, and I don't know about you, but I hate all that drama. I'm tryin' to have a good time."

I was more than surprised to see Debra there at Dog Days. After all, I had her on Snap. However, I never messaged her back because I was still conflicted about all the feelings I tried to process at the time. Even though she was probably one of the best-looking older women I had ever come across, I wasn't sure if I wanted to go there. I replied, "I heard that. Havin' a good time is what life's all about. Hell, I might get another drink after I get done with these two. You gonna be around once I reach my third?"

Debra looked from left to right with the ever-present grin she had and said, "I'll be here for as long as my friends are. They've cooled down since we've been on the boat. I'll be on that dance floor later, honey, if you're still around. That band usually plays all night long."

I told Debra, "Well, I don't plan on going anywhere. So I'll see ya later on. Plus, it would be nice to hang out with you and your friends anyway. I'm sort of a stranger around here, you know?"

Debra laughed and replied, "Find me on the dance floor then, honey. I'll be right by the music."

I told her I'd catch her later. The atmosphere of Dog Days was one of the most wonderful I'd ever experienced. I had the liberty that evening of looking out on a gigantic pool full of cool, streaming water all encapsulated around a brightly lit-up bar.

29 Palms

I saw Debra on the dance floor just like she said she'd be. Looking fabulous in a white ankle-high sundress in a straw sun hat that held all that streaming blonde hair of hers in order. She didn't notice me while she was out there dancing, and I pretended like I didn't see her, to be honest. While I ordered my next drink, I thought of the text Brooke sent me earlier in the day I almost dared not reply to. She sent me a quote that said, **"When a thing beckons you to explore it without telling you why or how, this is not a red herring; it's a map." —Gina Greenlee**

I'm assuming that map leads to something amazing.

It was this text invoking the thoughts I had before I entered the Stark Caverns. I wanted to deny the feeling rupturing within my heart when I saw it. It was like an irrevocable thought was placed within my heart that said, All I know is that my map leads to you. I don't know why nor how I find myself thinking about you from every moment I wake up to each time I lay down, but in my dreams we're together, and that's where every hope in my heart comes true.

I hated it. I hated having that feeling because it brought so much fear along with it. I didn't want to let myself go. Like all the girls I met along the way, they were all pretty, but they weren't beautiful enough for me to forget about her. In a way, I had already lost myself. I was just fighting to forget that I had. I loved her words, but they scared me so much. What if she thought I was crazy? I felt like my dad was right there with me in every moment, just like she was, but how could I tell her?

At that moment, at the pool bar, I couldn't help but reply to her when I said, Something's been doing that with me for sure. It might sound crazy, but I definitely don't feel alone on this journey. It's just weird how something strange has happened in each place I've been. I'm being lwd somewhere, wherever that is.

You're being what somewhere? But yes, it's the people you meet along the way that give you stories to tell.

I felt in my heart I was led toward her, but the damn shots kept throwing typos at me. *I really need to start proofreading my texts, lol. I feel like I'm being led somewhere, but I don't know where it's going to take me.*

It's okay, lol, where are you now?

I didn't want to tell her about the night before, but I had to let her know I was having a good time. *Lake of the Ozarks. It got a little wild last night, and it probably will tonight too. They have a bar inside of a swimming pool, lol, headed to Dodge City tomorrow.*

Well that sounds fun, lol; what state is that? And what's in Dodge City?

I thought, *Really, you've never heard of Dodge City? I guess not too many folks recall those good old days,* but I replied, *It's in Kansas. That's where the cowboys used to hang out, so I'm going to head into that town and pull my own guns out, lol.*

Well that sounds interesting, lol. My trip is coming up! The 24th-29th.

She brought up going to Vegas time and time again since the first night we met, but I could never remember what days she was going. I planned on staying in Dodge City next, the Stanley Hotel in Colorado, make a stop in Santa Fe, stay in Tombstone, then afterward, finally end up in Vegas. I wasn't sure if when I'd be staying in Vegas, she would be there too, but with all I had in my heart, I sent a wish out into the universe that when I was there, she'd be there too. It worked. I felt like hopping up on the bar at Dog Days and scream in triumph, but I didn't. With a bursting heart and the fullest smile I replied, *Really? I'll be in Vegas the 22nd to the 25th; that's what I booked anyway.*

Yeah, my birthday is the 26th.

29 Palms

I'd stay in Vegas longer if she wanted me to. I'd give up going to 29 Palms completely if it meant being with her longer. *It's my second to last stop, and yeah, I remembered you said you were going for your birthday, but I didn't really know when.*

What parts are you going to see?

Through my excitement, I sent a follow-up text at the same time she did. *What all do you plan to do there?*

I plan to go to the Hoover Dam, Boulder City, Grand Canyon, Fremont, and the strip.

I didn't do my research like she had. After all, I was just going off a whim, *I had the Grand Canyon and the Hoover Dam on the list, especially old Vegas; that's the strip I want to see the most. What are Fremont and Boulder City? Maybe that was a pretty stupid question; I'm sorry, lol.*

No, it's not, lol. Fremont is what's considered old Vegas. Fremont St. Then Boulder City is right below the Hoover Dam. We're also going to Lake Mead too.

Brooke sent me a picture and a video of a whole itinerary of what she'd be doing in Vegas from each day down to the time. I was so impressed by how ordered and precise she was. I felt kind of dumb too because I knew damn near nothing about any area I'd been to. I just googled it all on the fly. *You printed out a whole schedule? Lol, maybe I should've done that. I like the recovery day part of the list, lol; who are you going with? Old Vegas is what I'm most excited to see. I love the movie* Casino; *it's one of my favorites.*

I printed almost everything, lol. I have a folder for everything, and I'll bring it with us, lol. It's just me and my grandma. Old Vegas looks to be pretty fun. I'm not sure what I'm most excited for.

It was comical how inferior I felt compared to her at that point. All I could do was smile as I stared back at my phone while I thought, *She really does have it all, doesn't she? She's as sharp as a nail,* she has looks that could kill, and she has the greatest heart I've ever encountered. Except for my father, that is.

My father and I were the only people I could think of that truly had that innocent kind of heart, full of unadulterated passion, but there she was. She might've had a heart greater than even him and me. I tried not to fall too deep into my thoughts, so I re-gathered myself and kept everything as light as possible, and texted, *Is that how you do every trip? Lol, you don't just go with the wind?*

No, only for the trips that I have only a certain amount of time to be there for and there're places I want to see. I just make an "Itinerary" as a way to stay on track and not forget.

Things tend to get wild in Vegas. A hell of a lot more than they do in the Ozarks. I didn't even want to be a rock star that night, even with the cannonball splashes spraying out of the pool in sync with each live guitar riff. Talking to her gave me more of a high than partying ever could, but I had to ask, *Lol, you gonna let your wild side out? I know you have one.*

I don't know, lol. I'll definitely enjoy myself, but I don't know if Vegas will be that wild with them just opening back up, lol.

Covid made me sicker when it was hinted at more than it could've if I actually caught it. I hoped the restrictions wouldn't ruin the time her and I could have there. I joked a little when I replied, *Everybody is ready to get out of the house. I think it will be, lol; what happens in Vegas stays in Vegas.*

For sure, lol. I'm sure we'll find some clubs. Our hotel has a night club attached.

I could feel Debra's eyes from the dance floor peeling away at me like they were lasers. I didn't care. I turned away from her as quickly as I could. All I wanted to do was talk to Brooke. So I ran up a staircase on the side opposite of the dance floor to the rooftop bar where I could hideaway.

I eventually steered the conversation toward what her type was and what she looked for in a guy. She damn sure fit my type, and I felt I fit hers just as much. We were both two people who weren't afraid to see the whole world, all that was out there to see and offer, really was within anybody's grasp. In my heart, I felt like we were the perfect match, two dreamers with the same dream.

All of a sudden, some guy walked up singing a chick song called "Waterfalls" by TLC. He was dressed like the average frat boy with a ball cap to the back. He didn't just look tore up, but hella tore up, if that's even a word, really. I had to fight myself from busting out laughing. He looked at me with the same type of grin and said, "I'm not gay; you're gay, bro."

I couldn't hold it in anymore. I damn near spit my drink up everywhere as a shrill joker-sounding laugh erupted from my mouth. The frat guy laughed right with me, and once I could finally talk again, I said, "It is a good song, though."

The frat guy replied, "Yeah, definitely not a song you want to get caught blasting down the road, though."

I laughed again and said, "Yeah, man, that's definitely a headphone type of song."

The frat guy replied, "Hey, man, if you want, I'll help you get a babe out there or something, man. I'm great at hooking people up."

I told him I was all good. After he walked away, I started thinking about how weird and out of nowhere that had been. Any other time, I would've taken him up on the offer and had another crazy night like the one before, but I was already talking to the only "babe" I cared to talk to. Brooke replied, *I'd prefer the guy to be taller than me and have good hygiene. If he doesn't have those two going for him, then I don't even look his way, lol. Hygiene is probably my biggest requirement, lol, but yeah, it doesn't matter much to me what a person looks like.*

I had to keep everything light and continue with my jokes. She seemed to be responding pretty well to that. *Really? Lol, I'm pretty dirty from the road, so I guess I don't have much of a chance then, lol. So you're just more about personality then, right?*

No guy has much of a chance right now, lol, and yeah, personality is a lot for me. If I have to spend the rest of my life with a guy, I'm going to make sure I can actually get along with their personality before I even worry about what they look like.

I'd give anything to have a chance with you, I thought, but I knew I had to keep it light. *Well looks definitely matter to me. I guess I'm just a shitty person, but I just can't picture myself walking around with someone on my arm with a jagged edge for a smile, lol. Things like that are important: smile, looks, and personality for sure.*

I don't think it makes you a shitty person, but it's definitely rare to find the cute looks with a personality, lol.

I couldn't be light anymore with my replies. I had so much singing within my heart I wanted to say, but I knew I couldn't say it outright. I wanted her to get a sense of how I saw her, though, and I really hoped deep down she saw me the same way. *Yeah, it really is. When you do find somebody like that, you just recognize it as a rare thing like a real phenomenon. It's like a shooting star; you might see one or none your whole life. I think it's all about your energy though. It's like the universe reads what's in your heart, and it just takes you there, but only if you let it. That's kind of what happened with that car. I always wanted one just like it, and who would've knew in Stephen King's hometown I ran across the car of my dreams just like that. It's unbelievable.*

Yeah, that's why I look beyond physicality a majority of the time. It's definitely vibes. I guess that's what I was trying to describe above. Like your physical traits only get you so far with me, but if our vibes connect and just flow so in sync, then I'm definitely 10000x

attracted to you. But yes, your life is already written before you're born; you just get the pleasure of the unknown.

I couldn't have been any more attracted to another person even if they were the most beautiful Hollywood actress in the world. "The pleasure of the unknown," I like that a lot; I've had someone speak to me throughout dreams and tell me the same. You know how we've joked about the sugar mamas and daddy's out there? I had a chance for something like that while I've been here, and I found out that's not something I really want. I'd love to have the funds to travel everywhere I want to go, but it didn't feel right in my heart to me. This lady had condos about everywhere, but I'd rather do it on the fly off what I can do. I don't need what someone else can give me; I'm going to go off what the universe wants to give me. It's a crazy thing to see what it does from little things to big things. I've always tried to find my place in the world and never could, but now I realize that one place isn't my home. This whole world is mine and everywhere is my home; that's where I'm from. Sorry for the long text, lol. I know how your age group feels about paragraphs; they're very scary.

I like how you call me different than my age group, but then stereotype me with them, lol.

She had me on that one. *Lol, you are, but you're still influenced by their mindset.*

Example? Long texts don't scare me, lol. I send them myself.

She had me right up against the ropes with her cleverness. I don't really have an example now that I try to think of one; maybe it's just a feeling or stereotype I have. It's just something that comes to mind with people younger than me.

Well, I don't really find it fair to assume I'm like the rest of my generation. I'm far from it, honestly. I am very selective on what I choose to influence my perspective. I'm glad you discovered something else about yourself, though.

I thought, *if I had a kingdom of my own, I'd give it all to you. I wish I could take all of what I have in my heart for you and paint pictures across the sky with it. If I could, I really would. I'd do everything I could to give you everything you've ever wanted.* But I couldn't say that to her. All I could do was relay my dream for it when I replied, *It just isn't where my heart led me. I'd rather do it all on my own like an underdog ridin' high, lol. It's a lot more magical when you do it that way. Plus to me, if it isn't true love, I don't want it. If I don't have that feeling in my heart for that kind of love toward a person, I just don't want it anymore. I wasn't always that way, but this way sure feels a lot better. People laugh when I talk about true love, but it's something that I really believe in. People act like it's a fairytale and it isn't possible. It may not be for everyone else, but I'm going to make it possible, even if it kills me because that's what I want the most; I really do. I'm just talking. I'm not trying to lay the moves on you or anything. I know you're fine all by yourself.*

Well if it's something you're passionate about, then I think you should pursue it. Personally, I feel like when you want something that bad, it gets further away from you. Now, I'm all for waiting to give your all to one person, but I don't really strive to make it a priority to find it. I think life gives you what you want and need at the perfect time. So I know it'll come to me when I'm truly ready. But yes, I think true love is what everyone wants eventually.

She's where all that I was most passionate toward lied. I've always been passionate and loving toward my kids, but true love with a partner is what I've always been after the most. I've always wanted a bond that ran farther than emotions could ever be dreamt to run. Something that ignites eternally within two souls and is forever shared. Something time nor death could ever get between. It's possible; I know it is. It has to be.

All I could express to her was how I agreed with her, though. I couldn't let myself go all the way. She just wasn't ready to go there with me, and I knew that. I replied, *You're absolutely right about* that. I'm not looking for anything at all anymore. I just try to do right and love, as well as appreciate everything I gain or come across along the way. I just know when that moment does happen, it's going to be amazing.

Exactly. It will find you one day when you're really ready for it. Maybe you're not really ready for it now. Maybe God wants you to experience more self-growth than you had before. Maybe that's why you met me. For me to encourage you to take this time for self-growth to prepare yourself for that special love. You're a very passionate person, so you most likely love hard when you do love. You've got to be 100% ready for that kind of love, and so does the person you're going to love. Maybe you're ready, and they're not. Maybe they still have learning to do for their life too.

I left Dog Days while I could still drive, and when I went down the road back toward the Randall Hotel, the last text she sent me coursed throughout my entire body. She was absolutely right; only I felt like I was ready for it. I only wished she was ready for it too. She was everything I could ever hope to find in another person. All of these years of searching in the dark and fumbling around for what my heart always called out for the most was found with her. I wondered to myself, *Do I really love her?*

I wanted to say I did, but I wasn't sure what love even was. I just knew in my heart I wanted to find out. I'd never felt the way I felt about her toward anybody else. I kept thinking, *What do these feelings mean that I have for her? And why do I even feel them at all?*

When I first saw her, something happened inside of me that never happened before. Something unexplainable just clicked. It wasn't rational, and it didn't make any sense, but I had to figure it out. I had to discover the meaning of it all. She was the girl of my dreams and dreams were coming true left and right the whole trip. So what if this was it? I just didn't know, but I didn't want to keep it all buried in my heart anymore. How could I tell her, though? I didn't know.

29 Palms

    While I drove onward through the night, this song came on, and it felt like it played through my heart more than it was through the '69s radio. It was called "I'd Love You to Want Me." After I googled it, later on, I found out that it was by this guy called Lobo from back in the day. I got lost in that song through the night, and I drove onward thinking, *I really would. I really would love her to want me.*

CHAPTER XIX: RAMBLIN' GAMBLIN' MAN

29 Palms

There's something about being an outlaw, a dedicated renegade against the norm of things, that's always been so intriguing to me. Maybe that's why those old tales told about the West are so magical, so unreal to so many, compared to the life of servitude we all carry out in today's world. You know what I mean. We sell our souls for a dollar just to keep our heads above water.

When the cowboys rode across the plains, they lived a true life of freedom. Every minute, every day, was a gamble to them. It didn't matter if they won it all or lost it all; it was the thrill, the thrill of living, the joy of the ride giving meaning to each of their days. Their journey could end in a lover's arms or in a blaze of glory; it didn't matter. When each one of those old gunslingers bit the dust, they all knew one thing; that they *lived*. The biggest regret most of us have after we've been worked to death and we've ran out of time is the regret of not having the courage to gamble, to go all in, and dare to live. Not me, though. Racing through those dirt roads around Dodge City in that old '69, at this point, I was a cowboy, or at least I felt like one.

I even stayed at the old Cimarron Hotel the night before, one of the last remaining hotels of the Old West. It was a large, red-brick, two-story piece of time haunting the little town of Cimarron right down the road from Dodge City. While I stood before the hotel staring at the two-story balcony just above my gaze, it felt like I could almost see a bunch of folks up there playing cards in the evening, shooting slick remarks at one another as each hand was dealt. Most of the folks in the scene seemed humbly dressed in dirty, old, flannel-like attire, but a few folks wore top hats, making them stand out irregularly amongst the crowd. You could tell they didn't belong, but it was all about the thrill of the forbidden; it didn't matter.

Of course, there weren't card tables and top hats floating around up there on that old porch that day. I just have an illustrious imagination allowing me to time travel every once in a while in my head. The modern-day fell past the horizon and brought back a more adventurous time, even if it was only for a moment. Dreams are more immersive, though.

That night while I was asleep in the Cimarron, I found myself in a dream. I was around the same old Victorian-era furniture adorning the room, sitting in a plush red armchair staring at a kindled fireplace dancing before my eyes through thick clouds of cigar smoke. I noticed a figure in the chair across from me, whose face I wasn't able to make out beyond the almond scented clouds. The figure spoke, and he asked, "Well, how do you do there, friend?"

I wasn't startled by the voice at all, surprisingly, but I felt an air of comfort with the scene I was in as I lit up a cigar of my own. I replied, "It's been a long ride, but I've been doing just fine. What brings you all the way out here?"

The figure started to become clearer through the smoke. He had an old, dark vest on and sat there with his sleeves rolled up in a relaxed way. As a wide-brimmed hat started to appear, the figure replied, "Oh, an old sickness is what a lot of folks would say, but quite frankly, I much prefer the life of a gamblin' man to that of a life of service. Bothers me none. What would you consider yourself, a sick man or a gamblin' man?"

I didn't have to think on it, but the answer seemed to be there all on its own. I said, "Both. I'll tell you what, the ride is a gamble in its own, but the thrill seems to be the cure. Only a thrill never seems to last forever, and the sickness always makes its way back. If only a thrill wasn't subject to time. I don't think I'd ever feel sick again."

A large mustache and a goatee appeared on this western fellow's face as he replied, "That's where you're wrong, my friend.

Life itself is the thrill. I've lost it all on several occasions, you see, but I always end up gettin' my chips back. Here's the real daisy for ya, though. It doesn't matter if I'm holdin' my best hand or my worst. I'm still in the game. I still have a hand to play. You can win on the worst hand if you have the know-how to do it. The trick is to keep playing. I've never seen a man take the whole table after playin' only one hand."

I replied, "The thrill is the game itself then. Even when it seems like we're losing, there's still a way to win, right? And finding a way out of a loss sometimes leads to a greater thrill than winning outright. I think I'm getting it— yeah—I got it."

The figure replied with a puff of smoke, "No. You don't have it quite yet, my friend, but that's close enough. Living with loss is all a part of the game too."

I replied, "Wow, thanks. That gives me a lot to think about. What's your name anyway?"

The figure's mustache curled upward along with his lips as he held out his hand to shake mine, "You can call me Doc."

Doc was right. The following day, I could feel the thrill in life itself as the '69 gunned its way across the dirt and dust of the straightaway Kansas landscape. That day as I headed toward the Monument Rocks, it didn't feel like I was driving; it was more like flying. The rhythm and rolling of the wind carried me away toward something unknown. It was like nature decided to come along, and everything out there rode along with me. There was even a hawk overhead swaying from right to left above the '69 as its pipes thundered down the road. The sight of the hawk sent a single word from the past reverberating within my mind, *Vikare*.

Vikare is a name that's seldom been spoken for over a thousand years, but his legend is still remembered through other names. The tale goes that Vikare and his father once found themselves trapped in a labyrinth of their own making. They were in such a dilemma only one of them could truly escape this ancient maze of life, or whatever it could've been. So Vikare's father fashioned a set of wings to send him soaring out of the labyrinth toward the everlasting freedom they both so much desired.

    Before his flight, Vikare was told by his father not to fly too low, or he'd be swallowed up by the sea and not to fly too high, or he'd be ground into ashes by the sun. The legend ends with Vikare ascending too high in his flight, setting his wings ablaze, and plunging into the sea to his death, but I don't believe that. There's no limit to how high you can fly, and maybe Vikare left one labyrinth only to get lost in another. Maybe he's still out there searching for that one thing that truly feels real to him. Wings can tire after aiming for the horizon for too long, but strength is held through the pursuit of your one true heart's desire. I can understand that a lot better than soaring too high. I know I'd fly for a thousand years just to reach something like that.

    The sight of the hawk above injected a breath of inspiration and drive into my heart, blowing all of my fears and doubts away. I didn't know if I'd get what I desired at the end of my journey, but I told myself I'd never allow my wings to tire for it because whether the flight went through a storm or if my way was painted clear by the stars, it would all be worth it in the end regardless. I couldn't tell myself that before. There were so many times I wanted to shoot myself into the cliffs because the horizon seemed too clouded, but on that day, I could see the sun. I rode with the wind at my back, and the hawk flying before me. Then, appearing just within my line of view, there they were; those ancient towers once hidden within the sea.

    The archway of the Monument Rocks put me in the mind of a gateway. As if it were a looking glass, I saw the world within its eye and I felt a sense of all the worlds beyond the here and now, along with all that had come before. A voice came in the wind and said, *It's all here now, all manner of possibilities. Just keep your eyes to the sun and feel the depth of your dreams within you. Always believe in that. The wind may seem to be too much and the waves may drown you, but hold steadfast; when a paddle is needed, one shall fall. Keep the hands at work and never idle. True wings never tire until they've reached the end of their cycle.*

I wondered to myself as the typhoons of dust blew all around me, *How does one grow wings to fly? Are they always there or do they appear on their own?* Then, it all came to me.

Every soul that's ever been has the ability to fly, but there is no need for wings if there's no direction or destination in mind. Action uncovers the true will of every spirit. It's like digging in the sands of the desert. There appears to be nothing there, at first, but given time, as the knuckles bleed and the eyes can no longer see, you'll reach the bottom, and there your treasure will be. The excavation is complete. The tale is told and now you see where you were always meant to be.

I didn't know where I was headed then or where I should go, though, but in that moment, I couldn't keep myself from thinking about Brooke.

As much as I wanted to share with her how much I felt for her at that moment, I couldn't. *What if it scares her away and she never talks to me again?* I thought, *I'd better just keep it light.* So I sent her a picture of an obelisk-looking spire pointing toward the sky amongst the Monument Rocks. I texted, *Kind of a naughty picture too, if you look at it a certain way.* You know, because technically it sort of looked like a dick to tell you the truth. She sent a bunch of laughing emojis right after, and with a smile, I thought to myself, *Well, at least I could make her laugh today.*

29 Palms

    I peeled the tires of the '69 loose from the dirt and gravel surrounding the Monument Rocks and shot my way back toward the Cimarron as Led Zeppelin's "Immigrant Song" blared across the '69's radio. I'd already tossed a few coins atop the graves of some old cowboys earlier that day when I visited Boot Hill to pay my respects for the passage that would carry me farther out west toward the great Rocky Mountains. Those titans are a hell of a sight to see in person, but if you want to visit hell itself, I've always heard it's best to stay at the Stanley Hotel, which is where I was headed next. The only thing is, I don't know to this day if the hotel will give you more hell or the staff. Maybe everything that happened there really was all my fault. Who knows?

CHAPTER XX: CAN YOU HEAR ME KNOCKING

    The Great Rocky Mountains. I couldn't believe I was there at that moment, staring across a meadow of jagged giants crowned by a tundra running darker along the edges of each mountain as the descent of each grew deeper and deeper across the horizon. It was breathtaking and mind-boggling all at the same time. I thought to myself, *This snow up here is trippin' me out. I mean, I was just sweating my ass off in the '69 on the way here, but there it is right in front of me. Snow. How peculiar.* It just didn't make a whole lot of sense to me, plus I'm no scientist. I'd rather be the imaginative type and just get carried away by the wonders of nature rather than know how it all works.

I knew Brooke would appreciate that fantastic view just as much as I did. I sent her a picture and said, *How is that for a view there, ma'am?*

She expressed a deep love for the Rocky Mountains in our conversation. She thought it was as breathtaking as I did, and when she used that word right there, *breathtaking*, I thought to myself, *You're breathtaking, Brooke. All these beautiful things that I've seen all across nature, none of it means a thing. None of it comes close to comparing to you.*

In my heart, as I stood atop that mountain, I knew I'd throw that view away completely just to get a sight of her. I wanted to hold her in my arms and look deeply into her eyes and tell her how I felt about her without having an ounce of fear in the moment. It would be the greatest of eclipses, I thought to myself. When the sun and moon meet in unison, the stars glow brighter around them in an applause that would shake the whole world. Even if the word great doesn't even come close to the reality of it, that's just what it would be. I had to give her more time to see things that way. If she ever did. *Maybe that moment will happen in Vegas*, I thought. Only the days to come would tell.

After taking in the Rockies' grand atmosphere, I couldn't run away from the possible horrors awaiting me any longer. The Stanley was just below the mountains—waiting to claim me. *Nothing bad is going to happen*, one side of me thought, but my other half chimed in with, *Well, it's been a good run, pal. Who knows, once the hotel takes you like it has so many others, you'll make a bunch of new friends on the other side? Dying can't be all that bad.* I assured myself, though, that there was no way death awaited me at the Stanley, and there wouldn't be anything life-threatening about it at all. I was wrong.

The check-in process pissed me off to a degree of making me want to roar like a poltergeist across the place as the clerk told me the six hundred and fifty dollars I used to book a room in the Stanley wasn't going to be in the Stanley at all, but it would be in the lodge right next to it. Even though I was pissed, I still tried to stay polite when I said to the clerk, "That can't be right. I booked a room in the *main* building, not the lodge. There has to be some kind of mistake here."

The clerk replied, "As many other guests have. Unfortunately, the main building is closed due to the Coronavirus. We're directing all of our guests to the lodges surrounding the main building; you'll have a room right in this one."

I couldn't believe it. I wanted to snap, *Are you fucking kidding me? The main building is closed because of the virus, but you're still letting everyone stay in the lodges? Why even have the 'hotel' open at all? You guys are ripping people off! You're a dream killer, lady!* But I didn't. I accepted my fate and took the bare tray I was dealt, and the tray was quite bare indeed. I mean, the damn thing barely had any food on it at all.

The cable didn't work in my room, and on top of all that, it was 85 degrees in there and the A/C didn't work at all. It wasn't just my room either. The whole lodge didn't have air conditioning. I decided to bite the bullet and not make a scene about it, though. At least I could look out of the window and look at the outside of the Stanley as I cried over the shards of a childhood dream torn to pieces by the hotel's wonderful management team.

I decided to walk down to the store to get a twelve-pack of Blue Ribbon and some Wild Irish Rose to help me cool off. I was really pissed, but I couldn't scream at the lady clerk about it. She was very polite to me, and I just don't have it in me to come at people like that. I felt cheated and ripped off, but there was nothing like a few beers and some fine wine to bring in the "I don't even give a shit" attitude.

It worked. I really didn't care after the bottle of rose passed through my lips, and I pumped myself up full of Blue Ribbon bravery. I thought to myself, *You know what? Fuck it. I'm gonna at least walk around the main building and get a look-see of the inside from the windows. It's late enough at night. Nobody will be out and about on the grounds. Maybe try a door or two to see if one's unlocked. What's the worst that could happen?*

The Stanley Hotel looked creepier than ever on that eerie, windy night as the crickets sang their little warnings of, *Dude, this isn't a good idea; turn back.* Or at least it seemed like they were. Of course, I didn't try the doors to the front or the back, but the doors on the side porch—they seemed like fair game.

The boards of the deck creaked under my feet as I peered inside from window to window. It was pretty dark inside the hotel, but the foyer-like room I studied through the windows was dimly lit from the moon beaming down from the hollow night sky. It looked so empty and lonely in the foyer room from the window and all. *Did they move all the furniture out?* I thought, *They couldn't have. There has to be something in there.* And there was. All of a sudden, a girl appeared.

I jumped back from the window with a gasp that nearly turned into a scream, but then the door opened up, and a smiling girl popped her head out and said, "Hey, wanna come in?"

She was alive and wasn't a ghost—thank god—or at least appeared to be. My cool came back in an instant just about, and with shrugging shoulders, I replied, "Sure, why not?"

After I entered the Stanley's foyer, I noticed the girl wasn't alone, but there was a blonde-haired fella with her and a pretty, attractive girl with some ripped-up jeans along with her. Through my excitement I skipped, then jumped, and said, "I can't believe you guys got in. I was supposed to be staying in here tonight, but those assholes next door gypped me—guess it doesn't matter now because now we're in the main building."

The girl in the white sweater laughed along with her friends and said, "Really, man? That's bullshit."

I replied, "Yeah—I mean—we're probably really fuckin' up, but while we're in here, we should check out Room 217. That's the worst room to visit in the hotel." They seemed down for it, so off we went exploring.

The vacant piano in the Stanley's foyer seemed pretty ominous in the already very creepy surroundings of the darkened creaking room. I thought to myself, *Well, if I were by myself in here, I probably would've already pissed my pants and been out the door*; this was the most haunted hotel in America after all, but I wasn't alone. I was lucky enough to have a few new friends along with me.

While we walked through the lit-up hallways of the Stanley across the dark magenta carpet, I cracked a joke with the folks I hung with and said, "Yep, we'll probably get the cuffs slapped on us tonight, folks. If we do ,I'll just be like, 'Hey, thought I was bookin' a room here. I was just lookin' for my room, honestly."

The girls laughed, but the blonde-haired dude looked a tad scared after I'd mentioned the possibility of an arrest. It was definitely in the cards, though. Why fool yourself into believing that it wasn't? Best not to bring it up, though, I guess.

We all entered a room on the second floor after climbing one of the Stanley's many winding staircases, and one of the girls jumped on a bed with the other guy. I stopped and looked at them, surprised with a look that had to say, *Are you guys about to fuck?* I sure hoped not. Not with me in the room because I wasn't planning on joining in. With a confused laugh, I shuffled my legs as quickly as possible out of the room as they carried me back into the hall where the other girl was. I looked toward the end of the second-floor hall and saw the numbers 217 boldly placed to the right of a chestnut door. I looked back to the girl in ripped-up jeans and said, "Look, it's Room 217."

She smiled back at me, looking all mischievous and everything. I shot ahead of her toward the door and tried the knob. It was locked. I knocked three times on the door. They all started cracking up down the hall. I guess it was sort of funny, so I laughed myself. Then we all ran away up the staircase to the hotel's third floor to see what awaited us there.

All of the rooms were empty, and you could tell they were in the middle of being prepared for the reopening after the Covid restrictions were lifted. We eventually came across a pitch black room that had nothing but a wardrobe inside of it. Like a maniac, I walked into the room first and waved for the others to follow me, and I said, "Guys, look at this. What the hell is this?"

One of the girls screeched away laughing, "What the fuck is that? Maybe it's like a portal to another dimension?"

Maybe it was. It did put me in the mind of the wardrobe from the *Chronicles of Narnia*. Maybe one adventure would lead to another, and we'd all find ourselves in some cabin hot boxing a peace pipe with some little half-fawn half-man dude just trying to figure all our shit out together. Everything was normal though. I opened the doors to the wardrobe, and it was as empty as the hotel was. It was kind of a disappointment. I've always liked the idea of visiting Narnia.

When we continued down the hallway, I started thinking about the movie *The Shining* and of Jack Nicholson running down the hallway with an ax screaming, "Danny! Danny boy!" The thought of being in the actual setting of perhaps Stephen King's most famous novel felt so surreal to me. Then I thought about the twin ghost girls Danny saw in the hallway as he rode his big wheel through the halls, and I said, "Danny, come play with us."

The girls busted out laughing. Right after that, a guy came out from behind us and said, "Hey, you guys can't be in here." *Shit, we were caught.*

Since we were caught, there wasn't any point in freaking out. I knew the risk. Hell, we all knew the risk. *Might as well play it cool and not panic,* I thought, so I replied, "No? We're not?—Oh ok. It is pretty creepy. You don't ever get scared in here, man?"

The hotel guy replied, "Oh yeah, I do because I work here. It's always creepy—"

Stuttering, I interrupted, "Have you—have you ever seen anything in here?"

The hotel guy replied, "Yeah, man—yeah, especially where that basement parts at down there near the lobby—yeah, check out that area; it's pretty creepy—"

One of the girls interjected, "Can we?"

The hotel guy replied, "Right in the front. Right, where everybody comes in; there by the entrance—definitely check that out."

I replied, "Oh fuck—ok—Yeah, we'll definitely check that out."

The hotel guy started walking away, but I screamed, "Hey! Hey, man! Could you get us into Room 217?"

The hotel guy replied, "I can't. I have a job to do." As the girls laughed, the hotel guy continued, "I'm actually being nice right now."

As we walked away from the hotel guy, I replied, "Yeah, you are, 'preciate it, man. We'll check out the basement."

The damn basement was locked, though, or I thought where we went was toward the basement. There were so many old photographs adorning the walls as we headed down there, it forced me to keep in mind where I was and that something a lot more sinister than the hotel guy could be lurking behind any corner.

There was something more than us in those halls. It was as if something watched me ever so closely. It felt like a feminine entity of some kind. *Maybe I'm just getting paranoid*, I thought, but knowing what I know now, I believe something did pick me out in those halls that night.

We continued exploring the hotel until, eventually, we made our way outside to the courtyard in the back toward a fire escape leading to the rooftop. The others wanted to climb up to the top, but there was no way I was climbing around all the way up there. I was scared to death of heights. It was time for me to say sayonara to the rest and make it back to my room. I figured I'd already pressed my luck enough as it was.

When I entered back into the lodge by the Stanley, the lady clerk sat there at the desk staring at me as I walked in. In an act to seem as inconspicuous as possible, I said, "Whew! I started getting hot up there in my room. I figured I'd take a little walk and get some air. It's really pretty out there at night time."

The lady clerk replied with a kind smile. "I'm sorry about the air. A lot of guests are upset about it. You can always open the windows if you'd like."

I smiled with a nod and said, "Yeah, I'll try that out."

While I walked up the steps, I thought, *Yep, paid over six hundred dollars for a room you have to open the windows in so you don't suffocate to death. Hope they don't have laundry listed in the amenities. I'd hate to ask about that. They'd probably say, 'Oh, we don't have a dryer;*

that's what the clotheslines are for out back. Need some pins?' What a bunch of bullshit. At least I got an adventure in tonight. I continued to think there was no way the next night at the Stanley could top the first. Boy, was I wrong.

CHAPTER XXI: HELLRAISER

    Night had fallen at the Stanley again. While I sat on a bench, staring out into a bite-sized clearing that gave way to the lights of the trickling little town of Estes Park, my thoughts started to carry me away.

    I had gotten lost in the Garden of the Gods earlier that day, and I'm not trying to be poetic about it at all. I really did. I damn near died of thirst if that guy wouldn't have come along and saved me, but that place, it was just something different.

    The red rock towers abounding in that land of old invoked a sense of something ancient, perhaps prehistoric, within my soul. It was as true to a name as any place could be. It was magnetic and magnificent. There was magic in the air out there. I thought to myself, *Anu, who wound up the grand spinning wheel of time long ago and let it all go, you are here.* It felt like that old architect still resided there in a way. It was spectacular to say the least.

I sent a few pictures to Brooke of the amazing scenery, but it was quite a short-lived conversation. *What if she is starting to close the door again?* I thought. She'd been so open with me in her words during the whole trip, and it was like every syllable healed me in a way. When I talked to her, I didn't feel like I was this broken and shattered thing. I didn't feel like I was scrambling around in the dark for all the missing pieces anymore. Her words made me feel full. *But what if she stopped talking to me? What if—what if I lost her?* I thought. It was like my thoughts summoned her or something because while I sat all alone on that bench, that's when Brooke texted me.

It's a nice, lightly humid summer night here in Mobile, Alabama. I love summer nights.

I felt so warm and wanted. She must've been thinking about me the same time I thought about her. *How magical is that?* I thought, then I replied, *What do you love about them so much?*

The feel of the night. The true meaning of "the night is still young." Like I could conquer the world in just this night because we might only have this one night. The nights people step out of their comfort zone and just go for it. Do it like it's their last night. So you try everything to make it just one epic night.

We could conquer the world together, I thought. I replied, *I know about that, lol; you know you're really kind of a poet at heart. I think you hide that side of yourself from a lot of people. A lot more than you should.*

She started typing but stopped; then no response came at all. I figured she must've gotten busy or something, so I got up from the bench and walked the grounds again among the stars of the night.

Something made me stop in front of the hotel. It felt like—something was—like something watched me. I looked to my left at a corner window that had to have been on the fourth floor. There was something about it—something about that room. Someone was in there. The hotel was supposed to be empty, and even though I didn't see anyone in the window, I could feel someone there—watching in the darkness. Whoever or whatever it was staring down at me from that window wasn't a friendly fellow at all. Suddenly, I started to hear laughter behind me, and I turned around to see who it was. There, just ahead, was a group of four girls sitting cross-legged on the ground playing some sort of game. With a smoke in hand, I walked over to see what they were playing; it was a Ouija board.

I said, "Y'all are playing with a Ouija board right in front of the Stanley Hotel? That's a terrible idea."

One of the girls replied with a laugh, "Probably so—you wanna join?"

With enthusiasm, delight, and a drag off my smoke, I replied, "Well, absolutely."

All the girls in the group seemed to be around my age, except for one. She had long dark hair, and she put me in the mind of the Goth chicks that would linger in the halls skipping class back in my high school days. *She has to still be in high school*, I thought.

The rest of the girls seemed cool, but I could tell they weren't too much into guys, which was fine with me; I didn't care. I thought, *Great some outsiders and rejects just like me. We should get along just fine.* One of the girls offered me some liquor and beer. She said, "Here, you can have all you want."

I already had a couple of margaritas earlier with dinner and got around six Blue Ribbons deep after that, so I figured, *Why not?*

Talk to the dead and have a few drinks; what's the worst that could happen?

Shortly after a few shots, the girl said, "Ok guys, we're going to go ahead and do the preparation spell first so that we're protected from whatever comes through."

Then she lit the candles for the spell, and I thought to myself, *Preparation spell? That's an odd form of protection. We'd be a lot better off if I did a quick and simple banishing ritual. That'd do the trick,* but I just shrugged my shoulders and decided to go along with it anyway.

The five of us each placed a hand on the planchette. The girl who gave me a beer, whose name was Lindsey, started to ask the board, "Is there anyone here with us?"

No movement. Lindsey asked the same question again, and the planchette began to move. A N D Y. Andy. *Well, hello there, Andy.* Lindsey said, "Well, hi, Andy. Is there anything you want to tell us?"

The planchette started to move again. G O. *Go?* Lindsey asked, "Are you telling us to leave, Andy?"

The high school girl, whose name was Sarah, jumped back with a squeal damn near right into my lap. I thought, *Please. No. High school. Get off me.* Lindsey and the other girls panicked and told Sarah she had to keep her hand on the planchette. Whoever started had to finish. With a calmed but still trembling hand, Sarah put her fingers back on the planchette. Lindsey asked again, "Are you telling us to leave, Andy?" The planchette spelled out Y E S. *Yes.* Lindsey continued, "Why do we need to leave Andy?"

H E R. *Her? Her who?* I thought. Lindsey said, "Her who, Andy? Who is her?" The planchette forced its way to goodbye.

We all took our hands off the planchette. I looked around at a couple of calm and a couple panicked faces and said, "Ok—well, alright. Who's fuckin' with me? Was one of you guys moving that thing?"

The group let out a resounding no, but Sarah looked like she was in a complete panic mode; she didn't say a thing at all. Maybe she was thinking the same thing as I was; who was her, and why did we need to leave? Lindsey, however, looked pretty calm. *Too calm. Was she moving the planchette? Only one way to find out*, I thought.

Breaking the silence, I said, "Who's ready for another go? I know I am." Everyone reluctantly, except for Lindsey, placed their hands back on the planchette. Lindsey said, "You can ask it questions this time if you want." Sounded acceptable to me.

I started off and said, "Is there anyone present with us?" Y E S. Yes. There most certainly was. I could feel its presence in the air. It was much heavier than Andy's was. I barely felt him at all. Maybe Lindsey hadn't been moving the planchette. I then asked with a smile, "You're quite high up in the spiritual hierarchy, aren't you?"

The spirit replied with another yes like I knew it would. I asked if it was a female because it felt feminine. It responded with another yes. The lady spirit gave her name, but I can't recall what it was—probably for a reason. There was a lot wiped from my memory that night, and I feel like this lady spirit had something to do with it. The girls started to look real uneasy and freaked out except for Lindsey. I had to press further, though. I asked, "Is there someone more powerful than you here?" Another yes.

Then I said, "Can I speak with the most powerful being here?" The planchette shot toward no. One of the girls asked me, kind of joking, but I could tell she was serious about it, "Who are you? You're not one of the ghosts around here, are you?"

With a big grin, I said, "Well, of course not. What would give you that idea?"

She wasn't the first person who asked me if I was a ghost. Back in Dodge, an old guy walked up to me as I filled up the '69 and said, "I've seen you around town a lot today in this old '69 Caprice of yours, and I about damn near thought you was some kind of ghost ridin' around town listenin' to that old music. Why a feller used to ride around here about forty years back who looked a hell of a lot like you in a car that looked a hell of a lot like that. You ain't some sort of ghost, are ya?"

The man finished with a laugh, but I had to fuck with him—I mean, he opened the door up for it after all, so I didn't really have a choice. I replied, "Maybe I am. Maybe I'm just another ghost ridin' around in these plains."

Many folks take me for a ghost if they don't know me, and a lot of the time, I feel like one. Like I'm in the wrong time period or something.

Next, I asked the spirit, "Is the being demonic?" The planchette shot faster toward yes than it did earlier. That answer seemed to scare the shit out of everyone, including me. I continued to ask questions anyway. I gathered myself and didn't even want to know the being's name, so I asked, "Are you afraid of this being?"

The planchette would not move. It was like the spirit decided to stop talking to us. I asked, "Are you still with us?"

The planchette moved slowly toward no. I asked, "Who are you?"

The planchette started to spell out A Z A R—I started thinking rapidly, *It can't be; it can't be,* as the planchette continued to the letter I then A. As the planchette began moving toward H, I forced it toward goodbye, and I said to the rest, "Sorry, I don't know about you guys, but I was starting to get a little freaked out."

One of the girls replied, "Shit, I was freaked out when you started asking about demons and shit, man." *Perhaps that wasn't a good idea,* I thought, but it was something I needed to know. That's not why I chose to end the session, though. I knew without a shadow of a doubt I spoke to something from the other world—something different. I hadn't told that name to anyone. Nobody in that group knew the name of my youngest son. I hadn't said the name Azariah to anyone.

I couldn't understand—I still can't understand why the spirit brought up Azariah. I knew there was something different about my youngest son. He's like any other kid in a lot of ways, but mysterious in others. There's something about the way he looks at people that just put them off, and many folks have picked up on it. I even had a person tell me once, "If I didn't know any better, I'd say that little boy could see right through me. There's just something about his eyes. He's—I don't know—it's like he's been here before."

It was almost nice to hear someone I barely knew say the same thing I'd always thought. I didn't feel as crazy. It would be even wilder for me to say I didn't name him at all. His name came from somewhere else entirely.

Two of the girls left after the session. They still looked a little spooked, but the blunt they smoked calmed them down a bit, it looked like. Lindsay and Sarah stayed in the same lodge I got duped into paying for too, so we continued to drink with one another out on the grounds. Then it occurred to me—Brooke—did she text back yet? I completely forgot about texting her back. I guess I got too caught up in chatting with the dead. I looked down at my phone as I read her reply. **Not many people like to have deep conversations and deep thoughts. They don't want to think anything but standard. When I feel nights like this, it makes me think of me riding in a car with the rooftop down, riding through a tunnel, and just** *holding my arms open and head up—just embracing the night—letting it be me in just that moment—nothing else.*

She was so beautiful. Every inch of her, and I love her so much for it. I ran the scene she painted with her words through my head. It led me to the most wonderful, vivid imagery, and I cherished every second of it; I replied, Like a midnight rider, right? Just like the song, I like that. You ever find it odd that the most simple things can make you feel so much happiness and joy, but your mind and character are just as complex as they ever could be?

It's like at that moment, the world slows down, reality pauses, and you just feel—free. No matter how lost, you may think in reality. Those bursts of happiness prove that happiness is created within before shared with others. And not even materials can buy it.

She didn't reply to the strange words that fell forth from my fingertips at the end, but when it came to the rest, she was right. Brooke had a whole philosophy for doing things alone. I understood where she came from, I guess; I just couldn't ever understand why she emphasized doing everything alone. I wanted to ask, What about love, though? That means something too. Don't you want someone to care about you? You might need it someday. I guess that song by Heart sums up all of my questions. I didn't ask her any of that, though—I couldn't. I just replied, You always come up with the most beautiful thoughts. I'm starting to realize that myself. Materials don't mean anything. It's like where I'm at now; it feels so different than it does everywhere else. Do you think magic is real?

I believe being one with the Earth is real, and I've even experienced it. Like you feel connected to the elements. That kind of spiritual magic. Getting "powers" from the dead, eh, not so much.

I asked her about her belief in magic because whether she knew it or not, she was pretty good at it. The vivid scenes she'd paint through her visualizations were magic all on their own because they had an intense, psychological effect on the mind. They don't change the world, but they have a powerful effect on changing your outlook on reality. It's a very ancient and effective way of bringing your thoughts and feelings into a tangible form. If she only knew how effective her words were on casting a spell across my heart.

I could tell she didn't know what I talked about, and I didn't know how to create a response to tell you the truth. After all, Lindsay kept pouring vodka in my beer can, and I was teetering on the edge as it was, but I managed to reply, *I don't believe in death. Sure, people die, but we all live on in one way or another. Energy never dies; it is only transferred. Just because you can't see something doesn't mean it doesn't exist. When I go to each of these places, it's like the past is still alive in a way, and when I'm in that car, I feel like something else is there with me and that it loves me.*

I believe in a paranormal world, but I don't believe you can draw power from it. To me, the elements are what holds the true magic.

Nope, she didn't get it, only some of it. I had to stop texting her before I dug myself an even deeper hole. *I'm about completely tore up,* I thought to myself, *Damn it, Lindsay, why are you doing this to me?*

I looked over at Lindsay and Sarah, who I'd been talking with around the fireplace in the lodge's gathering room. I said to Lindsay with a laugh, "Oh man, I don't know how much more I can handle. How much vodka have you been pouring in that beer?"

Lindsay replied with a big grin, "Not that much. You'll be fine. Just sit here and talk with us. You want more?"

I thought, *Well, since your twisting my arm,* and replied, "Sure, why not?"

We sat there and talked for what felt like hours. Lindsay and Sarah were traveling across the states too. They said they'd even be in the Santa Fe and Tombstone areas just like I'd be in the following days. I couldn't believe the odds of running into two people that happened to be doing the same thing I was and headed to the same places too. It was crazy, and I was getting delirious. I confessed to them why I decided to travel so far. Through the fog, I can remember saying, "I just love this girl; I really do. I made her a promise that'd I'd go wherever my heart carried me—only—it's starting to lead me to her." I might've even cried (memory is pretty foggy) as I kept rambling on. "I don't think she feels the same way, though. It's like I'd bring the sun and the moon down and build her a whole new world just to show her how much I care. I'd do anything just to get her to love me back."

Lindsay replied, "Look, man, I think you're really overthinking things way too much. Just tell her how you feel when you meet up with her in Vegas. Who knows what could happen? Think poossiiitttive thoughts. Positive. It'll all turn out ok."

I hoped so much in my heart Lindsay was right. I really did. Maybe the most magical moment of all would happen in Vegas, and Brooke would finally give me a chance to be hers. *Maybe was more of a chance than not having one at all.* I couldn't wait to get to Vegas. I felt like I would go nuts with all of the feelings I had bearing down on my heart that I was damn near dying to let out. *Vegas. Maybe it really will all happen in Vegas,* I thought to myself. It was a thought that grew into a dream.

I'm not sure how late it got, but I couldn't even sit in a chair straight by that point. I managed to pull myself up out of the old Victorian lazy chair I'd been sitting in, and as I waved goodbye to Lindsay and Sarah, I said, "Well guys, I'm really—I don't know, man—I'm pretty fucked up. I gotta get upstairs, man—I'll see ya'll tomorrow."

They might've said bye too, or they probably just laughed as I stumbled my way out of the common room, ping-ponging my way across the walls as I went. Climbing the staircase felt like an Olympic feat. I climbed halfway and crawled the rest. Once I got to my room, I had to struggle to get the key in the door as I wobbled around screaming down the hallway, "Fuuuccckkk! Why me?!"

I may have woken a few folks up to say the least. Once I figured out the key card didn't go in the door, but over it, I got the door to open. The bed beckoned, and I completely collapsed into it.

The next day I woke up to someone prodding me with some sort of stick, or was it a flashlight? I'm not sure. They were saying, "Hey. Hey, buddy! HELLO!"

My eyes fluttered open slowly. I was back in the easy chair in the common room. *How did I get here?* I thought.

Three police officers were standing over me. My eyes immediately popped the rest of the way open. I was clueless. I said, "Ummm—What's—what's the fucks is goin' on?"

I couldn't even talk. One of the officers said, "Don't worry about that. We have a few questions about *what you did* last night!"

My mind rambled, *What did I do? I went to my room to sleep. I couldn't have done anything, but what am I doing back in the common area?* I continued to look around in a daze of confusion as I tried to get a grasp of what exactly was going on. One of the officers snapped at me, "Well, how about we help jog your memory a little bit, pal. What were *you* doing on that rooftop last night?"

What the hell is he talking about? I shook my head and said, "What?—what rooftop? I wasn't on a rooftop last night."

The officer put his hands on his hips for a minute, staring me down like I was the vilest thing on planet Earth. His two comrades looked like they were struggling to keep a straight face while their buddy got all worked up. They were about to burst wide open with laughter. *Is this a joke?*

29 Palms

The angry officer snapped back with a pointed finger, "Oh, you weren't on the rooftop of the main building last night? Well, tell me this. Why do we have a video of someone wearing the same cowboy boots that your wearing swinging off that tower up there screaming last night then?!" The officer crossed his arms; he continued, "Big coincidence if you ask me."

My thoughts raced evermore, *Was I swinging off the tower of the main building last night? Could I have? These boots of mine were handmade in Dodge City, so nobody else around here could possibly have the same pair—I'm scared to death of heights; what would make me climb up there?*

The officer continued, "And to make it even worse, you were caught in the kitchen last night trying to make a sandwich. You scared the hotel staff half to death. What do you have to say for yourself?"

I was in complete shock and was still halfway drunk from the night before. I leaned forward and placed my hand on my forehead as my eyes darted back and forth. *Where is my headband?* I had to say something, so I replied, "I don't—I don't know what I could've been doing up there. The last thing I can remember was going to my room and going to sleep. I'm scared to death of heights, man. Are you sure I was even up there?"

The officer shot back, "Well, you were, and we have a video. You scared that poor lady out of her mind last night. She thought you were going to jump."

Oh my god, am I going to jail? I'll never make it to Vegas if that happens, and I'll never get to see Brooke. The trip will be over. It can't all end like this. The officer shot me out of my delirium when he said, "My partner is going to walk with you outside. Me and Tom here are going to talk to the staff and see about just what we're going to do about this. *Don't go anywhere.*"

29 Palms

While Officer Brian, *Is his name Brian*, stood out on the front porch, I stared off toward the Rockies in complete shock. I looked over to Officer Brian wide-eyed and said, "Honestly, man, I don't know what I could've been doing up there. I can't remember anything about it. I had a few drinks, obviously, but I swear I went back to my room. Or at least I thought I did."

Officer Brian replied with a smirk, "It happens to the best of us. Everybody's just glad that you're ok. The staff is really upset about it all, though. We'll just have to see what they say."

Shit. "*We'll just have to see what they say,*" *he says. At least they didn't have a clue about what I did the night before. I could remember all that—but this. None of it makes any sense.* Deputy Angry returned to the front porch and said, "Well, today's your lucky day. You can go back upstairs and sleep it all off."

I almost wanted to wrap my arms around him and spin Officer Angry around in delight, but I didn't want to get shot, so I did as I was told and collapsed back into my sauna-like room for some more rest.

When I woke back up, I packed everything as fast as I could. It was time to gun the '69 out of that dreadful place and make my way through New Mexico and then on to Tombstone, Arizona—but my phone. *Where is my phone?* I flipped back through my bags immediately. I looked under the bed, over the bed, out the window, in the window, but no phone. *Where could it be?*

I carried on toward the walk of shame down toward the lobby of the lodge, where I heard a man speaking in a pretty angry tone, "Yeah, well, he's not welcome back. EVER! I want him off the premises right now!"

The man speaking talked to the lady at the front desk as she looked forward in a pretty sad and somber tone. When I approached the angry manager (I'm guessing that's what he was), he shot a glance my way looking like he'd chop my head right off if he ever got the chance. The manager stormed away from me and back outside, slamming the door on his way out. The lady at the desk had, *you're really in some deep shit*, written all across her face. I went up to her and said, "Um—yeah—hi—have you had anybody turn a phone in up here?"

The lady replied, "The manager took your phone down to the police station. You can pick it up down there."

Suddenly, Lindsay came walking into the lobby with a huge grin and said, "There you are! You're the talk of the town! Everyone's saying there was some crazy guy from Alabama swinging around on the rooftop last night. What the hell happened, man? I thought you went back to your room?"

Embarrassed as I darted my eyes back and forth from the desk clerk to Lindsay, I replied, "I don't even know, to be honest. I mean—I went back to my room, and next thing I know, I'm waking up with three police officers standing over me."

Lindsay laughed while the nervous desk clerk stared back at the both of us. Lindsay threw her arms up in the air like she threw confetti and laughed, "Well, that was a hell of a party last night then. Do you need a ride to the station to get your phone?"

Wanting more than ever to leave the Stanley behind, I replied, "No, that's fine. I'll just take my car down. I'm ready to get out of here."

Lindsay replied, "Ok—well, good luck. Maybe we can meet up later on down the road while you're in New Mexico." I bid my farewell while I thought, *Yeah, sure, so I can end up dancing around on another rooftop.*

While I stood by the '69 with the door open, I stared back up to the roof of the Stanley. I started thinking, *Wow. I can't believe I was really up there. What in the world would make me do that? I could be dead* *right now. All it would've taken was one slip, and—*There was something blowing in the wind on the flagpole atop the lookout tower on the Stanley's roof. Something blue, a blue piece of fabric flowing to and fro with the wind. *My headband.* My headband hung on the lookout tower's flagpole like someone placed it there the same way Neil Armstrong planted his flag on the moon. I thought, *That headband was the only fuckin' consistent thing in my life, and now it's stuck up there on the rooftop of the Stanley Hotel. That headband and I have been through so much together, and now it's gone.* I drove away from the Stanley before the hotel staff lynched me for my sins and headed toward the police station to get my phone.

My heart pounded so fast as I opened the door to the station. My mind raced with thoughts of, *Maybe I am going to jail after all? Why? Why did I do it? I had a clean record, and I've never been caught for anything, but now here I am. It's all just going down the drain like it always does.*

It didn't take long for the officer to bring my phone out. The officer handed my phone back to me and said, "Here's your phone, Mr. Smith. I have to tell you that you are no longer permitted on the grounds of the hotel. The management team was very adamant about that, and they have decided to press charges."

Charges? CHARGES! Oh no. I replied, "They're pressing charges? What sort of charges?"

The officer responded, "Trespassing charges for being on the roof. I have some papers right here that I need to serve you. The court date is at the bottom, and here is my card if you have any questions later on."

I was shocked. I replied in self-defense, "Trespassing charges? Honestly officer I don't even remember being up there." I paused in thought for a moment and continued, "Well, technically, I was a guest at the hotel, so I'm not sure how they could charge me with trespassing. I mean—I'm sorry about climbing around on the roof, but I didn't sign anything saying I couldn't go up there." Really nervous, I rambled on, "Am I going to go to jail over all of this?"

The officer kept a straight face, but there was a smile that crept underneath as he said, "No, you're not going to go to jail. Honestly, worst comes to worst, you'll just have to pay a fine—we didn't even want to press charges. I mean—we've all had nights like that at one point or another, but the hotel insisted that charges be pressed."

I replied, "But I don't even live around here. How can I make it to court? Will I have to fly all the way back?"

The officer replied, "The number to the clerk's office is on the back of the ticket. Most likely, if you just pay the fine, you won't have to come all the way back here and sit in court—you'll be ok. Like I said, we weren't even that upset about it. It's the staff that is in an uproar about the whole thing. I don't think they'll ever allow you back."

Good riddance, I thought. A so-called four-star hotel that didn't even have any A/C; they were a bunch of con artists anyway. I didn't want to linger any longer in the police station. I was just glad I got off the way I had and didn't get arrested over it all. I hopped back in the '69 and gunned it toward New Mexico. I was more than ready to leave Colorado.

While I drove down the road, I kept trying to process how and why exactly it all happened the night before. *Can I remember anything at all?*

I knew the only way to gain access to the rooftop would be by climbing up the fire escape, but you had to get into the courtyard at the back of the Stanley to get to it. I noticed while I walked around the hotel's grounds, before the Ouija board fiasco, the gate to the courtyard had been locked up, and there was a concrete wall at least eight feet tall surrounding the courtyard on all sides. *So how exactly did I reach the fire escape? Did I scale an eight-foot concrete wall so I could get into the courtyard?* That couldn't be, especially in the condition I was in. *So how did I get in there?*

Something or someone had to have opened the gate and let me in there. That's the only way I could've gotten access to the fire escape. Chills started to run down my spine, and even now, as I'm writing—the chills have returned. There's something more to that night, something I don't think I really want to remember. When I think about all of what happened, I get flashes sometimes of a woman. I can't make her out entirely in my mind, but she appears to be a young woman in an old-fashioned white gown of some kind—with me, standing there on the rooftop. It could just be my mind playing tricks on me, or maybe there was a woman with me that night. An old shade of the past coaxing me toward my death, saying, "This way. This way, Mr. Smith."

CHAPTER XXII: IS THIS LOVE

I stood at the edge of a cliff overlooking the Rio Grande gazing upon it all. The mighty stream of the river seemed to glisten and sparkle in a rhythmic pattern to a whispering song blowing through the wind as it carried the rays of the sun crashing into all of the nature lying beyond. The serpentine river seemed to slither its way across the landscape through the dark green brush laying upon bright sands toward a horizon of rocky giants standing over foot—bearing time immeasurable for all the times passing and all the time to come. It was a place unchanged by time. Backward or forward, it would always look the same.

I knew I wouldn't be standing there that day looking out across the Rio Grande if it wouldn't have been for Brooke. I think that's why she always came to mind with every sunset because her words set the sun of hope within my own heart, and I love her so much for it. It felt so pure, so unique; I had to find out what she thought. I shared that sunset with her like I had so many others. I told her, *It looks like a special kind of sunset to me; that's why I really wanted you to see it.*

Brooke said, **Stuff like that just screams 'free' to me.**

Freedom. What did true freedom feel like? To be free from all the pain and to truly be happy. What would that be like? Is that what love is? Maybe true love brought real freedom. I could only hope.

Brooke was so excited for her trip to Vegas. It was only seven days away. *Seven days and I'll get to see her again,* I thought. *The eternity of waiting to be in her company again will finally end,* but then something occurred to me. What if she didn't want to meet up with me in Vegas? What if her texts just grew into cold, short replies? *What if I become a ghost all over again and not get to see her at all?* I couldn't bear the thought of it.

So many girls are like that nowadays, especially to the nice guy. That's my biggest problem, and I'm a feelings catcher on top of that, so in that regard, I'm basically fucked. Nobody likes the nice guy with feelings. He's despised, hated even, and he knows it. So he hangs his heart from a tree and becomes the asshole everyone wants him to be. It's a shame really. What's toxic is low, and the expectations are even lower, so that makes the dynamic easier. It's more challenging to be with someone who thinks the world of you. I guess most women don't believe in themselves enough to live up to that. But that always makes me think, *Well ain't that the point of love? Behold what I behold. I see the world in you. Believe what I believe. You give life to me. Know what I know. Everyday my love for you shall grow. You're my world and you don't have to do a thing, but let it be known. You're already perfect; you just haven't been shown.*

29 Palms

While the Santa Fe sun finally set on another day, the '69 and I drove out into another evening of another day, and what a long day it had been.

I was exhausted from all the walking. It was hiking in the desert after all, and there were no trees to hide under beneath the blazing rays of the sun. *Thank god for cowboy hats.* I bought one earlier that day in town. It was sort of funny to me because I had this little side quest mapped out in my head of getting unique souvenirs from each area I wanted to visit in the Old West. It all played out through pure gut feeling, to be honest.

Somehow I knew I'd find the perfect boots back in Dodge. Then I'd get the poncho and hat there in Santa Fe, but the revolvers, I'd most likely find them in Tombstone. I had a picture of the perfect pair of guns all set up in my head. I passed by a few gun stores along the way, but all the pairs I ran across just didn't seem right. It was almost like a voice came to me and said, *Don't jump the gun just yet. The perfect pair you're looking for will be right in Tombstone. Just wait and see. You won't regret it.* It couldn't just be one revolver; the perfect pair was essential. I planned to keep one and give the other to my stepdad Tim when I got back because, after all, he loved the Wild West. I figured it was the least I could do for him.

Tim came into my life just when I was about to turn eighteen years old, which wasn't a good time at all, but I'm glad that it happened then rather than never. I didn't want to give him a chance at all at first. I thought to myself, *He's just going to be another asshole like the last one,* but I sure was wrong. He was the first guy my mom had brought around that would sit down to talk with me and actually be interested in what I had to say. We'd chill out and smoke cigars together, he took time out of his day to teach me how to drive, and it didn't seem like it was a burden on him at all. It was like he liked spending time with me. I had all of my uncles and cousins around, of course, and I learned a hell of a lot from them too, but it was just different having that father figure finally there at home.

He needed us just as much as we needed him. He'd just got through a nasty divorce and went home every night to an empty apartment; where, on the other hand, my mom had just left her prick of a boyfriend and did everything she could by herself to keep two crazy teenagers in line—especially me. We all came together at what didn't seem like the perfect moment, but with time, I saw it was. After almost forty years of searching, my mom finally found the person she could spend the rest of her life with, and we all grew to love one another like a real family should. Tim didn't replace my father, but I learned it was ok to love and look to someone else as a father figure without feeling like I was betraying the memory of my dad. In my heart, I thought, *Yeah, its ok. I think Dad would've liked him too.*

Tombstone waited across the horizon for tomorrow's adventure, but how could I gallop across that age-old land of the west without going on a side quest to some old long-forgotten ghost town? *That'd be a lot of fun,* I thought. *What's the worst that could happen?* A lot is the worst that could happen. A lot of extraordinarily fatal and torturous things are what could happen, and little did I know I'd soon come face to face with those possibilities.

I'm not going to say where precisely this ghost town is in New Mexico because I don't want to be held liable for some daredevil like myself going out there and getting themselves in a pretty unfavorable type of bind. The type of bind they don't find their way back from. I don't want that type of thing on me, man.

Maybe I should've stopped when I passed a sign saying something along the lines in bold letters, *state funding ends here*, or maybe I should've stopped when I heard the buzzards crowing overhead across the ever desolate nothingness. *This is a hell of a lot further out than I'd imagined. This might really be a bad idea, but I've come too far to go back now. I gotta at least drive through.*

Onward and onward, through the dust of the desert, I drove, but still no town. After a ways, I could see a tall, towering church seeming to look pretty well kept for being in an abandoned ghost town. The only thing was the so-called ghost town wasn't abandoned at all; there were still people living out there.

There were ramshackle little huts and old torn-up buildings just about everywhere, but the church itself looked better than a church you'd see in a regular town. None of it made any sense. I saw a man in a dingy old hat with some coveralls on raking nothing but dirt. *What the hell is he doing? Is he a farmer? How in the hell could you grow anything out here anyway?*

I started to grow pretty uneasy. I mean, after all, I had to stick out like a sore thumb. I was just some guy dressed like a cowboy cruisin' along out in the middle of nowhere in a '69 Chevy without a care in the world, only I was really starting to care about my safety. While I looked around all frantic from left to right at my weird spectators, I didn't notice how fast I was going or saw the massive dip in the road in front of me, but when I hit it—I knew. It seemed like the bottom of the '69's front end came crashing down into the road. I screamed, "Fuck! I did not see that there!"

As the shocks rose the '69 back up, it made a really strange whining noise, but it didn't sound like the normal whine a vehicle would make. It sounded more like a noise an injured creature would've made. When I drove the '69 up the hill after the dip, I parked in front of the church and hopped out to get a look at all the damage that had to have been done. *There isn't any damage at all, but how?* I thought.

I laid flat on my stomach on the old, crackled road to see if I could spot anything hanging down or leaking underneath. *Nothing.* Nothing seemed to be wrong. That is until I rose to my feet and saw the weird-looking preacher guy standing out on the front steps of the church straight as a nail with a bible clutched to his chest.

His eyes were dark and sunken above his bony cheekbones and the sagging skin of his neck. He reminded me a lot of the old preacher guy from *Poltergeist 2* Caroline kept running into. When Caroline saw him in the movie, she'd say, "Mommy, I want to go home." Well that's how I felt then. Only my mommy wasn't there, and I had the overwhelming feeling I needed to get the fuck out of there.

The bony preacher started to speak as a wide sneer spread across his face and said, "How do you do today, my child?"

I started thinking, *First of all, I'm not your child, bro, and if I were a child, you'd probably already have me praying naked in some dark, secluded room somewhere.* I collected myself as quick as I could and said, "Doing alright. I just had to pull over, you know, and check my car real quick."

Right after I spoke, I spotted a young blonde-headed teenage girl in pigtails wearing a dingy white t-shirt peeking at me from behind a rusted old pickup truck. She noticed I saw her. Her eyes widened as she put her hand over her mouth and went back into her hiding place. *Well, this is getting strange.*

The preacher continued to speak, "That is a rather fine automobile you have there. Will you be staying with us? I have refreshments inside if you need anything."

Refreshments? Yeah, right, I'm not falling for that shit, Jim Jones. I replied real quick, "Oh no! That's alright, man; I appreciate it. I just got lost, you see—but I—think I know which way I need to head now." Not knowing what else to say, I climbed back into the '69 as quick as possible and said, "Thanks anyway, though! Have a great day, buddy!"

    I didn't wait to hear a reply from him. I kicked the dirt and old pieces of cement everywhere as I hit the gas pedal and gunned my way out of there. *What are people still doing living out here in nothing but shacks and a bunch of dirt? I mean, hell, that church was kept up better than some of the churches you'd see around any other town,* and then it dawned on me. What if those people were running some kind of doomsday cult back there? *God, they could've knocked me over the head with a tire iron and drug me into some barn somewhere—yeah, that could've happened. Who knows what would've happened after that? Maybe they planned to harvest the innocent blonde man's seed and force me to impregnate all of their inbred daughters to bring forth the promised children of the next generation.* It's a long shot, but the fact is that *could* have really happened. It didn't, and thank god it didn't. It was really like some *Hills Have Eyes* shit, to be honest, or even worse, *Children of the Corn.*

    The rest of the way to Tombstone was a breeze, or a breeze is really what I needed the most because the farther I headed out west, the hotter it got, and the '69 didn't have a working A/C. Everything felt fine as long as I was running seventy-five down the interstate, but if I had to stop at a red light for a while, it was damn near unbearable. My phone even started to overheat it was so damn hot, and I couldn't wait to finally get to the lodging house in Tombstone, where I'd eventually catch some air.

    I pulled into the small little town of Tombstone just as dusk started to fall across the land. *Like a true cowboy chasing after the sun.* The town looked somewhat rundown on the outskirts. Many traditional-looking homes that looked a little too settled into if you want to know the truth. I mean, a few of them looked like they hadn't been power washed since the eighties. *Hmmm, it kind of*

29 Palms

reminds me of Zanesville, I started thinking to myself. As I drove down the road, though, the town seemed to go from the modern era straight into the eighteen-eighties. *Just my type of place.*

I could tell the lodging house had been there for a while when I parked the '69 alongside it. There wasn't much standing out about it, and it didn't give off an Old West type of vibe. It was pretty plain looking, and it sort of looked like a regular, everyday motel. *Damn it another motel. Hopefully, there isn't another dirty chick running around here that's hungry again. She'd be out of luck.*

Right across the street, though, was the most golden picture a modern fellow could ask for to get of the Old West. There was downtown Tombstone, and it was everything I dreamed it would be. All of the old structures were still intact. There was a long stretch of gabled rooftops with the same old, false front architecture displaying painted advertisements for saloons and gambling damn near everywhere. The deck boards lining the edge of the streets even looked to be all original even if they weren't, and horseshoe marks matted their way across the dirt roads sprawling across the whole downtown area. *A true vision to travel back in time*, I thought to myself. I had finally escaped the modern world.

After I checked into the lodging house and got all squared away, it was time for me to party like it was 1889. All the old saloons were still open! I couldn't believe it. From Doc Holliday's to Big Nose Kate's, and of course, Wyatt Earp's infamous Oriental Saloon, it was all still there. *This is an absolute dream come true. How good it feels when dreams do come true! Where to start?* Of course, I had to visit old Doc in his saloon down the road; I'd check out the Oriental later.

I couldn't help noticing throughout the town everybody was dressed up like a cowboy, but their cowboy hats weren't as cool as mine. They looked like the cheap toy store kind from Wal-Mart or something, and mine was done in wide-brimmed exquisite black felt, quite the opposite to theirs. With everybody wearing a cowboy hat—well, it made me not want to wear mine. I thought to myself, *I don't want to look like a tourist like everyone else around here. If everybody else is wearing a cowboy hat, it's not that fun wearing mine.* I didn't want to blend in with everyone else anyway.

On top of everyone wearing a cowboy hat, there were also the belt buckles. I've always hated the sight of someone wearing a belt buckle. I don't even know why, but I've just never liked it. Plus, most of the belt buckles these guys wore looked bigger than they were, and they had a staring problem. It was almost like their gaze said, "Oh, look at old Mr. Pretty boy here. Thinks he can just a come rollin' in town and steal all our woman. Well I ain't havin' it!"

I replied with a gaze that said, "Be careful how long you stand there and stare because your knees might end up bucklin' more than your belt there, my friend."

I didn't care too much, though. Fuck their staring. It was funny being in Doc's old saloon though because it was like being back in the 1880s in one way, but your listening to music saying "I can do it / put your ass into it" on the other. It was hilarious because it was like the place had an identity crisis or something. You could also tell who was local and who wasn't. The locals just walked around like Tombstone was any other place and there was nothing unique about it. It got me thinking about how all of us take for granted what's in our backyard. Your environment might not seem special to you because you deal with it every day, but that doesn't mean it isn't special. It's kind of that way with everything I guess.

The Oriental Saloon was even better than old Doc's. It made me feel like I went back in time. The lady bartenders were wearing the same old-fashioned blown-up dresses the dames back in the day used to. It all sparked that feeling of how fantastic old-fashioned romanticism had been back then and how, in the modern-day, all of that seemed to have gone away with the wind. There was music playing, but it wasn't the type of music I had in my head. In my mind, I saw a pianist wearing a black Kentucky bow-tie banging away at the keys of a piano. There were top hats and exquisite ruffled dresses waltzing or doing some other kind of corny dance, all across the dance floor in a blissful night of debauchery and extravagance. I don't know, I guess it was really just me trying to imagine what the place could've been like back in the day.

    Anyways, I wanted another beer. I tried to use my bank card at the bar, but some red lips that were finely worn by a beautiful brunette said, "Sorry, boo, cash-only bar."

    It didn't even bother me because tossing some greenbacks across the counter felt a lot more real than swiping a dirty old bank card. It just made the experience that more immersive.

    While I studied the crowd from the bar, I couldn't help notice the whole group was a lot older than I was, and there were only a few people around my age in there. It didn't bother me any, though. I was surrounded by countless sets of beautiful married couples that chose this as their getaway for the weekend, probably hoping to rekindle an old spark or something. All I know is it was beautiful to behold. No drama, just a bunch of people out to have a good time and letting themselves go with the atmosphere. It was all so wonderful, but I couldn't help myself from feeling lonely again.

    Maybe it was because everyone seemed to be a couple, and I was the only single guy there, I'm not sure, but the old feeling of being a ghost started to creep up again. It's not like I wanted everyone to acknowledge I was there or anything; I didn't need that. It was just standing there with the wish that I had someone I truly loved to dance the night away with. I've never had the chance to go out and do that with anyone. Never at a high school dance, never with my ex, and not now. Would I ever know what it felt like to just hold someone in my arms and dance? I really wanted to. I've always wanted to. Even if there would've been a girl there for me to dance with, it wouldn't be who I wanted. It wouldn't have been Brooke.

I sent her a picture earlier when I got into town, and I was so excited when I sent it because before I finally made it to Tombstone, I almost thought I'd miss the sunset entirely, and I wouldn't get the chance of sharing it with her at all. So I texted her, *See, I didn't forget.*

You almost did, lol; nah, you're good. It's beautiful. I'm glad you're loving the West.

She sent me a picture of her own of a girl laying on the inside of a beautifully decorated camper looking out of a window sipping on a cup of coffee and said, **This is going to be me one day; I can see it so clearly.**

I knew she would accomplish everything her heart could dream up. I could see it all just as clearly as she could. I replied, *That even kind of looks like you. So you're going to live the gypsy lifestyle? Lol.*

For right now. I see myself at least doing this until my late 20s. I think it's such a beautiful thing to have different sights to wake up to every day. Maybe even closer to my 30s.

I kept thinking, *I know you will. I know that you can do it,* as I replied, *It really is a beautiful lifestyle to have, and I know you'll really set out to do all that you dream about, and it's all because you really believe in yourself, so I know you'll really do it.*

Don't get me wrong, I'd love to share these amazing experiences with someone special. It's just not my choice when that'll happen, so I just go with what I got right now.

That's what I couldn't get. She told me time and time again she didn't want to be with anyone, but now she said she didn't have a choice when that would happen. Was she just not interested in me, or was she trying to tell me something more? Would she really end up giving me a chance after all this? There was so much I wanted to say like, *But what about me? I could be your special someone that you could share all of that with. If you'd only just let it be.* But I couldn't bring myself to say that. I wanted to tell her it all in person. I could only give her a sense of my worth, and well—yeah, I mean, I wanted to make her a little jealous too.

That's been the biggest lesson for me to learn. I'm just going with things as they come. I know without a shadow of a doubt now I have that one of a kind type of love in my heart to give, but I'll give it when it's meant to happen. The best kind of things happen when you least expect it I think. I'm going to have to watch myself when I get back to Mobile, though; I'm going to have a lot of fake people trying to weed their way into the picture.

Like who?

The truth was nobody messaged me at all. Of course, plenty of girls back in Mobile loved all the posts I'd put on Facebook of my travels. Most of them were girls who never would've given me the time of day before. So really, it wasn't a lie because I'd at least got their attention, but I didn't care about talking to any of them. I just wanted her, *I've been having girls message me that never wanted to give me the time of day, and now they do. You're not in that group. You at least text with me every once in a while, but we've been doing that.*

Well don't block them all out. You might find a genuine one again! But I would agree, just be careful who you let affect your aura.

I started to become disingenuous with myself and even worse with her. All because I didn't want to come off too strong, and I didn't want her to shut the door on me again. I didn't want a relationship with anyone, only her, but I couldn't tell her that yet. It just wasn't the right time. *I'm not going to, lol. I'm just not going to jump into a relationship with somebody right off the bat. After doing all this, I don't really even want to be in one anymore like I did. I'm fine by myself.* What I really meant was I'd have to find a way to be ok with being alone because if it wasn't her, I just wouldn't be interested.

Well I'm glad you're finally comfortable with yourself, also very proud that you have given yourself time to grow to this mindset.

When Brooke said, "you might find a genuine one again," she just didn't know. I've never found a genuine person to be with. I never had the high school sweetheart, never a girlfriend at all, until I met my ex, and love was dead in the water for our relationship from the start. I just settled for her because I didn't want to be alone anymore. It was one of the worst mistakes of my life, but two of the best things I could ever ask for came out of it. My boys. I've never felt true genuine love from anyone, and the only thing that's ever felt real to me is when I first kissed Brooke. That was real. To me anyway, and it had to mean something. I had to let her know a little bit without going too deep. I didn't get a response back when I said, *I've never really been in a relationship with a genuine person. The first person I was ever with was my kids' mom, and I just got kind of stuck with her. I never really fell in love with her. And yeah, I've definitely learned a lot. I'm showing people what I'm really made of.*

CHAPTER XXIII: SHOOT TO THRILL

Damn, was it hot out. Now granted, I had hiked across the desert in a cowboy hat with a black and white poncho wrapped around me, but believe it or not, everything seemed a lot hotter while I wasn't wearing the poncho, so I left it on. A guy passed me along the trail earlier and said, "Jesus Christ, man, aren't you hot?"

In full Clint Eastwood style, I took a drag off my hand-rolled cigar and said, "Why, of course not. I was built for this."

Only that was a lie, and I wasn't built for that type of heat at all. One hundred and ten degrees. That was just way too damn hot, and to be hiking around in the aridest heat imaginable without any water made me feel even crazier than I looked. The desert sure was a beautiful place, though.

29 Palms

Cactuses seemed to invade the desert landscape as far as the eye could see. It almost seemed like nature had made a city out of them because some of them looked to be around twenty feet tall—like a tiny little tower, and each of their arms seemed to spindle their way in a unique pattern to where not any one cactus looked the same. Some of them even had bright pink flowers blooming from them, which was a shock to me because I'd never heard of cactuses giving birth to flowers as pretty as those were.

Of course, there were lizards too—huge ones. They would dart out fast like they were trying to check out who invaded their territory, and it put me in the mind of that old Cheech and Chong movie where Pee Wee Herman tries to check the lizard guy in the back of the truck by saying, "Mmmmm, Mr. Lizard, care for a hamburger?!"

I don't think the lizards liked me a whole lot, to tell you the truth. After all, if they were looking for a hamburger, I didn't have one. I didn't even have any water. *Why do I always choose to go hiking without any water? It's the desert; what was I thinking?*

I wondered if cactuses really did hold water and how much I could get out of one if I cracked it open. Then it occurred to me. *Hey, wait a minute. The world's falling apart. We're in the middle of a global pandemic; we have all these problems going on in the world right now.*

Meanwhile, I'm just hiking through the desert, minding my own business dressed like a fuckin' bandito. I don't know what's going on anymore. Like the song goes, it damn sure was a "Cruel Summer." All I knew was I needed to get back to the '69 as soon as I could before I passed out from all the heat.

I had a pretty good time in Tombstone the night before, despite feeling all lonely and everything. I didn't even drink that much. I didn't care to. I was in one of those kinds of moods; if I would've kept drinking, I probably would've broken down in front of a bunch of people. It made me think about how much I'd been drinking the whole trip. I mean, I had a good time partying on the road, don't get me wrong, but after the crazy rooftop shit that happened at the Stanley, I started to come toward the self-destructing part of partying. It's kind of funny. When I feel like it's just me and I don't have a purpose, I just don't care. When my kids were around, I had something to focus on and take care of, but when it's just me—honestly, I don't even really even give a shit. It's always been that way.

I started thinking about those revolvers again, though. There was a gun shop not too far from downtown Tombstone called Poncho Vega's, and I just couldn't fight my gut anymore—something deep down told me the guns I'd been looking for were in there. So I did what anybody would; I figured I'd find out.

They were there. I almost couldn't believe it. Two Navy model conversion revolvers hailing back to 1871. They had notches carved into them from a few kills, I think, and there was a coiled-up snake on each of the wooden handles. *Ready to strike, I like that.*

I bought them both outright then and there. I'm not going to say how much they cost because that's my business, but I was ready to shoot them off all the same. Only the lady at the counter informed me I couldn't take the guns out of the shop because I was from out of state. They had to be shipped back to a Mobile gun store, where I could finally pick them up. It sucked after she broke the news to me.

After all, I wanted to shoot 'em up in the air as I drove off into the sunrise toward Vegas the next day. I figured the story I made was already crazy enough as it was. A guy just decided to leave his house one day and check out Savannah, only to end up traveling the whole country on a complete whim, all in the name of true love. Along the way, he bought a '69 Chevy and ended up becoming a cowboy, then gunned it out of Tombstone with a pair of old revolvers blazing his path toward the sunrise. That was me—I'm that guy.

I knew Tim would absolutely love the gun when I gave it to him. I imagined saying, "Here ya go. You got one, and I got one, desperado."

I was right about him loving the gun, though. Poor guy got so excited he almost shot his whole damn foot off.

I still hadn't visited the OK Corral shootout site yet, but when I did, it gave me all the magic I'd hoped for. There was a video at the museum that went through Tombstone's history, and it told of how it was a town just too tough to die. The place itself had many ups and downs, especially when Wyatt Earp and Doc Holliday rolled into the spot and had a war there with the cowboys. It was a small town, but a strong one. I liked to think the people living there over the years loved their home so much they went through whatever they had to in order to keep it alive. There's a lot of wisdom you can get from that. Like the town, you might not be the biggest or the best, but if you keep your wheels rollin', you never know what you'll find. A journey only truly ends if you let it.

I didn't pick up on anything at the actual site where the shootout took place, but around it, I could just feel something in the air. A particular type of heaviness—I don't know, like the troubles of the past still weighed down and plagued the air a little bit. I wondered how an event that happened so long ago could still hold weight in modern times. It's almost like people have something more to them, some type of energy, and when they push pure, raw emotions out, it somehow leaves a fingerprint forever scratching its way throughout time. It sounds kind of nuts, but I don't really care. I've felt that way about a lot of places. Some of them seemed completely ordinary on the surface, but they weren't. Something had happened. Something still lingered there, but for what? I've always wondered.

29 Palms

I went to the old Boot Hill Cemetery next. Throughout the West, there are countless cemeteries like it and they're labeled as "boot hill" because the people buried there were shot and died in their boots. There were so many people who died around 1882 buried there, and a lot of them were unknown. Most of them were probably just some poor fella who decided to waltz through town to get a beer and ended up getting himself shot out of nowhere. There were even a few babies buried there, and when I looked down on those graves, my heart felt so heavy. Such a young, new, blossoming life lost. Death is hard enough to cope with, but when a child dies, that's another thing. It's always been something I haven't been able to mentally handle thinking about too long, especially then when I didn't know how my kids were doing.

I passed by the graves of the Clanton and McLaury boys too, who died in the OK Corral shootout. They were all buried right next to each other. They might've been the bad guys in the story, but everyone can be a bad guy in one way or another; most of us just keep that part of ourselves hidden. Any one of us can be the greatest hero or the worst villain in each of our stories. It all depends on which one you feed the most—devil or angel, good or evil—we're all a little bit of both, and it's all a matter of choice. There are two sides to every coin, and deep down on the inside, we're all Harvey Dent. Nevertheless, I dropped a few coins on each of those villains' graves anyway. I guess that was my way of paying my respects to the old desperados who never got a chance to leave Tombstone.

I wasn't sure what else I would do with the rest of my day after I left Boot Hill. I saw most of what downtown had to offer the night before, but I sure wasn't done with soaking up that Old West atmosphere.

I started strolled along Downtown Tombstone's dirt roads, and I thought about how I didn't get a reply back from Brooke when we had last talked. It's not that I got upset about her hitting me back; it was just the dreadful thought of her going cold again is what got me. *What if when I'm in Vegas, she doesn't even talk to me? What if I just end up becoming a ghost again?*

I couldn't bear the thought of it. It clawed at my insides and made me want to cry. I've always been good at hiding my emotions, so as I passed people along my walk, I did my best to smile along the way, even though I tortured myself on the inside. I couldn't help it. I went ahead and texted her anyway. *I just wanted to tell somebody you're the only person I really text, but I'm sort of proud of myself about last night. I didn't try to stand out in any kind of way. I saw people that I was attracted to, but that didn't mean much to me because none of them are what I want. They just didn't seem special to me.*

I was really trying to give her a hint in a subtle way that I didn't want anybody but her. It probably wasn't the best hint to give because I really wasn't thinking straight when I sent it. I just wanted a reason to text her. I wanted to talk to her so bad because, honestly, I stood at the edge of the cliff of desperation, and when you're there—well, you might as well just jump off or leave it be altogether.

She ended up replying not too long after. **I'm glad you're proud of yourself! I hope you do find someone special to share days and nights with while you're on the road, though. I know you don't feel alone anymore, but letting there be a person you make memories with in one city is just part of the journey and story!**

You're the only girl I want to make memories with, I thought. The fact was I did still feel alone. Loneliness was a shadow always following close behind. Being out on the road helped me run from it, but the shadows always managed to catch right back up. When I texted Brooke back, I said, *I don't know. I think this journey has changed me in a lot of ways. I'm still scared about being alone forever, but I'm not going to latch on to just anyone so I don't feel that way anymore.*

I'm not better than anyone, but I'm just too different from everyone else to make an intense connection with anyone, I think. It's always been that way, but I don't think it's a curse anymore. Me being made the way I am has to add up to something; I just have to find out what.

Then I sent her a picture of another Wild West sunset, but before I could wait for a reply, my phone started to ring—it was my mom. I answered her call and said, "Hey, how ya doin'?"

Mom replied, "Oh, I'm fine. So where ya at today?"

I replied, "I'm in Tombstone right now, just hanging out on a bench downtown. I really think you and Tim would love it here. It's like going back in time or something. I got the guns today, by the way."

Shocked, mom replied, "Did you really? Oh, he's going to love that. How much did they cost?"

I laughed a little to myself while biting a nail and said, "Oh, not too much. I'll be headed to Vegas tomorrow. I'm gonna try to enter the city in a helicopter. I think that'll be pretty badass. Then I'll be headed to 29 Palms." With a sigh, I continued, "I can't believe the trip is almost over."

Mom replied, "Well, hell, take some pictures while you're up there. I'm wondering how much has changed in 29 Palms since me and your dad lived there. We used to go to this bar called Gabby's all the time. Let me know if that's still there—and I'm still trying to find our old address to where we used to live. I'll be surprised if that's still there."

I wanted to know so much more about her and my dad's time together there. She usually didn't talk about him much when I'd ask, or she would just end up saying she couldn't remember. I tried to get more out of her when I replied, "I bet you guys had some really good times out there."

Mom got excited when I asked. I could tell. She replied, "Oh yeah, we did. A lot of your dad's buddies used to come by all the time to party at our place. There was this one guy who used to come over with his girlfriend—oh, I can't remember their names. They used to call him something—but anyways. That guy passed out one time, and he had this really hairy back, and your dad and the rest of 'em shaved his whole fuckin' back while he was asleep—"

"What?"

"Yeah, his back looked all fucked up, but his girlfriend had this big mole on her face, and they started to try to pluck it off, and I thought that was just going too far, so I made 'em stop."

With a big smile on my face, I thought, *Sounds like something I would do, besides plucking a mole off.* Then I replied, "Wow, that's crazy. I didn't know he used to do crazy shit like that."

Mom replied, "Oh yeah, they used to get in trouble all the time. I remember this one party we had—we were somewhere. It was either in our apartment or someone else's—no, it wasn't in our apartment, but anyways, we had a pyramid of Heinekens stacked to the ceiling, and we broke open a bunch of these glow sticks and had the shit everywhere."

She had told me that story before. I just wished she would've told me more of the good things about him over the years instead of all the bad things that had happened in their marriage. I still didn't know how I'd feel once I got to 29 Palms, and I told Mom that on the phone. She hasn't ever been the type to go into talking about deep feelings. It always sort of seemed like when I'd open up to her about certain things, I wouldn't get much of a reply. I knew it wasn't because she didn't care. I just think it's because she didn't know what to say. I knew she cared, though. She was just a woman living a hard life with a lot of heartbreaks. Working like a man and raising two boys on her own didn't allow her to have the time to sit back and think about the deeper things, and I think that's why, a lot of the time, she just didn't know what to say.

My mom and I had a great relationship with one another then, but it wasn't always that way. While I was growing up, it always seemed like we were always at odds with one another. I hated the way she would always demand when or when I wasn't going to do something. I hated being told what to do, and how she came across, it felt like it never mattered how I felt about anything, so I rebelled. I'd rebel against her in any way I could. Everything came to a boiling point when I was eighteen years old, though. My mom and I got into such a bad argument I packed my things and left. I ran away. I never really wanted to hurt my mom as deeply as I did from going where I went, but I had to. I had to get my answers. I had to find out why everything had happened that night. The night I lost my father, I lost a part of myself, and the only way I thought I could get that part of myself back was by getting those answers. It was time for me to come face to face with the past. It was time for me to find Christina.

CHAPTER XXIV: NO EASY WAY OUT

My first time on the road felt like driving into the heart of fear itself. There was so much ahead of me. So much that could go wrong, and for all I knew, once I crossed the bridge from Cincinnati into Kentucky, that might've been the last time I'd ever see Ohio.

I visited everyone before I left—everyone except for my mom. I was tired of arguing with her all the time. She never wanted to listen to me about anything anyway. All she ever wanted to talk about was how irresponsible I was and how I needed to start getting better grades in school. *Who cares about school? Not me. I can't even remember the last time I went.*

She wouldn't care about me being gone anyway. She was always more focused on work. Plus she just got married on top of that. Tim was pretty cool and I like him a lot, but I'm not too sure if I fit into the picture of my mom's new life. Matter of fact, I feel like my spot in the family portrait expired a long time ago. Maybe that's why she was always bitching at me. Because she's just tired of having me around and wants me to go. She was never as hard on my brother as she was me, so that had to be the reason, right? Because I was eighteen and it was just time for me to go. As jealous of my brother I could be at times, he was the hardest person to leave behind.

Of course, I'd never let him know that. It was more fun picking on him all the time and driving him nuts than to let the kid know I actually loved him, even though I'd let it slip every once in a while. I took him to see *The Green Hornet* a few days ago. Seth Rogen's movies are funny as fuck, especially *Pineapple Express*. I didn't even get high before watching it, which took a lot for me to do. I guess I wanted to get the most I could get out of the evening. After all, this could be the last time I'd ever see him.

I took him to get something to eat after the movie, and believe it or not, it felt really good to make him happy for a change. I was so used to seeing him rolling around on the ground throwing some crazy kind of tantrum from some prank I pulled, or if he wanted some snacks and Mom didn't have any, he'd always do the same thing. The shit was funny, plain and simple. The kid never took anything lightly, but the other night he had a big smile on his face. I could tell it made him feel really good I was nice to him for a change. He kept talking about how mean girls can be at school sometimes, and I figured it was probably because he was a fat kid. I used to be that kind of kid too, that's until I stopped eating.

Look, I'm not going to lie, on some days I would eat, but I'd usually just make myself throw it all right back up anyway. I didn't want to be a fat kid anymore. Girls always laughed at me if I'd try to get their number, so I figured it had to be the weight, right? I dropped from two-eighty to one-ninety in just the past six months, but it still doesn't matter. I still can't get a date with a girl. Don't tell my friends, but I'm still a virgin.

When it was time to drop Pavin off at Mom's, I told him I loved him and always wanted him to remember that. His face warmed up so much with a smile when I told him that, and he said he loved me too. I started to feel guilty about leaving, but he'll understand one day. Plus, he has a lot more friends than I've ever had, so he might not even think about me that much after a while. That was the thing. Everyone had something. Pavin had his friends, and everyone else had their families. I was just sort of floating around out here without any kind of purpose. I've felt that way for a while now. Sort of like, after a while, people would end up forgetting about me anyways. I knew they all loved me, but I didn't add much to any of their lives anyway. It wouldn't matter in the end if I disappeared.

I sort of had to leave town anyway. After the stickup kids from Jewett Drive caught me slippin' the other day at this abandoned house I stayed at, I knew shit was getting hot around town. It was kind of my fault, though. I was sort of chillin' with them a few nights before, and we were makin' these king drinks, right? Where you mix Yeager with some Monster—but anyways, I started braggin' about all this money me and my boy Dom made around town, and they caught every word of it. I didn't think it would matter because I felt I could trust 'em, you know? We pretty much grew up together, but when I had that sawed-off shotgun in my face, I knew none of that shit mattered. They didn't get nothing really because they got kind of outnumbered at the spot. After it was all over, I figured I needed to take the cash I had and hit the road. Nobody had a clue I was leaving, and I wanted to keep it that way. So really, I would've been dead in the water anyway if I would've stayed, but getting answers, that brought some meaning to leaving.

I think my grandma sort of caught on to my plan, though. She's always had a *knowing* way about her when it comes to things that haven't been told. I didn't even really care if she knew, though, honestly. I asked her plenty of questions about my dad over the years. She was the only one who would even talk about him anymore, and we'd talk for hours. I felt like I got to know so much more about him through her, and when we'd talk, it would almost seem like, in his own way, he'd join in on our visit too.

She told me about the last Memorial Day my dad came out to her house. She painted the scene so vividly with her words I could almost see it in my head as if I were there. She told me it was a very bright and sunny day out; with the birds soaring through the air, spilling their beautiful songs throughout the wind. She lives way out in the country on a few acres, so the deer were even grazing their way around her yard. She told me she walked outside and saw my father standing there gazing up at the sky. She asked him, "What are you looking at, Rob?"

He turned to look at her with this big smile on his face, and then he pointed to this tree and said, "Look at that tree, Mom. It bloomed flowers. Is it the first time it's done that? I've never seen flowers on it before."

I guess it hadn't because she said, "Wow, no, I've never seen flowers grow on it before. Isn't that something?"

My father turned away from her and walked over to the tree and picked one of the bright pink flowers growing from it. Then, he walked over to her with it in his hands. He handed her the flower and said, "Every year after this, I want you to look at that tree with its blooming flowers and remember that I love you, Mom."

Every year after that, the tree bloomed flowers for her, and it always reminded her of him every time she looked at it. He just wasn't around to pick them for her anymore.

I could tell from the look on grandma's face she knew what I planned when I'd asked her if she had any idea where Christina was now. She didn't have an address or anything, just the state and the town. She also told me Christina had married some old guy and moved out of Zanesville to start a new life in Kentucky. I guess she had divorced the guy by now, but that wasn't much of a shock. That was all I needed to know, and since I had Facebook, it wasn't that hard to find her.

When I saw her again for the first time in so many years, I didn't know how to feel. I looked at the person I felt had taken everything from me. *You killed my father. He was my best friend, the realest friend I've ever had, and you took him away.* That was all I could think at first, but then I felt this longing deep down within myself. A longing for the impossible wish of getting everything back to the way it once was. If there were a way to fix it all to where none of it had ever happened, I'd do it. No matter what it would take. I'd do it. I didn't feel burning hate for Christina as I sat there staring at her picture. I wasn't sure what to think at the time. All I could wonder was where the hate had gone.

While I scrolled through the rest of her pictures, I started to run across pictures of Josci. I hadn't seen my little sister in so long. *Does she even remember me? I remember her. How could I ever forget?*

How could I ever forget the happy little girl in her little dresses who used to run from me in grandma's house as we'd dash through the halls laughing. She'd carry her little baskets out to grandma's garden they planted together and have that delightful little smile pouring all across her face as she picked little dandelions and hummed little tunes to herself. She always had this loud, obnoxious laugh that would get me every time. I missed her so much. She's the only one who could understand all this pain I feel inside. Nobody else could. She was there with me. Even if she can't remember, it was just her and me. We were there.

I had to see her again no matter what the cost was. I didn't care if my family ended up finding out where I went and decided to disown me for it. I had to go. I never had any other choice. After I made my mind up to risk it all, my relationships with everyone, maybe even my own life, it didn't take much after that. I was a dead man either way. I went, and then I was gone. I was bound for Kentucky.

The whole drive there, my mind kept running over all the possibilities of what could happen when I got to Christina's house. Would she scream at me and tell me to go? Would I not get any answers out of her at all? Would Josci even be there when I got there? I didn't know.

I was pretty sure I had the correct address, though. The reverse phone number lookup seemed to be pretty accurate, and if it weren't the correct address, I'd find them somehow. It felt like all I'd been through since my father died had culminated to this point, this one moment, to where it would all come to rest and finally settle. After a three-hour drive, I finally got off the interstate, and the GPS said Christina's house was only twenty minutes away. It was all or nothing. I'd either be crushed or finally set free.

I passed by her house once without even knowing it. I looked right at it and thought, *That place looks a little rough. I sure hope that isn't it*, but the GPS kept going haywire on me, so I passed it right up. Eventually, I just gave up on the GPS after it kept telling me to go right then go left onto roads that didn't even exist. I knew I was on the right road for sure, so I figured I'd just do it the old-fashioned way and just go off the mailbox number: 1063. I knew it couldn't have been too far down the road after I pulled into an old gravel turnaround and made my way back up the road, glancing my way over at one mailbox after another. *1063. There it is*, but it didn't look like anybody was home. *I wasn't expecting this. When will they be home? How long will I have to wait?* I was out in the middle of nowhere, and I wasn't sure what to do, so I did all I could do. I pulled up into the driveway and parked anyway.

There might not be a vehicle here, but someone might still be home. Maybe it's just Josci in there. I put my large, dark, woolen pea coat on as I got out of my Nissan Altima and approached the door. It was chilly out for it being nearly in the middle of February. I started to knock on the door. Then I waited. I knocked again, but no answer. My heart started to drop. They weren't even home. I headed back to my car as my heart began to slow for a minute after beating with anticipation for the past three hours, but then a van started coming up the road, and it began to slow at the mailbox. Then it pulled into the driveway.

My heart started to race with a steady mix of fear and another wave of stampeding anticipation as the driver got out. It was Christina. She was nearly just as I'd remembered her before, like she hadn't even aged much at all. She still had her short red hair, but she didn't come off as sweet as she used to be. There was something more hardened about her character. I got the sense that whatever had happened over the years to her had taken a toll on her, and she came off a lot tougher than she used to be. Christina walked up to me with a pissed-off look and asked, "Who are you? A caseworker?"

I couldn't find the words to say. I couldn't believe it was her after all this time, and after all the thoughts that ran through my mind on what I'd say to her once I saw her again. Christina retorted back, "Well can't you talk? Who are you?"

I had to say something. I started stuttering at first but managed to say, "You-you-you don't know who I am?"

Christina widened her eyes and shook her head. I could feel my body begin to tremble as I said, "It's-it's me. It's me, Hawke."

Christina's mouth popped wide open in shock. She started to come toward me, but then the van door popped open, and a twelve-year-old, blonde-headed, blue-eyed little girl popped her head out with a big smile. It was Josci. Christina looked at Josci and said, "It's your brother, Jo."

She screamed, "Bubby!" as she ran to me and I caught her in my arms. *She did remember me. After all this time, she really did remember me.* Holding Josci in my arms for the first time in eight years made me feel perhaps the warmest I had ever felt in my life up until that moment. I didn't even notice Christina there anymore. I thought, *She loves me. She loves me, and I love her too.* All I could do was smile and fight to hold my tears back as I said, "It's been a long time, huh?"

Josci popped her head away from my chest and looked up at me like she was in complete awe, and said, "Yeah, it has! What took you so long?!"

I was in complete shock. It felt like such an unreal moment to finally have my little sister back in my life again. Over the years, I tried to push her out of my mind and not even think about her, but even if we didn't grow up together, she was there the whole time, always in my heart. The reunion felt so surreal and extraordinary I started to feel more comfortable. A little bit anyway. Christina said, "Well, you can come inside if you want to."

Josci grabbed one of my hands with both of hers as she jumped up in excitement, "Yeah, come inside and see the house! I want to show you my room!"

I couldn't deny her that even though part of me was afraid more than ever to go inside. I couldn't help but fall into the grip of Josci's little hand as she and Christina led me inside.

Christina had a little boy by this time too, named David. He was only a little guy and was around the same age I was the last time I saw his mother. He looked like he didn't know what the fuck was going on, and I didn't either. I expected to confront Christina right there on the spot as soon as I saw her, but I couldn't do it. It was like most of the anger I felt toward her went away as soon as I laid eyes on her, and the little bit of it that might've been left was melted away after I caught Josci in my arms.

After Josci and her brother showed me their rooms, I sat down on the couch, trying to process all of what was going on. Christina sat in her chair along the other side of her coffee table and said, "Well, I'm surprised to see you here. Does anybody know about you coming down?"

I looked up at her as I met her eyes and said, "No—no, nobody knows that I'm down here."

That was probably a stupid response, I thought to myself. *If she has the slightest inkling to make me disappear, I just assured her that she could completely get away with it.* She stared back at me for a minute, and then she said, "Well, I'm glad that you're here now. We have a lot to talk about."

Then she lit up a smoke, and I felt a tinge of relief she had because that meant I could too. I needed a smoke right then. It would probably be the only thing that could keep me from completely losing my shit, so I lit one up. I started to speak, but all of a sudden somebody started walking up the steps. It was some older guy with gray hair who had a mullet-like haircut wearing an old Marine ball cap. The man said, "Oh, hey there, Chris. I thought I heard you and the kids up here. Who's this?"

Christina replied, "This is Hawke, my oldest son. Hawke, this is Jim. Him and his wife Kim live with me. Kim's not here right now, but you'll meet her when she comes back later on."

Kim and Jim, huh? The classic rhyming couple. I exchanged a few pretty awkward greeting words with Jim as he stood at the top of the stairs, and then he started to talk about an argument him and Kim had earlier. Apparently, he got a little too boozed up and pissed her off so bad she had to leave and cool off for a day or so. After Jim went back downstairs, Christina looked at me as she rolled her eyes and said, "I don't give a shit what those two have going on—Sorry about that. I still have some old pictures of us when you were a little boy if you want to see them."

I decided to just go with it. It all started to feel natural in a strange kind of way, and I couldn't believe how casual she acted with me. It was almost like we were sort of picking up where we had left off. I wasn't ready to bring up all the questions I had for her, especially with Josci and David still awake and with the weird guy Jim hanging out in the basement; it just didn't feel like the right time, but I was there at Christina's finally, and that's all that mattered. I was with Josci again. Having her sitting on the couch, resting her hand on my arm and her head on my shoulder, I felt loved. *She loves me. She does. She really did remember me, after all.*

Christina started showing me old pictures she had when we were all a family. It brought back so much for me. It took me back to when I felt the happiest and safest I ever had in my life. I saw pictures of my father I never saw before of him holding me in his arms and of Christina holding me in hers. *I felt so good back then. I really did. That was me before I was broken, before everything became broken. That was when everything felt just right to me. Why did it all have to end? Why couldn't it have lasted forever?*

Christina even had a lot of my dad's old things still hanging around up in her house. She had this blue glass cup sitting by the door, and she pointed it out to me and said, "Remember that? Every time your dad would walk in the door, he'd always drop his change in there. I still use it. It just didn't feel right letting it go."

She had a lot of other things of his lying around too. Old Marine stuff like his badges, blankets, sword, and hats. While she showed me all of this stuff I wished I had over the years, I wondered why she kept it all. If she meant to kill him, why would she keep it all? It didn't make any sense. She even had all the old movies I used to watch as a kid still there. She pointed out the movie *Liar Liar* and said, "We used to watch that one all the time. Do you remember the claw? Your dad and me used to always get you with the claw."

I remembered it all, that's for sure. I loved reliving those memories with her as we went through her pictures and walked down memory lane together, but they were tainted memories. Memories of some of the greatest joy I'd ever felt, but the greatest shadows of my pain clung to each and every one of them. It was all tainted by what had happened. Before Josci went to bed, she grabbed my hand again. She hadn't let go of me all evening. She looked up at me and said, "You're not leaving, are you? You're going to stay, right? Mom, can he stay?"

Christina looked at me, then Josci, and replied, "Sure he can. He can stay for however long he wants to."

For however long I wanted to. Apart of me didn't want to stay. How could I? But how could I leave? As much as I didn't understand it, a part of me liked being around Christina again, and how could I leave Josci? I just got her back, so how could I leave? I didn't want to break her heart. *She loves me. She really does.*

After Josci and her brother went to bed, it was just Christina and me alone in the living room. She sat cross-legged on the floor, not too far from me on the couch. She broke the silence first when she said, "I'm sure you have a lot of questions for me."

I didn't even know where to start. After having her bring back all those old memories I had of her, I felt so conflicted inside as I sat there looking at her. She looked right back at me, but I couldn't feel any hate toward her. There was so much I didn't understand. I asked the only thing I could, "Why-why did you do it?"

Christina never took her gaze off me as she said, "Hawke, I never wanted to hurt him—"

I interrupted her, "Everyone said that you planned it all out, and you wanted to kill him that night. You called and told him to check the mail so he'd be out there."

Christina started twitching her lips around as tears welled up in her eyes, "That's a lie. I don't know why everyone told you that. I can understand why everyone hates me—why you hate me, but I loved your dad, and I loved you. I still love you both. What happened that night should've never happened, but it did. I know it did, and I can never take it back—"

Tears started to roll down her face as she looked back at me. I couldn't understand why, but it bothered me to see her cry. I almost couldn't stand it, but I had to ask, "Then how did it happen?"

Christina's body started to tremble as her tears came rolling down. She burst out, saying, "We were having problems, Hawke. I didn't know what to do. He wanted to work it out, but I needed time to think."

Her body started to rock back and forth as she sat on the floor. "I just wanted to get some of my clothes so I could stay with a friend for a few days."

She started sobbing even more as she said, "He wanted to talk—he wanted to work it out. I know that he didn't want to be left alone anymore, but I still needed time. He tried to get me to stay, but I wouldn't—I-I told him I'd call him tomorrow, but when I tried to leave—before I knew it, he was right in front of the car and—"

Christina burst out bawling as her head dropped toward the floor. I couldn't stand to see her cry. My heart started to blister in anguish for her, and I couldn't understand why. She was the reason why I had to grow up without a father. I loved my father more than anything in the world, and she took him from me. I didn't have a choice in how my heart felt for her, though. I felt like I had no choice in what I did next. I took her hand in mine and pulled her up to me. She looked up into my eyes and wrapped her arms around me. Then her face fell into my chest as she burst out bawling again.

My arms stayed hanging at my sides while her arms were around me. For a moment, I felt like a little boy again. It felt so good to me when she used to hold me back then; she was the only woman that ever really did, and I started thinking, *Am I betraying my father? Does this mean that I never really loved him if I don't hate her? It's not ok—it's not ok what happened.*

Then through her bawling, Christina said, "I never meant to hurt him." I brought my arms up and wrapped them around her. As if something deep rose within me, I said it. I said, "I forgive you."

Christina raised her head to look into my eyes, and she said, "I love you." *She loves me, but why—why does she love me?* I thought, *Why does it have to be you? You're the one person that showed me more love than anybody. Why does it have to be you?* I couldn't make any sense of it, but it felt good for her to tell me she loved me, and I didn't know why it did. As a warm wave washed over me, all I could think was, *I hate myself for not hating you,* and then I said it. I broke down in tears, and I just said it. I told her, "I love you too."

I decided to stay the next day. I didn't know for how long, but I couldn't leave. I felt like once everybody found out, *and they would find out*, nobody would understand the way I felt about everything. I didn't even understand how I felt about it all, but I couldn't deny what I felt in my heart, no matter how much everyone thought I should hate her. I knew at that moment for sure I had the same type of heart my father had. He wouldn't have wanted me to hate her. As much as people out there want to call people like him and me soft, we're really not. It's easier to hate someone, especially if they do something that's damn near unforgivable, but to people like us, like him and me, it's much more natural to love. I knew he wouldn't want me to hate her, and I know deep down in my heart he would've understood what I did. It's just not in my nature to hate someone, even if I want to. I just can't do it.

    I didn't just stay there for another day or a week. I lived with Christina for a few months. I felt like I found a purpose there with Josci. I could finally be the big brother to her I had always wanted to be. I didn't forget about my brother back home, but he and I got plenty of time together, and if he couldn't understand then, he would one day.

    Everyone, all of my family, found out eventually when I finally decided to come clean. After all, I was a registered missing person. I told them it all even if they would hate me for it. I didn't care what they thought about it. They all even had the nerve to say Christina and I had something going on, which hurt me more than ever. I had hurt them by going missing, but as soon as I popped up again and everyone knew where I was, they had to accuse me of something like that. I knew they would never understand; that's why I didn't want to tell them. The only one who listened to what I had to say was my Uncle Josh. He's always been more like a big brother to me than an uncle, but I was glad I had someone in my life who at least tried to understand, even if he didn't completely.

    What eventually made it all come crashing down in Kentucky was when I got into an argument with Christina's new boyfriend over the phone. He wanted to fuck me up real good, he said to me, and I started to fear for my life again. So I left. I didn't have any money to make it back, so a few of my family members came down and got me back to Ohio. The hardest part was leaving Josci. She didn't want me to go, but I knew I had to. My time with her couldn't have lasted forever. Nothing ever does. You only wish it could. I broke her heart and left her crying in the yard when I pulled off to meet my family in town.

I cried all the way there thinking, *I failed her. The last thing that my father told me was to look after her, and I failed her. I'm not any good for anything. I broke her heart and probably my brother's back home over all this. The purpose I have here is to be a brother, and I can't even do that right.*

When I got back to Ohio, my mom, Tim, and Pavin were gone—they all moved to Alabama. They stopped to visit me in Kentucky on their way down for the move, though. They tried everything they could to talk me into going with them, but I couldn't do it. I couldn't bring myself to leave Josci. It wasn't just because I loved her. It was because she was the only purpose I could find for myself in the world. Without her, I didn't feel like I had a purpose. My brother had so many people in his life he could go to, but she barely had anyone.

I moved in with my cousin Justin once I got back to Ohio. He tried to help me the best he could to get me back on my feet. He and his brother Zack were always like my big brothers too, just like Uncle Josh was, only I knew they couldn't understand any of what I did, so we just didn't talk about it. I spent months smoking and drinking every paycheck I had away until my brother, Pavin, returned home for Christmas. It was great to catch back up with him and to find out how he was finally doing. He was in middle school then, and I couldn't believe how much he changed since the last time I saw him. He wasn't a little boy anymore, but a teenager, and with all the growth he had made, we started having the same type of talks we still have today. We created a bond stronger than ever when he returned to see everyone for Christmas, but when he had to go back to Alabama, I felt like falling apart.

29 Palms

On New Year's Eve of 2012, I did fall apart. Everyone went out to the bar, and I wasn't old enough to get in, so I was back at the house by myself. Everyone might have left, but their liquor was still there, a whole counter full in fact, and I just lost it through all the booze. I called my mom up crying and told her how sorry I was for everything and how I never meant to hurt her by doing what I did. I just had to do it. It didn't have anything to do with her. I knew she loved me even if she didn't know how to show it. She never really had time to show it even if she did. She worked her ass off like a man her whole life to give my brother and me the things she never had. It all came at a cost for all of us, though. I loved the things she could provide for me, but I would've loved it so much more if we would've gotten more time together. I told her it all on the phone that night. I poured my heart out, and at the end of it all, I said, "I'll do it. I'll come to Alabama."

It wasn't a week later, and she flew me down. I began starting a new life in a new town down there in Saraland, Alabama, but it didn't help anything at all. All of the people I'd had around growing up were all gone. All my friends, all my family, everyone. I still had my mom, Tim, and Pavin, but they all had their own lives with jobs and especially friends. I've never been too good at making new friends. People usually don't give me a chance. That's until I met my kids' mom.

She gave me a chance, and we started off as great friends, but I never really wanted to date her. I just clung to her so I wouldn't have to feel lonely anymore, and it was a terrible thing to do because before we even had our first son, I knew we weren't right for one another. She wouldn't touch me, and when she did, it never really felt like she loved me. Maybe she did, and I just couldn't feel it because I never really fell for her. There was nothing that felt real about it, but she gave me a direction. She gave me both of my boys, and through them, I truly had a purpose. I found a reason to keep living and to keep pushing forward. Without them, I probably would've given up on it all a long time ago, but from having children with someone I never fell in love with, I created a prison for myself. I yearned through pain for years wishing I could find the love I so deeply desired.

After years of trying to make it work, I knew it never would. So we had to end it. That was the only thing we ever got on the same page about, was finally ending the relationship. After we did, though, she started using my kids against me, and her true character began to show, and I believe that's why I could never fall for her at all because that part of her was always below the surface. She took the boys from me, and I lost my purpose. I lost it and was on the brink of losing it all completely until that one night. That one night, I finally experienced a kiss more real than reality itself, and I felt the potential spark for the love I'd always truly wanted. It was my kiss with Brooke—and there I was in Sin City of all places in the summer of 2020, ready to meet her again at last.

CHAPTER XXV: WELCOME TO THE JUNGLE

Get to the chopper!! Was all that I could hear and I was gunnin' it like the Bandit; Burt Reynolds would've been proud.

The entire day had been filled with a blistering heat as I sped the '69 through the Arizona desert and onward through Nevada. *One hundred and twenty degrees with no A/C.* To make it even worse, I nearly blew myself up earlier that day. One hundred and twenty degrees was just too damn hot for a fifty-year-old car with only half of an exhaust system left and a radiator puking green slime-like antifreeze everywhere at every stop. I forgot to mention earlier; apparently, the entire exhaust system hung onto the bottom of the '69 by a thread the entire way from Maine to Nevada. There was barely even a crossbar underneath holding it all up. That's probably why half of it became disconnected in the ghost town incident, I'm guessing. Who knows when that happened? To top it all off, the radiator fan was hardly working, and the wiring system was completely fucked. When I got it checked out, the mechanic asked, "Hey, buddy, are you the one that wired this car?"

I told him, "Hell no, I didn't. I just saw it on the side of the road and bought it."

The mechanic replied, "Who in the hell did you buy it from? Whoever did this wiring job needs to be shot."

I replied rather nonchalantly as I flicked some ashes off my smoke, "I don't know; it was some old guy in Maine who looked like he was in the mob or something. I didn't ask any questions. I just liked the car and bought it."

The mechanic looked up at me from under the hood with bulging eyes like I was nuts or something and said, "You mean to tell me, son, you made it all the way from Maine to Arizona in this car right here?!"

The mechanic shook his head and placed his hand on his forehead, "That's a miracle. A real goddamn miracle."

I thought, *I'll never make it to Vegas in time,* and said, "Well, I have about a hundred miles to go till I get to Vegas. I mean, it made it this far, so—do ya think it'll make it the rest of the way?"

The mechanic shut the hood to the '69 and said, "You're nuts, kid, and ya got a hell of a lot of luck considering you made it damn near all the way across the country in this car right here. It shouldn't even be running." He shook his head again, completely perplexed as he continued, "If you really need to get to Vegas, it might just make it, but you sure are damn nuts, kid, if you even try it."

That was the thing. I had to try it. I didn't have any other choice. The chopper was supposed to leave at 8 p.m. I didn't want to put the '69 through anymore wear and tear—I really didn't. It felt like, throughout my journey, the '69 and I bonded very deeply just like two people could, and I trusted it. I knew deep down in my heart we could make it, and we did. Barely, but we made it. Almost.

I had nothing but sweat and adrenaline pouring out of my body as I raced onward through the outskirts of Vegas toward the helicopter's hangar. It was 7:53, but the hangar was fifteen minutes away; if I didn't get there in time, the chopper would leave without me. I called the clerk at the terminal and got her on the phone. After she greeted me, I screamed into the phone, "Yeah, this is Hawke Smith! I know my chopper leaves in about eight minutes, but I still have about twelve minutes until I get to you. Can you hold the chopper?! Please?! I'm just about there!"

The clerk replied as calm and as casual as ever, "Why, of course, Mr. Smith. We just encourage our passengers to be here by 8 p.m. The actual flight doesn't leave until 8:20 p.m. So rest assured, the helicopter will still be here when you arrive."

What an asshole. I mean, here I was trying to get there as fast as I could to get to the helipad, thinking it would leave without me, and I still had damn near half an hour before the chopper even took off. After I got off the phone with the clerk, I sighed and tried to relax. Then I started to wonder why I got myself so worked up to begin with. After all, it wasn't the end of the world where torpedoes were slamming into the ground all around me with people half on fire running around screaming, "Damn President Trump! Damn him! He's brought an end to us all!"

No, none of that was going on. It was just a helicopter ride over Las Vegas, but I had to enter the city that way. I couldn't have done it any other way. No—no other way at all. Vegas is like a fine wine or a beautiful woman. You gotta handle her a little differently.

When I finally arrived at the airport's hangar, I climbed out of the '69, more relieved than ever to have finally made it. I stood there for a minute as the cool night air of the Vegas wind wrapped around me, soothing me with its touch. As I took a deep breath with my eyes closed, I started thinking, *Much better. Much, much better. I feel so much calmer now.* Then, almost instantaneously, my eyes popped open, and I ran for the hangar office's door. It was time to fly.

Not right off the bat, though. I still had ten minutes to spare after all. I walked smoothly up to the counter in pure gentleman-like fashion, completely masking the fact I'd nearly gone mad just a few minutes earlier. I smiled at the lady clerk at the counter and said, "Well, hello there. The name's Hawke Smith, and you are?"

The lady clerk replied with a bright, friendly smile crowned with burgundy lips as she pointed to her nametag, "I'm Rachel. I see you're going out on the 8:25 flight. Your pilot will be ready to instruct you on a few of our safety measures in just a few moments. We have a glass of champagne ready for you while you wait."

She pointed to six glasses of champagne that pretty much filled up the counter. *Six? Why six? And why did I ask for her name when she's wearing a nametag? I'm a dumbass.* I looked around behind me from left to right at the empty lobby, and then I leaned up on the counter toward Rachel and asked, "You said a glass, right? Why do you have six? I'm the only one here."

Rachel grinned a little and said, "Well, we had a few last-minute cancellations this evening. We had a whole party of five cancel for the 8:25 flight, so it appears you will be going on your flight alone, Mr. Smith." She laughed a little and continued, "You and the pilot anyway."

8:25 flight? Didn't she say 8:20 earlier? Oh well, I have to ask, "So what are you going to do with the other five glasses?"

Rachel laughed a little again and said, "I guess we'll just throw them out."

No, no, no, don't throw them out! I had to save them. I replied, "Well, I mean—I could—you and me maybe—"

No, I could tell she wasn't going to drink as soon as she pushed her brow down, looking all confused, but I had to try at least. It was champagne, after all. Save the fine wine. That's a good cause. I looked around behind me at the empty room again and continued, "Look, all I have is a ten in cash. You can have it—if you—what I'm trying to say is I've been on a highway to hell all day and—I'm not gonna lie, I could use all six of those right now. I'll drink 'em. So what do ya say?"

Rachel appeared shocked at first. Then she muffled her laughter right before she replied, "You can keep the ten. Just do it fast before anybody sees you."

I snapped and then made the finger bang at her. *Finger bang? What the fuck was I finger banging at people for? What am I, possessed?* I swallowed all six glasses of champagne faster than Sonic. Rachel gave me a look that said, *This guy's fucking crazy*, all over her face. Just as I went to talk to Rachel again, the pilot came in and said, "Flight's ready."

With a red face about to burst, Rachel said, "There's the pilot. Good luck in Vegas, Mr. Smith. Have a safe flight."

While I started to make my way out, I spun back around toward Rachel and mouthed the words, "Why did you do this to me?" With a big smile painted across her face, I'm pretty sure she mouthed the words back, "You did this to you. Not me." I waved my hand at her as I walked out of the door toward the helicopter. Now it was time to fly.

As the helicopter ascended into the night sky, I almost couldn't believe I was even on it. *How did I even get here? In this moment?* It all just seemed so wild, so free, so outlandish. The whole ascent could be viewed from nearly all corners of the helicopter. This pilot sure knew what he was doing; I could tell, or I at least hoped he did. Maybe he had some champagne too; who knows? All I did know is Vegas was just ahead. There was no mistaking it.

The darkness of the desolate desert wrapped its shadowy arms around the city as if it were cradling something hidden, something special, that had just a different level of exclusivity to it. There in the middle of all the darkness, the city of Vegas glimmered. All of the lights looked like stars that had fallen from above, making their presence known in every manner of uniqueness the mind could possibly conceive of. I could see gold, blue, pink, and green colors flashing together below like some sort of dazzling kaleidoscope intending to draw you toward either an instantaneous rise or a dramatic fall. It all lay down there, and I was on top of the world. The power of all the lights felt invigorating: it felt raw; it *hypnotized* me.

It was either just me or the champagne kicking in, but I needed a song ready before we went over the actual strip. I screamed over the sound of the helicopter blades, "Hey!—Hey, man! Can you listen to music up here?! Like, can you play a song or something?!"

The pilot replied, "Sure, what do you want to hear?"

I bounced up in delight like a kid and said, "Play 'Hypnotize' by Biggie. Yeah! Yeah! That'll do it!"

The pilot gave me a thumbs up and said, "I like your style."

There it was, the Vegas strip. The golden lights of the Y-shaped Mandalay Bay awaited us first as if it were the first guardian of many to welcome my gaze to the up-close and above splendor of all the stars lying below. The crisp blue lights of the

Luxor straddled their way on the edge of the Mandalay, calling my mind back to times long forgotten and past from its grand pyramid-like architecture. *Reminds me of Egypt. I'm going to make it there someday. I just know I will.*

There was a building of emerald waiting further amid the chopper that's mere glow beckoned toward me and hypnotized me even more. As we continued to fly toward and then past all the violets and the yellows and the blues dancing around everywhere, my eyes could see it all—a true neon jungle for the taking. Where the greatest of dreams could come true or the greatest crash you could ever imagine lie in wait like a leopard; it was all there. All matter of possibilities. It was here I could become a star in my heart overnight. Only winning millions of dollars didn't interest me at all because the chance to hold Brooke in my arms would make me as rich of a man I could ever hope to be. Everything that came before, especially the road running behind me, led me to this moment. I'd either win my greatest heart's desire to be loved and to truly love, or I'd lose it all completely. It was worth the gamble. She was worth the gamble. So I didn't care.

After the helicopter landed back at the terminal, I prayed and prayed in my heart the '69 would start back up so I could finally make it to the Flamingo apartments, where I had booked a room. I stuck the key in the ignition, and before I turned it, I put my hand on the dash and said, "Just a little further. I promise tomorrow I'll get you in the shop, and you'll be as good as new. Just start for me. Just one more time tonight. I know you can do it."

The '69 started up as smooth as a brand new car would've. You know, like I hadn't put it through all manner of living hell just to get there to Vegas. *Is this car like Christine from that Stephen King novel?* I thought.

I couldn't have been more relieved to have finally reached my room as I dropped my bags on the floor and flopped down on the couch. *Vegas. I finally made it.* I still couldn't believe it. As I sat there sinking into the zebra-colored furniture, my phone started to go off. It was a text from Brooke. **I'm finishing homework and packing as we speak. I'm so excited.**

My heart would always dance around with so much joy when she'd text me out of the blue like that. I'd think, *She's thinking about me. Me of all people.* I couldn't believe it. It just made my heart feel so full. I replied, *I bet you are, lol. There is so much to see around here.*

Where's my picture???

I hadn't sent her a picture yet. I did take a few from the helicopter while I was up there, but I didn't want to bother her. I told her about the helicopter ride and sent her a few of the pictures I had taken while I was up there. I told her about all of what happened with the '69 on the way, and she couldn't believe that. I knew I'd have to get a rental the next day, but there was no way it could be a minivan or anything like that. I had to ride in style, and I did just that.

The next day I dropped the '69 off with one of the best mechanics Vegas had to offer. He was some bald guy whose shop was called the Silver Arrow, I think. He was a cool guy, but he didn't like spending time answering questions. Short man syndrome, I presume.

Shortly afterward, I held the keys to a 2019 all-white convertible Ford Mustang. A hell of a cruza if I had to say so myself, and to feel the cool air of an A/C unit blow across my face again felt better than sex, damn near, I have to say.

On my way to Lake Mead, I pulled off the side of the road to take a video to show off my new ride. Everybody loved the video I took of the helicopter ride, if everyone means like thirty people, but the show had to go on, and I wanted to make a few pricks back home jealous. In the video, I said, "So I decided to drop the '69 off to get the restoration work completed on it—to really, you know—wake that ghost back up if you know what I mean—really bring it back to life. But until then, I'm stuck with this fuckin' thing and—I don't know. I was havin' a pretty good time, but now—now it's just all going down the drain."

I rotated the camera around to show off the Mustang's front as I walked around it and opened up the door. I continued, "I mean—what am I supposed to do now? Whole trip's fuckin' ruined."

While I sat in the driver's seat, I began to let the top down and said, "You can't have a super good time everywhere you go. I mean, sometimes things go to shit, and sometimes—ya know, I don't know. But—yeah." With a huge grin, I said, "What am I supposed to do now?"

People thought it was hilarious. Most of the time, people don't get my sense of humor, and a lot of the time on Snap I probably look like a maniac to most, but it's all in good fun. I'm an underdog, after all, and an outsider on top of that. So when I'm shining, why not show it?

Lake Mead was indeed a sight to behold. It had to have been nearly the most incredible desert oasis you could ever hope to set your eyes on. From my boots in the dusty gravel to the horizon stretching out ahead, I could just see forever approaching a vastness like no other through the tattered greens of tiny bushes spotting the rocky terrain of canyons and mountains. Glimmers of crystal seemed to bounce to and fro across the darkened hue of the lake shining with the eloquence of the finest lapis lazuli one could ever hope to find. Lake Mead was magnificent and appeared to be a true reflection within desolation of all that lie possible in the above realms and to those below. It looked ancient to the eye, but it was pretty new. That lake wasn't even there before the thirties. I guess we can work wonders in nature if we really want to or by complete accident on some occasions.

I couldn't get enough of the view at all, so I started following the road along the lake to take in all the vibrant colors of the waters bouncing back toward me. I raced along the desert landscape in full top-down galore. After I turned on Michael Jackson's "Beat It," my engine revved up just as much as the Mustang's had. It was time to see how fast this thing could go.

I could feel it all, living in the moment—not a care for the future or the past because whatever had come and gone, I beat it, and whatever was ahead, I knew I could beat that too. The wind blew through my hair as I punched the gas pedal further and further toward 110 miles per hour. *Nothing is going to stop me. I can do it. I'm somebody, even if people treat me like I'm not.* I felt like I was winning in life for the first time, with no worries, no tragedy, no heartbreak, just me, the wind, and Vikare flying above.

I texted Brooke and gave her the god-awful news that the Hoover Dam was closed. I knew it was one of the places she wanted to see the most once she got to Vegas. I thought, *There go the Covid regulations once again, swooping in to tear apart everyone's hopes and dreams; what a surprise.*

She wasn't too happy about the news, but I told her about how beautiful I thought the lake was, and the whole time, my heart kept racing while I sat there along the lake talking to her. She couldn't wait to be in Vegas, and I couldn't wait either, but my fear kept creeping back in this time through the darker side of the familiar voice. It said, *You've come all this way for some girl that you've only seen in person twice in your life. You're an idiot. She's going to get here and not even give you the time of day.* I told myself, *No, no, she will. I'll get to see her again. At least I hope I do. If—if she doesn't, I don't know what I'll do. If she doesn't give me a chance after all this, I don't know what I'll do.*

I had to turn my mind off. I couldn't handle those thoughts. They were breaking me down too much. So I pushed it all out of my mind and tried my best to focus on the present. After all, the Vegas strip waited for me, and I intended to make my debut at the Hard Rock.

The cabbie didn't drop me off right at the Hard Rock, though. I just had him drop me off at the Excalibur instead because I couldn't take any more of his talking. I was in a deep part of my mind at the time and still wrestling with my inner fears. I tried as hard as I could to not let them tear me down, but I couldn't keep those nagging thoughts out of my head. *Her texts are getting shorter. You're a nobody to her—you're not anything to anybody.* I didn't want to believe it, but after a while, with thoughts like that creeping in, you start to lose energy fighting it all.

Meanwhile, the cabbie said, "So I'm sleeping in this car right here, you know, man, with my feet all kicked out the window, and all, and this guy comes along and tries to rip my shoes right off my feet! Can you believe that? My shoes! Then he pulls out a blade and wants my wallet, but luckily for me, I'm a black belt. I've been a black belt in karate since I was four years old, man. My great uncle on my momma's side was Bruce Lee's brother, but nobody believes me, man, because I'm a Mexican, you know? Like Mexicans can't do karate? We got UFOs that fly over Mexico city all the time, man; I've seen a lot of unbelievable shit—" I had to interject, "Hey, wait, man—what's that over there?"

The cabbie replied, "What's what over where, man?"

Damn near maddened by my thoughts with his constant rambling; I pointed over toward the castle-like structure. "That thing over there. What is that? What's the sign say? Excalibur? Ok—yeah—I couldn't see it through those trees. Just drop me off right here. I wanna check that out."

29 Palms

The cabbie bounced around in his seat as he said, "Yeah, man, the Excalibur—like knights of the round table, right, man?" He began to laugh hysterically and continued, "You about to get into a sword fight or what, man?!" He kept laughing and laughing, and I thought, *Ok, what the fuck is this guy on right now?*

I couldn't take anymore, so I handed him some cash for the ride and said, "Sure am. I'm a hell of a lot closer than you think—here, keep the change. See ya later, and watch out for the UFO behind us. It's been following us the whole time." His laughing stopped immediately. He started bellowing, "Say what, man—" but I closed the door before he could finish. I wished the guy luck. I really did, but I had to get out of that cab.

There it was, the Excalibur. It looked pretty grand with all of its outstretched turrets and towers, but it didn't come anywhere close to the castles of the old world. It still looked incredible to me, though. After all, someone used their imagination to build that thing, just like all the other structures along the strip. If something is truly made from the spontaneity of one's imagination, its magic will never cease to die, but all these buildings and structures weren't made from the heart; they were built to reel people in and their pocketbooks. I knew from those first thoughts coming into my head my stay in Vegas wasn't going to turn into the next *Hangover* movie. I didn't feel great on the inside out there around everybody else. With each step, I started feeling more like the stranger in a strange land all over again. I didn't like it. I just wished I would've stayed by the lake for the sunset. It felt so much better out there that day than it did on the strip.

If I could've smacked myself out of my depressive decline in front of everyone, I would have. I just kept trying to tell myself, *Come on, you're in Vegas. You've come all the way across the country to get here. This place is in so many people's dreams. So many people work their asses off just to get here. Suppose you can't enjoy it for yourself. Enjoy it for them. Everything's going to be ok.* I kept repeating those thoughts over the shadows of fear that kept creeping in. I thought to myself; *I got this. I got this. I'm going to enjoy today and not worry about tomorrow. Just take in the atmosphere and have fun in the moment.* With that thought in mind, I went up the escalator to the Hard Rock's bar.

    The Hard Rock looked just as you would expect it to. There were pictures and odes to all the old rock legends everywhere. Those guys back then were like gods. Their guitars would roar through the air like thunder, and the rumble of their melodies felt like it could tear through the atmosphere and rip apart the sky. They truly changed hearts and minds with their tunes. It was a different kind of music vibrating through the soul and aiming its way right into the very core of your being. Peace, love, and harmony are the simplest of words, but the greatest of things to center a movement around. That's what the '60s were about, "breaking on through to the other side," just like Jim Morrison said.

    I struck up a conversation with the male bartender after I took a seat. *A male bartender, well, that's quite a buzz kill.* I've always liked talking to women bartenders more than the guy ones. I don't hate other guys or anything, but most of them always bring up boring shit like sports or cars. I've never really got what the big deal is with sports. I mean, where's the fun in sitting in the same spot for four hours drinking beer after beer yelling at a guy on TV to go when you don't even go for yourself? I've always hated it. It bores me to death, in fact, but this fellow wasn't too bad. He filled me in on all the Covid regulations, which was a level up from sports talk, in my opinion. According to him, there weren't any live shows going on, and you had to wear a mask in all the casinos. I started thinking, *Fuck me. Vegas too? All over a virus with a 99 percent survival rate, I just don't get it.*

After the Covid talk, I ordered a long island and some nachos. Then another long island. Then another and just one more, I said to myself. After I asked for the check, I changed my mind, "Stop, wait a minute. Give me a tall Blue Ribbon and a shot of Crown Apple before I get on out of here."

I left the guy a twenty for bothering him again. I felt kind of rude toward the end, but the buzz kicked in, and I was ready to see some lights—every single one of them.

There they were, all of the lights. I could see the bright blue of the Paris hot air balloon over the top of the ever-encroaching night sky. I could see the red, white, and blue of an Eiffel tower replica just beyond that, and then the pink light of the Flamingo jutting across the new resort in old-style, vice lettering, I think it's called, but I don't know to tell you the truth. It just sounds smart describing it that way. Truth is, I didn't even know what half the buildings were called all around me—I was like the biggest dumbass in Vegas. I google mapped everything later of course, to write about it, but honestly, I didn't know what the fuck was going on.

To my left, the Bellagio fountains laid assault upon the night sky through bursting fireworks of water falling as fast as they rose. Just ahead was Caesar's Palace. That was the casino that got me out of all the others. I've never been much of a fan of Caesar, to tell you the truth. I despise him and he's always seemed quite distasteful.

To be honest, I've never even seen a picture of what Caesar's Palace looked like, but in my imagination, I thought it would look like one of the temples in Baalbek or something, you know? It kind of looked better in my imagination to tell you the truth, but the inside looked pretty nice.

Of course, your average casino folks were scrambling all around inside. There were a lot of old folks in there from the looks of it. I found myself in a terrifying sea of gray and thinning hair. To my left, at the slot machines, this old lady who looked pretty fed up with life slammed her card into a machine. Every play or so, she'd take her oxygen mask off and take another puff off her cigarette. Her eyes started to roll at another loss, I'm guessing. *She really didn't give a shit.* She probably thought, *Well, I'd be damned if I give any of those goddamn grandkids a cent of my hard-earned money. That little bastard Tommy won't even come cut my grass, so fuck 'em all.*

When I walked further into the palace, this small bald guy with a huge gut popping out at the bottom of his purple t-shirt started walking toward me. He sort of reminded me of a pint-sized version of the bad guy from the movie *Lovely Bones* or something. I guess his glasses alone brought all that to mind. I kept thinking, *Don't look at his gut. Don't look at his gut*, but I couldn't help it; it was just there, bouncing like some sort of ball. The chubby little guy pushed his brow down at me and said, "What are you staring at?! You staring at me?"

He had me, but I didn't want to admit he did. I tried everything I could not to laugh as I replied, "What? No—I was checking out that chick behind you. See that blonde right there?" I pointed toward this beautiful blonde with long, curly, flowing locks. Apparently red was her favorite color. Red dress, red nails, red lipstick; I knew what she was trying to do. She was trying to light a fire in a man's soul looking that damn good, and it worked its charm on me, I gotta say. The little guy said, "Ooooh, are you talking about that babe right there?!"

I replied, "Yeah, that *babe* right there. You know she was sort of eyeing you too. I think she might be following you or something."

The little chubby man's eyebrows lifted across his forehead as he made an o-shape with his lips; he said, "Oh wow, she was looking at *me*?"

I lit up a smoke and replied, "Yeah, she was looking at you. You should go talk to her. You know, like flex out your chest and just let her have it, man."

The little chubby man replied, "Wha—what do ya—what do ya think I should say?"

Trying not to burst out in laughter and delving fully into mischief, I replied, "Man, I don't know; let me think. Ummm—honestly, man, the purple shirt isn't going to help your case. I mean, you look like Barney a little bit—"

"Hey, what are you—"

I continued, "Just hear me out—I'm just being honest. Ok—well you see a chick like that, right? That's what you call very high maintenance; she's a handful, and money is going to be the only thing that's going to catch her attention. So she's at the roulette table, right?"

"Yeah—"

"Well, you go over to the roulette table and try to look like a high roller—that's what she's looking for. If you got the dough to place a big bet, show off some steam, man. Just go all the way. Go with a number that speaks to you. Believe in it, and if you win, she's yours. If you don't—well, then she's not, is she? Worth a shot."

The little man replied, "But-but what do I say?"

I replied in kind of a precise way, I gotta admit, "That's the thing. It doesn't matter what you say. Most folks don't care about what you say or what you think; they just want a piece of what you have—not everybody, but most—if you can go over there and win—

you could say whatever you want, and it wouldn't even matter. That's a gold digger right there."

The pudgy man looked at red riding hood in her dress and then back to me and said, "Ya really think it'll work?"

Honestly, I did. I think I had her pinned down pretty well. I hate to judge people like that, but some people you just have to watch out for. I'd love it if the world was filled with people that aren't out to get one another, but that's just not the case. You gotta trust that alarm system you have sometimes.

Now the chick in all-red in Caesar's Palace was beautiful. I had to give her that, but she was the average high-maintenance type, and that's always looked pretty ugly to me. I like the type of down-to-Earth girl who isn't afraid to be herself and drink a little; who doesn't have a problem with wearing a t-shirt but still knows how to clean up like a queen. That's my type, and she gets bonus points if she's not afraid to say fuck or cusses somebody out every once in a while. I admire a girl with spirit.

The little guy did follow my advice and go to the roulette table, though. I'm not sure how high he bet, but I think he had a lot of money to blow for some reason. I wasn't even sure if he won—I stood off a ways watching it all go down—but he must've won something because the red nails of red riding hood ran their way right across his back. I felt good about that. Most likely, he was probably a virgin; who knows? And I might've helped him get to the next stage of manhood. Maybe little red riding hood liked 'em short anyway; who knows? Maybe she dressed him up like a baby and fed him cereal later on—who really knows or wants to? Not me, really. I was getting bored, and I didn't feel like gambling, so I went back outside.

After Caesar's Palace, I continued my stroll down the strip. As I went further and further down, I started to notice the big crowd of people became a small crowd, and the small crowd turned into nobody at all, and there were hardly any lights left either. I could see the Stratosphere in the distance, but besides the passing cars on the road, there was only me. Well, just me and this raving lunatic up the sidewalk.

At first, I thought the guy was just dancing around acting goofy, you know. I mean, who hasn't been there before? But when you see a bald guy dancing naked in a trench coat a little less than half a mile in front of you, that's someone acting more than goofy. That is a picturesque example of someone technically losing their shit.

I almost couldn't believe it. *What the fuck is this guy doing?* He was just twirling around, batting the edges of his overcoat around like they were wings, screeching like some kind of bird. Then suddenly, he flipped his trench coat off and threw it out into traffic at a passing car. They pounded on their horn and screamed, "What the fuck is wrong with you, asshole?!"

The bald man screamed something back in some unknown foreign language; it sounded like, I wasn't sure. Then he shook his thing—you know, his dick—around at all the passing traffic. There wasn't much for him to shake, though, I have to admit. I mean, I wasn't trying to look, but suddenly I could understand him completely. If I were in his predicament and had to use tweezers every time I had to take a piss—well, quite frankly, I'd use every drug known to man to get that type of shame out of my mind. From a google search I decided to conduct later, I found out that scientists commonly label his condition as micropenis syndrome. Apparently, one in every ten thousand men are afflicted with it in the United States. I guess my personal problems weren't as big, or small in the bald guy's case, as I thought, but with his new course of action taking a more sinister turn, I jumped the concrete barricade to my left and bolted across the street as fast as I could. Whatever demons that guy battled, he'd have to do it alone.

I was more relieved than ever when I finally made it to the Strat. I waded my way through the screaming valets and sports cars toward the glass front doors of the casino. *Where would I start?* I didn't care too much to play any of the slots, those things are rigged the most, in my opinion, but I was up for some blackjack at the bar. The blackjack was computerized there too, but I didn't care. There was a bartender there and a lady this time at that. She looked to be the librarian type, sort of like Janie from *Not Another Teen Movie*, with her dark hair pulled back into a ponytail. I ordered a cranberry vodka for a change on this go-around and started to play some blackjack. Gambling has never really been my thing, not with money anyway, but this was Vegas. How could I be in Vegas and not gamble? After another vodka and cranberry, the bartender asked, "Hey, sweetheart, are you ok?"

I lifted my head to look around, but I was the only one at the bar. I replied, "Who me?"

"Yeah—you look like you're upset about something."

Sometimes when I get caught up in my thoughts, I forget to keep my happy face on. I couldn't believe she caught on and actually cared. I kept thinking about Brooke at the bar.

She was supposed to be in Vegas tomorrow, and I kept thinking, *What if she doesn't even try to hang out with me when she's here? What if she goes cold on me and pretends like I don't even exist?* The possibility of that happening tore me apart on the inside. It felt like I lay on the ground with chains wrapped around my ankles, dragged back down toward the dark. I didn't want to go back there. I've always been afraid of the dark. I couldn't stand the thought of not seeing her. Talking about it with someone, though, would be better than dealing with it myself. I decided to open up to her when I sighed, "I just got my mind on this girl. That's all."

The bartender replied, "Oh, you have a girlfriend?"

I replied, "No, she's not my girlfriend. We're more like friends, but I really care about her. I think I might love her, actually, but I'm not sure if I even know what love is."

"Well, love's nothing to be sad about."

I took another sip of my vodka cranberry and replied, "It is to me. I've never felt like this before, and what worries me the most is that I don't think she feels the same way about me at all." I continued to just let it all go. I had to let it out. "It's just that I've traveled this whole way, and at first, it wasn't about her at all, but somehow, with each passing sunrise and with each passing sunset, all I could think about was her. I didn't even want to think about her at all, but I couldn't help it. It's like the thought of her just came with all those things—I don't know—she's-she's going to be here tomorrow, and I'm just so afraid that she's not going to want to see me at all."

The lady bartender leaned up against the counter toward me and sighed. "Love can be a really tough thing. I've had plenty of guys break my heart over the years, but—I'm not saying I'm glad that they did, but—you can't put yourself in a big worry about it. What's meant for you will come to you. You just have to trust in it."

That made me even more afraid. What if my heart led me toward the wrong place? What if I were to end up at the end of the road more broken than I was at the start of all this? *That can't happen, it can't. I don't want to go back in the dark.* I lifted my head up again to meet the eyes of the bartender and said, "I am trusting in it. I'm trusting in my heart. I'm just so scared that it's not going to work out. Like it's going to turn into some kind of tragedy or something at the end."

The lady bartender replied, "Well, if your heart is leading you to her, then follow it. If it doesn't work out this time, then maybe it will later on? Just show her that you care and see what happens. It can turn out bad, but there's also a chance it could all turn out good too, right?" I nodded my head and said, "Yeah—yeah, I think it can. I hope it'll all turn out alright."

CHAPTER XXVI: BLINDED BY THE LIGHT

    Damn, there it was, the Grand Canyon. The drive there took a hell of a lot longer than I thought from Vegas, but it was one hell of a scenic route to behold. It was dry and barren, don't get me wrong, but some of the mountains I passed along the way looked incredible. There was even one that looked like some sort of long-forgotten juggernaut that just fell across the wasteland. The top looked like a spine of some sort and the summit ran across the edge of the sky. I named that place the dragon's spine. I might've taken a picture of it, but I'm not sure. Pictures never do a thing justice anyway.

    The roads running through the desert aren't too twisty either, like the ones around Lake Mead. I damn near flipped the whole convertible going as fast as I was on those roads, but on the route I took to the Grand Canyon, I could really put the pedal to the metal. I gunned it all the way there, blasting Skid Row, Guns N' Roses, and of course the good old-fashioned *Rocky IV* soundtrack. "No Easy Way Out," that's my song, and it all gave some flavor to one hell of a ride.

      I never felt so minuscule, so irrelevant, and small than when I saw the Grand Canyon for the first time. It just seemed so impossible. Like *how? How did this occur right here?* This natural work of art seemed to have chiseled its way up, and then through, and across as far as the eye could see through red rock etchings, giving rise to subterranean mountains and peaks for the eagles to perch upon. Looking at the Grand Canyon for the first time probably feels the same if you were to take your mind, rip it up into a bunch of little pieces, and throw it all up in the air like confetti. Unbelievable just isn't even the word. Nothing out there can match it, and pictures don't do it justice at all. Absolutely mind-boggling. The true essence of the Grand Canyon can only be experienced in person, I have to say.

      The air even felt different out there. I knew I was in Arizona, but it didn't feel like Arizona at all. The air felt so crisp, so clean, and so light that it made me feel the same way along with it. It was like the natural magic in that place had a cleansing type of energy to it that would fly through your soul as fast as the wind blew through the pines. The leaves rustled, and the canyon seemed to hum along with it all. I wasn't sure if everyone could hear it, but the sound of the canyon had a very ancient feel to it—like it whispered the same way a sea shell would when you place your ear up to it.

      You might only be able to hear it if you close your eyes or if you clear your mind completely, but I can almost swear the wind harmonics blowing through it all was akin to the sound of angels singing just below the surface of the sun as it all shined down from above. It was just as magical of a place as Niagara Falls, and I could never go to either of them enough even if I tried. I could've stayed out there all day, but I had my heart set on going back to the Strat that night back in Vegas. Of course, I was there the night before, but I hadn't gone to the top yet, and what would be more glorious than gazing upon the setting sun at the highest point in Vegas? Top of the world, they say. That's just where I had to go.

It felt like I brought the eighties back every time I'd turn up the radio while I cruised down the Vegas strip. I felt forever young, in the heat of the moment with a beating heart, all on a quest to know what love is like a foreigner or some stranger in a strange land as I spun the wheels of the Mustang back toward the Strat. I was in my fancy clothes this time, though, Hollywood style; the top of the world deserved nothing less.

It might not have been the fanciest outfit, but for a chrome-colored dress shirt with pinstripe dress pants to match and black snakeskin shoes to mark each step, I felt like a high roller even if I wasn't one. I'd already bought my ticket for the top of the tower the night before, so I was ready to go, and what perfect timing? The strip's neon lights were starting to turn back on, and the sun set behind me. Top of the world, here I come.

I felt so dashing and full of myself as I leaned up against the railing of the escalator toward the elevator that went to the *top*. I couldn't smoke in there, which made me feel less cool, so I just sort of bit my nails casually through all the anticipation. I thought, *Damn, I'm not egotistical or anything, but I look good right now. I mean, Grandma tells me so all the time, so it must be true, right?*

I entered the elevator and looked at my Michael Kor's watch, thinking, *Yeah, this thing was a hundred bucks. I'm Mr. Flashy today. I'm the man of this town right now. I'm that guy. Like James St. Patrick off that show* Power, *only I'm just some white geek from Ohio, but I'm doing it right now. I really am.*

When the elevator doors opened up, I was there, in the moment, with the clouds waiting right outside the doors ahead. When I walked outside and felt the Vegas wind rushing through past my face and all of the lights below glimmering closer and closer with each step, I looked toward the sunrise in the clouds beyond and thought to myself, *Is this heaven? Is this what heaven feels like?* It all seemed so beautiful, and I made it to the top of the world; the only thing was—I was all alone.

I started thinking, *Here I am. I traveled all the way here in my fancy clothes and my fancy cars, but what does this shit mean? Does any of it mean anything?* I didn't really know. All I knew was none of the materials meant a thing at all. I'm not gonna lie. I got all dressed up and excited over this fantasy I had playing in my head of Brooke being at the top of the Stratosphere when I got there. How magical would that have been? I'd just walk out there, and then there she'd be already watching the sunset, and I'd say, "You know how long I've waited to see you? A lot longer than you think. Try a whole lifetime," and then it would all just happen. Everything would be ok, and all that came before would finally mean something. All the tears, all the terrors, all the battles, would've all been worth it because all of it would've brought me to the top of the world for a happy ending after all. It wouldn't all feel like a big tragedy anymore. Everything would just be ok, but it wasn't, and it didn't feel that way at all. Brooke was already in Vegas, and I hadn't heard a word out of her at all.

I already rationalized a lot of it in my head, so it didn't bother me as much as you might think. She'd been planning this trip to Vegas long before she ever met me, and it was a trip she took to let loose, not to just meet up with me, plus her grandma was with her. Her and I being in Vegas together at the same time just sort of happened. I never planned to travel the whole country; that all happened pretty much on the fly. Of course, I decided to extend my weekend trip outside of Georgia to impress her, but when I made her the promise I would go as far as I could go, I saw that as a way to show her I was different. That I meant what I said, and most of all, I wanted to show her I wasn't just telling her what she wanted to hear, but we really did share the same dreams.

29 Palms just seemed like the right destination to end it all in. Out of all the places I'd been so far, 29 Palms was the one place I'd always wanted to see the most. It was where my dad used to live. I knew he loved it there, or at least I thought he did. I always wanted to visit it because part of me still believed deep down inside it would bring me closer to him in the end no matter how far away he seemed to be. I could get a piece of him back there; the only thing was, none of that had been on my mind at all since I finally let go and admitted to myself I loved Brooke. Sure the pain was still there, but all the light Brooke had brought into my life seemed to make it all so much better. Just the mere thought of her made me feel so warm inside. Nothing had ever been able to touch me like that.

I stood there and gazed out across the neon lights and onward toward the glowing horizon. I thought to myself, *She might be here to see the Vegas sunset wherever she is, but she's not at the top of the world with me. So I guess I'll just bring her to it.*

I sent her a text that said, *If you want to link up while you're in town, just let me know.*

Then I sent her a picture of the glowing Vegas sunset lying across the surrounding desert mountains and said, *Top of the world.*

She replied a few minutes later. **That's so nice!! Where is that? And I will let you know! We're at Fremont Street now, but I'm sure I can meet you on the strip or something one night!**

I tried to be as calm and cool as possible without allowing my bleeding emotions to infect my message. *I haven't been there yet. It's at the Stratosphere, though; you should check it out while you're here.*

Yeah, that's where we're going on my actual birthday! I have the tickets for the rides.

Fuck, I should've known. I mean, she did send me her whole schedule for the trip about a week or so ago, but I didn't want to be the stalker type of guy that would be like "wherever you are, I will find you." No, nobody wants to be that guy or should be, really. As bad as I wanted to see her, I vowed not to follow it. I'd just continue to go to the places I wanted to visit on my schedule, and if I just so happened to run into her, all for the better. I looked for a real magical moment after all. Not a predetermined "Well, she's going here at this time, so I'll go there too" type of moment. I'm trying to make a true love story, after all, not the next Halloween movie, but I already planned to go to Fremont Street that night anyway. If I'd see her there, then I would. Either way, I was bound for Fremont next.

The sun had already set by this point, and night had fallen across the streets of Vegas as I let the top down on the Mustang on my way to Fremont Street. Of course, I changed into a more casual outfit back in my room. If I ran into Brooke on Fremont, I didn't want to look like I got all dressed up and ready to get married or something, so I just strapped my cowboy hat back on and hopped back into my boots. I thought, *Damn, these boots and hat are starting to grow on me. I almost don't even miss my blue headband anymore. Fuckin' Stanley hotel, what was I thinking?*

I let the top down on the Mustang to the broad, encompassing view of neon lights yet again as I hit the peddle through the Vegas strip on my way to Fremont Street. I blasted that old "Sister Christian" song by Night Ranger along the way. I wasn't sure why that was the song I picked for the ride, but it was the one that popped in my head, so I figured I'd just go with it.

It felt truly remarkable skating across the streets of Vegas in that convertible, but I started to really miss the '69. In a strange way, that car would always play the perfect song to match my mood, and I have to admit, around each of those sunsets, it seemed like this one song would always play around that same time. "Sister Golden Hair," I think it was. I'm sure that was the one. It seemed odd for that song to reoccur and pop up in the times it had, and it would usually be when Brooke was on my mind the most. It's like I lived every word of that song in my heart, and every syllable matched the way I felt inside.

I've been a depressed person most of my life, stumbling around grasping at pockets of happiness here and there as I've gone along, but with Brooke, she was the one thing I could think about that would just make all of my sadness go away. My kids made me happy, don't get me wrong, but it made me sad to think of them. It's like it wouldn't make me happy anymore, and I'd just want to lose my mind. It's like the love I had for my children just had another tragedy attached to it because they were taken from me, but with Brooke, she didn't bring me close to thinking about any tragedies at all.

With her, I could truly feel the sunshine beating within my heart toward her, and it made all the darkness run away. She was my guiding light through all the darkness, and I thought to myself, *Maybe I've chased after that light too much. Am I running toward my deepest heart's desire, or am I just running away from the shadows?* I didn't know. All I could do was go where my heart led me, and hopefully, just maybe, all the shadows would go away forever. I wanted to see her more than ever at that moment, but when I stepped out on Fremont Street for the first time, I tried not to expect too much at all.

Welcome to Fabulous Downtown Las Vegas. The lights didn't just glow on Fremont, but they danced. The brightly lit up bold signs of the Four Queens and Golden Nugget stood at the gate, beckoning me toward the Fremont Street Experience. The golden lights of the Four Queens blinked and crashed toward the surface in perfect harmony to Sam Boyd's Fremont Casino seemingly engineered toward drawing you into an ablaze of fire that would leave your pockets asunder. *Spectacular.*

Every color I could imagine glittered its way across the old Vegas metropolis through a rhythmic wave-like pattern all around me. It was like all the colors would creep away, but then they would stampede their way right back toward me, each bringing a magnetic wave with the sole desire to pull me within an electric current created by some kind of madman. It wasn't just an adult playground, but it was a carnival. Maybe a carnival for lunatics, who knows? All I knew at the time was Dr. Thompson was right. Vegas was by no means a town for psychedelics. Forget about all the lights of the casinos—what swept me off my feet was the gigantic video screen, dubbed Viva Vision, running like a subway train down Fremont Street.

Jesus, what's going on here? Above me, I saw rocket ships shooting off into space, and meteor's exploded all in some kind of grand symphony in tune with some space opera playing all above in perfect synchronicity to AC/DC's "Shoot to Thrill." *No, not a town for psychedelics at all.*

I couldn't imagine anything like that. It sure would be terrible to be swept away into a multicolored rainbow that in one moment feels like you became some sort of Laffy Taffy of a human being, completely losing grip upon yourself as everything you believed made you yourself is swallowed up in the jaws of some terrible kaleidoscope dragon that's sole intention is to incinerate every inch of your identity, only to bring you right back down into the midst of a roaring crowd with scrambled emotions and a complete lost sense of reality. *No, that would be absolutely terrible.* Who would put themselves through that? Honestly—not saying I did—but I would.

There are always varying different odds to everything. You could have a good trip too. Just imagine feeling every part of the rainbow melding within your soul and every color around you cooling and swirling within your body, each representing a different aspect of love running up through your veins and bursting through the entirety of your being in some sort of orgasmic supernova. Flowing with nature like it's electric. The wave may shock you, but it'll have you feeling more alive than Frankenstein, I can guarantee that, but in a place where street performers are running about in Chewbacca costumes screeching around with light sabers and strippers decked out in BDSM gear snapping whips; most likely it would lead to a bad trip, but you could have a good trip too, just sayin'. Vegas is about gamblin', right?

I didn't have any acid with me, though, or mushrooms or DMT; gee-whiz, *that'd be a doozy,* but there was plenty of weed around. It was like my most favorite smell floated through the air and wrapped me up in its warm embrace like a smiling cartoon cloud. I could almost see the Cheshire cat from *Alice in Wonderland* perched upon the sign of the nearby weed store, ushering me toward all of the perfect bliss and harmony of the true golden nuggets. They had Grandaddy Purp, AK47, Sour Diesel, Bubble Gum; you name it, all of my best friends from the old high school days were there waiting for me. Absolutely wide-eyed and astonished, I approached the guy at the counter and said, "Oh my god, ok—do these actually get you high, or is it that CBD bullshit?"

The man gave me a very serious stare knocking me slightly off-balance at first, but then he smiled and asked the guy behind him stocking shelves, "Hey, did you hear that, Mike? Fabio here wants to know if our bud really gets you high?"

Fabio, really? Kiss my ass. Nobody has called me that since that pack of lesbians tried to murder me on that cruise ship a couple of years back. How was I supposed to know the biggest chick had already taken the girl I made out with in the bunch? Oh well, let's hear about this, bud, Mr. Mike.

Mike, apparently that was his name, turned toward me with a smile so big his cheeks practically touched his forehead. He had a deep, devilish, crimson glare to his eyes informing me right away he had to be from Ohio because you only get a look like that in your eyes if you're on numerous different illegal substances all at once, and that's what we Ohioans are known for. Can you blame us? It's boring as fuck there.

Mike seemed to be pretty high when he looked at me and said, "Does it get you high?" Mike chuckled, "No, not that shit right there—I mean, it's all CBD sort of—I mean, that's all we got, but it'll relax you."

Mike knelt and pulled a bag of pre-rolled *cigars* out from under the counter and said, "These right here, though, are for premium relaxation, my man. It's CBD, you know—I mean, that's all we can really sell here, but if you really wanna see the true colors of the lights tonight, man, I'd recommend going with one of these pre-rolls, my dude."

I stood there for a minute in deep contemplation over the words of Mike. *Deep relaxation—if I really wanted to see the lights, he says—hmmm.* I looked into the red floodgates of hell appearing to be Mike's eyes and replied, "Ok, I'm sold. I'll take three—nope, scratch that, four. And by the way, is that a brownie? I might as well check that out too. I mean, I haven't eaten anything all day." I stopped myself for a minute, and then it occurred to me, so I had to ask, "Wait a minute, will any of this shit make you fail a drug test?"

A slow, rumbling, drawn-out laugh crept out from between Mike's lips as he said, "What? These? No way, man, it's impossible. My P.O. tests me all the time, and I always pass with flying colors, man. You should be good to go, brother." *Perhaps the only test you've ever passed*, I thought to myself, then I slammed my money down on the counter and said, "Fine, I'm sold. Give me the best that you got."

And was it the best he had or that I ever had for that matter. I wasn't sure if it was the drink I had just bought from Fat Tuesday's that had me feeling so sluggish, the pre-roll, or maybe it was the brownie? Damn, that thing was huge, but it was so good. After a couple of bites, I felt the same joy and splendor I felt like I did when I was a little boy after eating a whole box of Little Debbie cakes. *Wonderfully wonderful*. Before I knew it, I was lost in the midst of the crowd.

There were men and women of all sorts of shapes and sizes all around me wearing surgical masks on all fronts. *Masked raiders. They're here to take their fill of Vegas and plunder it for all of its riches; I just know it, or maybe—maybe they're here for me? They're all—all of them are staring at me—Jesus Christ, this is some really strong CBD. Am I going to be ok? Oh no—Oh my god.* But then a voice came and said, *Just cool it, man. You're fine. If anybody knows that you're buggin' out, man, nobody really even gives a shit. Look at that guy right there; he's literally rollin' a blunt right now in front of everybody. Nobody cares.* Then an even worse thought crept into my mind. *What if I run into Brooke while I'm like this? That would be fuckin' terrible.* I knew at that moment I had to get a grip on myself immediately. If anything, I would refill that gigantic Fat Tuesday's cup in my hands with some shock treatment to reset the balance. There was no other choice.

That seemed to do the trick for the most part. I'm not sure if it reset the balance, but it helped me not really give a shit, at least for a little while. The crowd was still a little overwhelming, though, and especially the robot screaming at the crosswalk, "Wait to cross 4th Street! Wait to cross 4th Street! Wait to cross 4th Street!"

I mean, the thing wouldn't shut up, and I have to say if I would've had my six-shooter on me, I would've shot that thing to smithereens. Sure everybody around would've panicked, but I could've calmed the crowd down. I would've just simply said, "Look, guys, I did us all a favor. Now we can cross 4th Street whenever we want. That thing was askin' for it."

I'm sure I would've got my dick knocked into the dirt by a few of the boys in blue before I would've ever had a chance to open my mouth, but it still would've been quite tempting nonetheless. I didn't like that thing.

While I stood there waiting to cross 4th Street listening to that *thing*, I couldn't help but notice this beautiful blonde woman in front of me. She had on these tight white capris that her ass was just screaming out of. I mean, it wasn't Brooke, but I had begun to get in the mood a little as the alcohol and whatever that guy gave me at the smoke shop worked on me. I must admit I was getting in the mood—until I wasn't.

Suddenly, the back of her white capris started to turn brown, and I almost couldn't process it for a minute—*Why are her pants changing colors?* I thought, but then it dawned on me, *Oh my god, that girl just shit all over herself.* I mean, it was unbelievable. There wasn't even a sound or anything, or maybe there was, and it just wasn't audible over the reoccurring, "Wait to cross 4th Street!"

I wasn't standing too far behind her either, and I started looking myself up and down, just hoping this lady didn't just shit all over me. Then the smell came, and my eyes started to water with tears from the stench. I thought, *I have to get out of here before I throw up.* I turned around and ran away as fast as I could. Away from her, away from that *thing*. I went inside the nearest casino, I think it was the D, toward the nearest bathroom in case I ended up spewing brownies and shock treatment everywhere.

I didn't, thank god. I have an iron stomach, it seems, and I would've hated to bump into Brooke with throw-up residue all in my mouth. After all, if I could've caught her without her grandma around, I planned on going in for one, and if I overstepped my boundaries, she could've just smacked me. I actually wouldn't have even minded. I love women when they're angry, after all.

While I walked out of the D's restroom, this older guy said to me, "Hey man, you can do what you want, but these folks around here in this casino might kick you out without having a mask on. They're making everyone wear one in all of 'em now."

The mask bullshit. I replied, "Oh yeah—shit, I forget. You know what, man? I bet the FBI's most wanted is really lovin' this shit. They can pretty much go anywhere now." The old man laughed his ass off at that one. I love making people laugh, so I rambled on, "I'm serious—I mean think about it. If Bundy was still alive and on the loose there would be no catching that guy. We'd forget about Covid real quick with that motherfucker runnin' around. Hell, for all anybody knows, I'm a wanted man. I mean, I'm already dressed like a fuckin' cowboy."

He just kept letting it out. I mean—I didn't know it was that funny. Perhaps he went to that smoke shop too; who knows? I got out of there, though, before the guy had a heart attack.

Another older guy, who I think was homeless by the looks of him, even said something about the look I flaunted around all over Fremont. He jumped up in my face with a jack-o-lantern-like smile and screamed, "Well, goddamn, there he is, Cowboy boots wearin' jack, hahaha. Well, I'll be damned, boy, it lookin' like those old boots right there done brought you clear across the country, whaddya say?"

Little did he know they actually had. I've always liked the name Jack, though. It's always resonated with me in a peculiar way, so I replied, "I'm the fastest there is, man. I pretty much ran across the country in these things." I pulled out a twenty and said, "Hey man, cowboy boots wearin' Jack, I like that. I'll give you twenty bucks if you spread it around and tell everybody that's who I am."

The old guy snatched the twenty and started skipping and jumping down Fremont screaming, "See that boy right there! That's cowboy boots wearin' Jack. Cowboy boots wearin' Jack, mothafucka!"

I took a draw off the third pre-roll I had available and waved toward the crowd's shocked pedestrians and made my way down the rest of Fremont.

When I got halfway through my pre-roll, I started to feel super relaxed again and decided to lounge back under Fremont's lights and get lost in the Viva Vision above. There were swirling glorious colors of pink, green, and majestic blue coagulating and waving around into one another in all kinds of geometric patterns that seemed to have been a part of some deep and profound DMT trip. *Wow, it's so amazing.* "Hurdy Gurdy Man" danced through the air as the light show drew me in further and further. It almost felt like the essence of my being had evaporated into a sea of rainbows. It felt so luxuriously pleasing I nearly lost myself. After watching the light show above, I made another round toward Fat Tuesday's for another drink.

I tried as hard as I could not think about Brooke while I was on Fremont. Maybe that's why I decided to say fuck it and just let go to set my mind at ease, but that wasn't working either, and with the amount of alcohol I had in my system, I started to feel pretty emotional. She didn't even reply to my last text about coming down to Fremont Street. I was pretty sure I played it off cool and didn't come across like I was going down there just to see her, but I had a feeling she took it that way. In actuality, I already planned to visit Fremont anyway that night, but I also have to admit, knowing she was down there made me want to go even more. *She isn't worried about seeing me at all. What have I done to myself?*

There was always the age gap there I'd always forget about. She was only nearly twenty-one, and I was twenty-seven, but what about all of the other stuff? No matter how hard either of us would try to keep everything light, we would somehow end up in these really deep conversations, and despite her age, she sort of made me feel stupid by some of the advice she would give. I'd think, *She's so much wiser than I am,* and she even said a lot of people told her that she had an old soul and she acts way older than what she is. It should be hard, but it's easy for me to admit she's a lot more level-headed and responsible than I was by a long shot. Plus, I just couldn't get over the way she made me feel. *There has to be something to it. It has to mean something—my feelings just run too deep for them not to mean a thing at all.* I looked around Fremont while I sat propped up against the wall, thinking about it all. Just like that, all of a sudden, I didn't even want to be there anymore. I couldn't keep my happy mask on any longer. When I started to leave, I had begun to accept defeat. *All of this is just going to end in nothing. She's never going to give me a chance.*

I texted her, *It might be early, but I hope you have an amazing, unforgettable, twenty-first here in Vegas on the 26; just make it as special as you can and live it up to the fullest.*

While I sat there staring at my phone, twirling my fingers around it slowly, tears began to fall on the screen, and thoughts started to tear across my mind. *Will this lonely life ever end? Will I ever* be free? Sometimes it feels like I can't—like I can't breathe. It feels like I'm always drowning, and there's nothing to hold onto. It's like nobody will have me, and I can't figure out why. I wish it would all just take me. Sometimes I really do, but it's just not that easy. I don't know if I belong here, but if I do, something's gotta give. I don't want to go back in the dark again.

Regardless of how emotional I felt, I still tried to hold onto hope. The hope she would want to see me the next day. There's always hope, isn't there? Even if it seems like there's not? I stumbled my way back into my room toward the bottle of Ciroc waiting for me on the counter. I turned the bottle up and let as much liquor I could handle pour down my throat, bringing me toward a dreamless sleep. One more day in Vegas and then off to 29 Palms. How am I going to be able to leave here without seeing her? How can I even go back home after all of this? I collapsed under the covers and drifted off into a deep sleep. Maybe tomorrow. Maybe—just maybe— tomorrow.

CHAPTER XXVII: THRILLER

The next day I woke up in a glimmer of haze from the previous night. I immediately checked my phone to see if Brooke had texted me back; she hadn't. I felt my heart sinking back toward despair, but then I thought to myself, *Come on; this is your last day in Vegas; just try to enjoy it as much as you can. Nature has always made you feel better, right?*

It sure did, at least while I was out there. I wasn't sure where to go at first, but I ran across a park on Google called the Valley of Fire, or something like that. Everyone online said it was beautiful. *I need some beauty in my heart right now. Maybe there will be some magic out there somewhere today?*

There was. It might've just been me, but it seemed like what I saw out there in the Valley of Fire that day was a mix-matched montage of all the nature I had seen before, all coming together in one moment to celebrate the new day along with me. Sure there weren't any trees; those things are few and far between in the desert, but there sure was some magic in those clouds.

For some reason, the clouds seemed to be hanging so low they appeared to be just above me. Like if I wanted to, I could reach out and grab a handful of one. *Maybe heaven isn't too far away, and in a funny kind of way, it's always just within your reach. What if heaven wasn't a place but was a mind state? Where you're just happy all of the time, not caring anymore about the sorrows of the heart, and just living in love throughout life? Could I ever reach a place like that?*

These clouds weren't the regular bulbous-shaped clouds you see in the sky every day either. They looked like paint strokes of the most brilliant white you could ever imagine swirling across a blemish-less blue sky. That was the thing. The blue of the sky even looked different, like the depth of the ocean was placed up there with all the hidden stars above stretching onward toward infinity, never-ending in all of its vastness. It all looked so alluring and wonderful amongst the red rock canyons and titanic rock outcroppings strewn across the white sands of the desert floor.

That was another thing too. The sand even looked different in this place, and the heat didn't make you feel uncomfortable either. It was a soothing kind of warmth, and the smell of the air was greater than that of the frankincense or myrrh once burning within the altars of the holy temples in the land of before. *This is a sacred place—an abode of the great spirit above.* I believe whatever it is up there led me to that place on that day. It was like it all had a message that said, *You haven't even begun to witness all the wonders that lie out there in the world. There is love in the land outside of yourself, but there is even more within—untapped and universal.*

I already knew that. That message had come to me so many times before. Through books, through movies, even through Brooke, but I've always wondered, how can you find true love in a lonely heart? If everything is meant to be done alone or finding something within yourself, then why does my heart yearn so deeply for someone to hold me in their arms and for me to hold them in mine? *Is my life meant to be carried out all alone?* That thought has always brought me so much sorrow. It makes me wonder why I was even put here. Heaven seems so close, but hell is even closer. It's like the anguish of the thought of being alone forever is going to burn me up completely and swallow me up one day. I couldn't stand it. I couldn't stand that thought, but there was just me and nature yet again, except for one other thing. In the distance, there was a hawk. *Was it the same hawk from before or a different one?* Vikare, I thought. *There he is again. Vikare flying above.*

    I wasn't too sure what to do after the Valley of Fire. I still had so much to do with the day, but where to go, I wondered? I didn't have a clue. I didn't care too much for the Vegas Strip. Fremont was spectacular; that's where the true magic in Vegas lies, but that was a nightlife kind of place—but then something occurred to me. *Isn't Zak Bagan's Haunted Museum here in Vegas?* I've always loved watching his show. I gotta admit I was pretty skeptical of him at first, but if anything, his show is entertaining, whether any of it's real or not. Who knows? The only way I could find out if there were any sort of truth to any of Zak's claims is if I at least checked out his museum. I wasn't sure what I was getting myself into, and some of it I can't even remember at all. It's like my memory is fragmented from the whole experience, but I'll never forget how that place made me feel. I couldn't even if I tried.

    On the exterior of Zak's museum, it looked like a regular old house to me. It had a dark red roof with a beige stucco exterior— *was it stucco? I don't know. I'm not an architect,* but as I said, it looked pretty regular and no goosebumps at all outside. Of course, the place had set up precautions because of the Covid you had to follow if you were going to participate in a tour. *Gee, how shocking?* I would've never expected that at all. I didn't care too much at this point, though. I just wanted to get a taste of the place for myself. So after waiting for about twenty minutes or so, they let four other people in and me. Everybody else got the regular pass, but I already reserved the R.I.P. pass online, and with that little dandy in hand, I'd get access to six extra rooms in the place. Little did I know, since I was the only one that had a pass to the six extra rooms, I'd be the only one that would be going in them, without a tour guide, which adds up to nobody but me. Or at least that's what I try to tell myself.

While we all waited in the lobby for the tour guide to arrive, I immediately noticed a shift in the atmosphere. I wasn't sure if it was from all the oddities and antique toys lining the dark shelves of the dimly lit room or if it was just me, but I couldn't deny it either way. Something—something had changed.

When the tour guide appeared, I became awestruck on the spot by how gorgeous I thought she was. Her hair wasn't bleached blonde, but it was white enough to look like she was some kind of princess or something, even if she wore all black. I couldn't help thinking to myself, *I like your style Zak Bagans. Not only have you surrounded yourself with demonic artifacts that could swallow your soul at any second, but you've also surrounded yourself with beautiful women that have the potential to steal a heart right away.* I couldn't help but respect it.

The beautiful tour guide informed us all we couldn't take any pictures, videos, Instagrams, or whatever else you can do with a phone along the tour, so I figured I'd just put my phone on airplane mode. It wasn't like anybody was going to text me anyway. I started to follow the tour guide into the gates of hell afterward, and this is where everything starts getting a little spacey.

I can remember all of these creepy-looking photographs lining the museum's halls toward each room. Everything was very dim-lit. Every hall, room, nook, and cranny in Zak's museum. I figured that was intended to make the tour even creepier, but I have to say the whole place could've been lit up brighter than a Christmas tree, and you still wouldn't be able to escape all the heavy energy the place gave off. It was like the deeper I went, the heavier the air felt, but I didn't feel drained at all. It was more like my senses were heightened on all levels, and I had this—not a staticky feeling, but more like—a feeling of being supercharged. Almost like if a battery was already on 100 percent and electricity started shooting right out of the socket. It was the most concentrated energy I had ever felt in any kind of place. Not all of it was dark either. Some of what I felt there didn't belong to a good or evil domain, but it lay somewhere in between—like it was the cosmic glue between various quantum realms. It was magical, to say the least.

 I can't remember the first room completely, and honestly, if I did, I wouldn't describe it all anyway. There's no fun in giving it all away, but the first room I found myself in making me feel uncomfortable was the doll closet.

 It was one of the first exclusive rooms my pass gave access to, and I have to say unimaginable fear crept all around me when I was in there. Various shelves lined the closet, and all of these dolls from different time periods lined each and every one of them. There were dolls from the Victorian era, the early twentieth century, and onward through the 1950s. They didn't just feel like dolls, though. No, these things weren't just toys, but they were alive, I swear it, but they didn't feel threatening to me. Maybe it was from whatever kind of energy I felt bursting throughout my body, or maybe it was my amulet. I blessed the thing everywhere throughout my journey. It's the only one of it's kind throughout the whole world. To be honest, it's kind of an antediluvian design, you know, before the flood and all. I had an idea kings and queens back then probably wore something like it, but who knows? Seems like a cool idea to me. Maybe the dolls and the things in that place recognized that. The tour guide noticed but never asked. I would've played it off anyway.

I remember Belle Lugosi's mirror too in that place for sure, and of course, I had to look into it. I felt sort of silly doing it at first, but I felt a presence in the air demanding respect. It didn't want to be taken lightly at all. On the surface, all I saw was my reflection in the mirror, but I could feel something beyond that surface. It was like the mirror had a greater depth to it than you could fathom, and even if the tour guide hadn't told me Lugosi once used it as a scrying mirror, I would've thought the same. In my mind, I thought, *Yes—yes, there have been things that have appeared within these depths before. Some of them were people, but others—the others—some of them had never even lived at all.* At least that's the feeling I got anyway. I can be kind of weird sometimes to tell you the truth.

The next thing I remember is being in some kind of room. Oh, how I wish I could remember what it was, but I can't, no matter how hard I try. It was where one of the exclusive rooms was to my pass, though. After the tour guide gave her exposition on the history of whatever items were in the room, she pointed at this little square in the room's darkest corner. She said, "Through that crawlspace is another room, and that is for the eyes of our R.I.P. guest only."

I looked at her like, *What the fuck, through there?!*, but then I managed to say, "You want me to go in there?"

She let off a big grin as she waved toward the dark square in the wall and said, "Yeah, sure. Just crawl your way through the tunnel, and there's a room full of surprises waiting on the other side."

My mouth went agape as I stared at the hole. I looked back toward the tour guide and replied, "Uh—yeah—no. I don't think that's going to work for me."

She nearly laughed and said, "You mean you don't want to go in?"

"Nope, I'm good."

There was no way in hell I was going in there. Was she crazy? I started to regret getting the R.I.P. pass altogether. I thought, *I would be the only guy on the tour with the R.I.P. pass, so I have to do all of this scary shit all alone. What was I thinking?* It got even worse than that.

Dr. Kevorkian's room was entirely different from all of the other rooms I can remember in the place. There wasn't anything scary about it, though. I have to admit, I had no idea who this doctor guy was when I walked in there, but when I saw his van, dread fell over me.

It wasn't a terrifying sort of dread. The sight of the van brought on an intense sorrowful feeling, though. It wasn't the first time I've felt that kind of dread, but this—this was just different. I got this image in my mind of the van parked out in a dark wooded area on a crescent moonlit night. There was a woman with dark hair lying in the van with tears streaming down her face back there. I wasn't sure if the sorrow came from her, but her hand was gently trying to grasp for something, but nothing was there. Pain streaked all across her face, but it wasn't from physical pain—no. It was worse than physical pain; it was pain bleeding from her heart. It felt like she didn't want to die, but there was nothing here for her to hold on to. It was like she just didn't know what else to do. I don't know if that scene was from my imagination, but I felt that deep sorrow within myself all the same. It was like it all played through my head; I just kept thinking, *If I would've known you, I would've been your friend.* A friend can't fix everything, but sometimes one person's words can make all the difference in whether you punch your ticket out or decide to buy another for the next ride.

The doctor's room left a lot of pain reeling within my heart, but the tour continued, and I think this is where the basement came in.

At the top of the basement's steps, right in front of a DO NOT ENTER sign, the tour guide started telling us all about what went on down there. Apparently, the house hosting the museum itself belonged to some sort of cult back in the day that used to conduct demonic rituals down there in an old ritual room they constructed. I can't remember all of what she said because her voice seemed to be going in and out as I stared down at the bottom of the steps, just knowing what was about to come next, and what do you know, she said it, "And this right here is exclusive for our R.I.P. guest."

Fuck me, why do I do these things to myself. I slowly looked up at the tour guide to meet her wide grin as she stood there with the door propped open with one hand and ushered me down the steps with the other. My thoughts started to race. *Well—damn it. I did pay for the pass, and I already skipped one of the other rooms—FUCK—I guess I'll just have to go down.*

I took in a deep breath as I approached the darkened steps leading to utter and perpetual darkness. I took my phone out in an attempt to turn my flashlight on, but then the tour guide said, "Uh uh. No lights."

I tried to give her the most pleading look I could, but it didn't work. I had to make the descent into darkness all alone.

The air grew heavier and heavier with each step, and the atmosphere started to cool. Not to a chill, but there was a shift, to say the least. I could hear the spirit box's static sound reverberating all throughout the dark hall toward a candlelit room. It looked like some sort of shrine was down there, and I started to feel something encroaching upon me all throughout the air. It was like beasts of an unknown nature held a clutching grasp out toward me—only—only it didn't seem like they could get to me, and it even felt like—this might've been all in my head—but it felt like my amulet started to heat up.

Nevertheless, I felt trapped in an abyss with Qliphotic demons on all sides. Those things—their names should never be spoken. There was no escape, and the hallway behind me had disappeared, and the very room I stood in started to become overcrowded. It was like the Goetic beasts all around me in that room weren't ushering me backward but forward down the other hall to the ritual room. I stood at the archway of that deep, chasmic tunnel that led—somewhere—to a place existing in between realms. For something—for some kind of reason—I could feel it. I started to make my first step down the hall, but then the all-too-familiar voice came to me and said, *No. No, don't go down there. You can't.* There wasn't much else to what it said, and for a minute, I thought, *There you are. Whatever you are, that is.* I hadn't felt whatever that consciousness was for some time, but I knew to listen to it. I got the hell out of there.

That is, out of the basement anyway. I can't remember much of the tour after being in the basement, but I did feel something after I got back upstairs. I almost thought it was all in my head, but after a while, I knew it wasn't. I felt this terrible burning sensation at the bottom of my right leg. I didn't feel any kind of physical pain in that whole place until I got down in the basement by myself, and come to think of it, the same leg I stepped across the archway with was the same one burning. I'm not sure. Either way, I still can't explain what caused it, but whatever it was, it had something to do with what was in that basement.

I do remember being in the room with the dybbuk box at the end of the tour. However, my memory of it isn't all the way there either. The feeling I got from that room wasn't anywhere near what I felt in the basement, but the closer I would get to the box, the edgier I felt. Maybe it was from how legendary of an artifact it was, and it was just my mind playing tricks on me, but I could almost swear there was a name ringing in the air. I can't remember the name, and I'm glad I can't, but it had to have been a very ancient name—something from before trapped in that box for who knows for whatever reason. Maybe it was one of the Grigori of Mount Hermon trapped within that cabinet, but I'm not sure. They used to say Azazel was imprisoned in the ancient sands of long-forgotten Dudael—brooding somewhere and biding his time within the Earth. He was the father of warfare, they used to say, or maybe it was all just a story. Who knows? But whatever was in that box—was brooding its time too—like it was waiting, but for what?

I remember standing in front of the dybbuk box, staring deep into its doors. I could see something—something rather strange within it I couldn't make out. Something—but then, all of a sudden, the doors appeared to slightly open. It alarmed me immediately. At that moment, I knew if I saw the whole breadth of what the box held within it I'd probably be cursed forever. I stepped away from the box immediately in shock. I had to get away from that thing. *Was it all in my head? Or was it starting to open itself?*

I asked the tour guide, "Hey, this might sound strange, but have you ever seen that box over there try to open itself?"

The tour guide replied, "Yeah—it's been doing that lately for some reason. It's like it's being agitated by something."

29 Palms

I started thinking, *Is this lady just fucking with me, and they have some kind of little magnet under that rectangular little altar block, or did those doors just try to open themselves up?* I didn't know, and I didn't want to know. Not to say I'd never go back, of course; I would. There was just something about it, but at that moment, I was just ready to get out of there.

It felt like my mind and body were reeling once I got back outside. It was like the supercharged feeling I had in that place was still with me, and being back out in the sun just intensified it for some reason. It almost felt like I did a shit load of cocaine or something, but I could still contain myself without completely losing my shit. I do have to say, though, because people might wonder; I don't think I was possessed or anything in there or cursed. My life hasn't taken a terrible turn for the worse, and I haven't nearly died in a plane crash or have burglars invade my home like Post Malone did after he went to the museum. Everything seemed to carry on like it always had afterward.

Once I got back in the Mustang and started cruisin' my way back toward the strip, something suddenly dawned on me; my phone was still on airplane mode. My mind had been racing so much after I left the museum I didn't even check it or try to play any music. Once I got to a red light, I went ahead and turned airplane mode off. My phone started going off immediately. Three missed texts from Brooke came across the screen. My heart leaped with so much joy; if I were a rocket, I would've shot right through the stratosphere. I had to find somewhere to pull over to see what she said. Once I found a good place to park, I read her text that said, **I'm just now seeing this; sorry, we've had a busy day! We went to Lake Mead! But thank you, it really means a lot. I'll be at the Gold Spike bar at midnight if you want to party with me. Where did you go today?**

She finally replied to the text from the night before and she sent me a pretty picture of her own of Lake Mead. I was in complete shock. I could feel my throat lock up a little bit and I felt so much pressure and anxiety release from my chest; I just filled up completely with something unexplainable I'd never felt before. I thought to myself, *She is going to give me the time of day after all. Oh my god! It really was all worth it. All of it. Is this true magic? Am I really going to get to see her tonight?*

    I couldn't believe it. Even if I never planned on it, my whole trip across the country culminated up to this moment. This grand, wonderful moment when I could finally tell Brooke how I felt about her and just hope and pray with everything I held in my heart she felt the same. *Did she feel the same way? I might just die if she does, but nothing would be more wonderful in the whole wide world than for me to be hers and for her to be mine.* I was ecstatic and petrified all at the same time. In just a few short hours, I'd know for sure if it was all for nothing or if it was all for everything. I couldn't wait. I couldn't wait to see her. *Would this finally be the moment I've always waited for? To finally be set free in my longing to get lost in the embrace of true love?* I didn't know. I didn't know, but I'd soon find out.

CHAPTER XXVIII: MORE THAN WORDS

    I didn't pull up on Fremont in the Mustang where I was supposed to meet Brooke. I offered for her to go on some top-down cruisin' with me all over Vegas during the conversation I had with her earlier, but she didn't want to leave her grandma alone. *Fuck.* I mean, I guess I understood. Her and her grandma traveled to Vegas together, after all, and honestly, if my grandma were with me, I wouldn't have ditched her at a hotel for some hot chick either. There's no way—actually I'm lying my ass off to tell you the truth. I would've left my grandma in a heartbeat at the hotel if the shoe would've been on the other foot, and Brooke was the one pulling up with a convertible to take me cruisin'. I would've been like, "Hey, Grandma, you want a drink or something? I got some fine tequila right here if you wanna try it. It's a Vegas exclusive; you're going to absolutely love it!"

I'd get her so damn drunk she wouldn't want to leave the room, but apparently, Brooke's grandma knew how to get down. I wasn't sure, but I hoped it would just be Brooke meeting me at the Gold Spike that night. I had to talk to her alone.

On top of all that, I got all dressed up into some pretty nice clothes, if I say so myself. I didn't go too overboard, but I put on this blue silk-like button-down shirt matching my eyes' color, the color they'd been that night anyway. I wore some casual-enough-looking jeans, though, to level everything out and not look like I tried too hard, but I couldn't help it; this was the moment. The one moment that would matter more than any other, and it was all right there within arms' reach. I still couldn't believe it as I stood outside puffing away on some smoke, trying to calm my nerves as I waited for my Uber driver to arrive.

When the driver finally dropped me off at Fremont Street, all of the lights danced around with even more flair than they had the night before. I couldn't help but wonder if they were more active and alive all on their own or if it was because that's how I truly felt on the inside at that moment. It was like my heartstrings pulsated within each wave and movement of every color, and the environment and I were all tuned in to the same frequency. I was ready, the fullness of the moon in the night sky was ready, the crowd was ready, all of Fremont was ready. It was time for me to see Brooke again at last.

I was a little early, though. Brooke told me to meet her at twelve on the dot at the Gold Spike and the clock ticked about a half an hour or so before that. I didn't want to be in the club before she got there. That would've been pretty awkward; what would I say when she walked in? Something like, "Oh hey, I arrived a little early; don't mind me. It's just that I couldn't wait to get here and see you. Happy birthday!"

Absolutely not. That wouldn't work at all. All of the self-help videos I've watched over the years on YouTube clearly stated you should never be early, but make it a little late so you don't look desperate. "Chicks hate a desperate guy," they'd always say, but it's a hell of a lot harder actually being in the moment and on the brink of partying with that one girl you've always wished for in your heart. I still had a little time to burn, so I walked along under the multi-colored lights of the wonder screen above as the glitz and glam of Vegas moved through the air and the sound waves pulsated all around me.

I was hypnotized at the moment as I walked along, but then my ears started to catch the sound of something in the air. The words to a song I hadn't heard in years started spilling through the night. It was a song called "More Than Words," and the lyrics floated all around me.

That song stopped me right in my tracks. It was a song my dad used to play on his guitar for my mom. I could almost see him all over again in my mind, sitting there cross-legged on the floor playing his guitar and singing that song to her. I never saw him sing it myself, but Mom told me he liked that song a lot. I thought to myself, *Dad, are you here? Are you trying to tell me something? What are the odds of me hearing that song again right before I meet up with Brooke? Was this all supposed to be a sign? That I've finally reached the end of the road and found true love?* I couldn't wait anymore—I had to find out.

I was a little too impatient, of course. I got to the Gold Spike, and Brooke was nowhere in sight. I walked up to the bouncer at the door first, who agreed to let me in after telling him I was meeting someone, but only if I put a mask on. She wasn't in there yet, of course, and I started to feel so stupid for not just waiting a little longer for her to get there.

    I went ahead and just stood outside to wait for her anyway. I didn't care how it would look. I couldn't run around Fremont Street anymore like some kind of maniac just trying to burn the time away. I pulled out my phone and started scrolling through Facebook, and then I went ahead and clicked on Snap. Brooke posted a few things I hadn't gotten a chance to check out yet. I started tapping through her story until a picture of her in her hotel room appeared. She stood in one of the rooms at the Oasis posed up in a sunflower-colored tied-up tank top with some little white shorts showing off the complexion of her golden tanned legs. She had this ribbon running across her chest for her birthday that ran from her shoulder and went down around her waist. It felt like an elevator kept going up and down throughout my body as my heart started to race and a smile spread across my face. Then I heard someone behind me say, "Hey there."

    I turned around suddenly to face her. There she was. She wore the same outfit she wore in the picture. *Incredible.* Everything about her was incredible. My eyes probably popped out of my head like some kind of cartoon. My feelings on the inside probably showed all over my face, but I didn't even care. I spoke up suddenly and said, "Hey there, how you doin' tonight? It's nice to see you."

    I wanted to hug her so badly, but her grandma was pretty much right on her arm. *Oh, boy, what's she still doing up?* Brooke had a nervous look on her face as she looked me up and down. I could tell it wasn't the same kind of nervous feeling I had; it seemed more like she was apprehensive. The excitement I hoped she'd give didn't seem to be there at all. I tried to ignore my feelings of fear creeping up inside of me. Brooke looked to her grandma and back to me and replied, "We just got done pre-gaming a little bit back at the room. Did you just get here?"

I was too early. Did that seem creepy? I replied, "Yeah, of course. I haven't even had a chance to check this place out yet. You ready for some more drinks?" With a laugh, I continued, "I guess I gotta catch up."

They were both ready, and I was too, much more than ever. The anxiety monsters tore me open from the inside out, and I needed something to calm me down. A pitcher, maybe, or perhaps a whole truckload of cranberry vodkas would do the trick. I was so nervous I cut right in front of her grandma at the door. I thought, *Fuck, that was really rude of me, but I gave her a chance to walk in first, and it looked like she wanted me to go ahead first, so I did.* I just tried to brush it off. I thought to myself, *Well, I hope they're not that sensitive. I don't think Brooke is, but her grandma—who knows?*

The three of us started to walk down the red-carpeted hallway that had matching drapes hanging down along it toward the outside patio to the bar—it was huge. There was this big soundstage front and center to all of it. The bouncer had informed us as we seated ourselves at a table we couldn't get up and walk around any because of the Covid regulations and we were all supposed to remain seated. Brooke got sort of a twisted look on her face and looked at me with a look that kind of said, *Well, that's a load of bullshit.* I read it immediately. I threw a leg over my knee and looked to Brooke and said with a smile, "Well, now you know what I've been dealing with this whole time."

Brooke leaned forward and said, "I know, right? We had to wear masks on the plane when we were headed here. Everywhere you go now, it's all about Covid."

I laughed and replied, "I know what you mean. This might be the new normal now, you know? I had hoped Vegas would be a little different, but it's worse even here than other cities. Oh well—we can still have a good time, though, right?"

Brooke looked toward her grandma as a mischievous smile spread across her face, and she threw her hands up, saying, "Well, I still plan on having a good time."

The waiter or bartender or whatever walked up to us in full surgeon-like gear with the first few drinks we ordered. Brooke damn near downed hers immediately and ordered another before the masked mystery person even had a chance to go to the next table. I intended to keep up with her; I wasn't about to let her outdrink me, so I had ordered the same thing she got. From the way she drank it, I figured it must've been a hell of a drink. After the bartender left to get the next round of drinks, I asked Brooke, "So you're finally in Vegas. What do you think about it so far?"

Brooke replied, "I love it here; I was so ready to get out of Mobile. We're going to check out the dispensary tomorrow. Might as well." With a laugh, she continued, "It is Vegas, right?"

She started to warm up to me a little bit more; I could tell. When I first saw her outside of the Gold Spike from the edgy looks she gave me, I started to wonder if she wanted to even hang out with me at all. I couldn't help catch the vibe she only got ahold of me because she didn't want to hurt my feelings. Something in her demeanor started to change, though. Of course, she talked to her grandma too at the table, but when she would look at me to talk, she got this really warm look, and the sweetest smiles would come across her face. It made me feel like she wanted me there. I tried to keep my emotions reined in for the most part, but I couldn't hide the fact I was happy to be there with her too. I just didn't want to show her how happy I was.

It was hilarious when she brought up the dispensary. I tried teasing her a little bit when I replied, "Ready to get out of Mobile? But why? It's a great place to live. That place is full of dreamers and amazing people to talk to. Why would you ever want to leave there?" I started to laugh because I could tell she picked up on all the sarcasm. I continued, "You're going to the dispensary tomorrow too? Hope it's not too early; you'll probably end up passing out."

Brooke shot darts out of her eyes at me at that and downed another drink. She laughed and raised her voice a little when she said, "I can handle my own. You should know that, and Mobile is terrible. The only fun thing about it is Mardi Gras, and this year, I'm finally going to be able actually to enjoy it. Grandma's had me a spot reserved in her organization practically since I've been born. I'm ready for it."

The thought of seeing her in a dress at a Mardi Gras ball completely captivated me. She'd be the brightest star in the crowd; I just knew it. The last ball I went to, I didn't have any fun at all, really. It felt like I was the only guy there without a date. So I drank as many free drinks as I could and ran out into the streets of downtown Mobile, full tux and all, to join my brother at the Saddle Up Saloon. I couldn't take it in there anymore. It depressed me way too much. I thought to myself, *It would be a dream come true to lead you out onto the dance floor at a ball. You're the girl of my dreams, and I just feel so full whenever I'm around you. How can I tell you that? I wish I could. I just wish I had the words for it.*

I tried not to get lost in my thoughts as I replied, "Yeah, Mardi Gras balls can be a lot of fun. I mean, I didn't have the best time at the last one I was at. I don't want to go to one by myself again. Sometimes all the people there can be a little overwhelming, you know, but there's always the free drinks, though, right?"

Brooke took another gulp of her drink. Some of it poured down her chin a little, and I thought, *You're a maniac, but I love maniacs. You got a lot of spirit.* She aimed to get as drunk as possible, and it took everything I had to stay caught up with her. Brooke set her drink back down and replied, "You worry about what people think too much. So what if you were single there? That shouldn't stop you from having fun. You just have to get lost in the moment and not worry about anything else. That's what I try to do anyway."

She was right; I knew she was, but when you've lived a life where most of your memories are of being alone, you always crave for that moment when you truly have somebody. You desire more than anything in your heart just to be wanted by someone. After I met Brooke, that someone just wasn't anyone anymore. That someone I'd always been searching for had a face, and it was her. That someone couldn't be just anyone anymore; I wanted it to be her. *If only I could just tell her that,* I thought to myself, but it didn't feel like the right time or the right moment at all like I expected it to be. *Just go with the moment. She's here, you're here, and Grandma's here. Just enjoy it as much as you can.* I downed my drink and replied, "Yeah, I know what you mean. That's what I've been trying to do on this whole trip, and it's helped me out a lot. There are just so many places out there that each has its own vibe. It's just incredible everywhere out there. You'll see it when you go out there yourself."

Brooke's eyes lit up at the thought of that, and she replied, "Oh, I can't wait; I still want to get a van and convert it a little bit to travel across the states that way. That's what I hope I get out of going to Europe next summer, though. I'm going to stay over there for as long as I can after I finish school. Six months maybe. I'm just ready to get out there and see the world."

I could see her doing it all. It was like for me to imagine her accomplishing her dreams was better than picturing myself living through my own. I believed in her so much. More than she could ever comprehend. I knew she would actually end up doing it all too; I just wished more than anything to be alongside her to watch her truly live through it all. We both had the same dreams. Why do it all alone when it could be done together? I just wished she could see that, and I could tell it all to her. I just didn't know how.

The bartender came back around, and I decided to get us all a round of shots along with some more mixed drinks. I started to feel really buzzed, and I could tell Brooke was too. She raised in her seat and started twitching around, and said, "I wanna get up and dance. Look at this DJ; who's he yelling at?! Nobody's even out there!"

She started screaming at him to play some sort of song. The guy just waved his hand at her like he wanted her to shut up. That pissed me off a little bit. I mean, here we were ready to have a good time, but you couldn't get up from your table and do anything; it was ridiculous. I pulled out my phone and started looking up other bars. All of a sudden, Brooke shot at me, "What are you doing?"

Pretty surprised, I looked up at her and said, "I was just looking up other bars that we could probably go to. I mean, you can't even dance here. There's a place down the street that I went in the other night that would let you move around."

Brooke didn't want to leave, though. I didn't care; I just figured we could've had a better time if we got out of there, but it was her birthday, so if she wanted to stay, we would stay. Once the shots came, I tried to pay for them, but Brooke said, "No, no, no, you don't have to do that. I got this."

I was pretty shocked and said, "Oh, so you're going to buy me a drink then? Ok, I like the sound of that."

Brooke gave me that deep kind of look I always cherished seeing as she smiled and handed her card to the bartender. We both slammed our shots, and Grandma did too. I thought, *Goddamn, Grandma, I can see where Brooke gets it from now.* After I took mine, I said, "Damn, I'm getting a little buzzed. I'm not trying to get too fucked up. I don't want to end up on any more rooftops."

Brooke leaned forward and laughed, "Are you talking about that hotel you went to? I still can't believe you did that. What made you even go up there?"

I couldn't fight the mischievous grin that had to have appeared on my face when I replied, "I don't even know, really. It's not like I planned it out or anything; it just happened. Plus, it wasn't even my fault anyway; those girls got me drunk. They knew what they were doing."

Brooke widened her eyes at me and said, "Uh-huh, I bet."

I leaned back in my seat and shook my head, "No, but really they did. I'm banned for life from that place. The little bellhop guy didn't pull any punches with me. He said don't ever, ever come back here again—ever. Everybody was so angry, and it wasn't even my fault."

Brooke laughed at that and started downing another drink. The three of us started talking more about Vegas and what they had thought about Lake Mead, and how spectacular the city was. Of course, I had to tell them about the helicopter ride and how crazy it felt to be up there above everything among all those flashing lights. I told Brooke she should check out doing a helicopter ride while she was there; after all, it wasn't that much, and it's nearly impossible to take in the full Vegas view if you don't go up in the air to see it all. The night went by great, and we all had our fair share of drinks going around. Eventually, Brooke got up to go to the restroom. As much as she drank, it was only a matter of time; I just knew it.

While she was gone, it was just her grandma and I sitting there, and I don't know why I said what I said, but I just had to. Her grandma seemed sweet, and for some reason, I figured if I couldn't get Brooke alone to tell her how I truly felt, maybe if I told her grandma some of what I thought about her granddaughter, she could help my case. She seemed to like me, or at least I thought. I just couldn't hold it in anymore when I said, "You know I've seen a lot of sunsets on my trip, and I've tried to share every one of them that I could with your granddaughter. I guess they just made me think of her. Sunsets are nice, but she's more beautiful than all of them."

Her grandma didn't say anything back at all. She just stared at me and smiled. There might've been a lot of reasons why she didn't say anything back, but for some reason, everything came crashing down inside of me during that moment of silence. I started thinking to myself, *She's going to tell her what I said tomorrow, and none of what I've done or hoped for will go in my favor at all.* The whole night had been great, but the all-to-familiar voice was there with me chiming in throughout the night. As I'd watch Brooke laughing and talking with her grandma, it would say, *Hawke, it doesn't have anything to do with you. When she tells you she's not ready, it means she isn't. She's just focused on having good times in her life right now. Look at her, isn't she having fun?* She was. I felt so happy for her, and my heart felt so full from being alongside her at that moment and sharing in her joy, but once the last call was made and we had to part ways, the longing came rushing back.

I sat slumped against some building on Fremont waiting for my Uber, and on the inside, I just knew. I knew I had lost myself to a fantasy. It wasn't that what I felt for Brooke wasn't true; it had to be. I felt it throughout every fiber of my heart, but I knew at that moment, at the end of my journey, Brooke and I wouldn't end up together. I knew the journey would end the same way it had started; I'd be all alone. *I don't want to go back in the dark.* I couldn't fight the feeling and the fear of it all. I should've been happy. I would be bound for 29 Palms, California, the next day. The one place I'd always wanted to see the most in the world, but it didn't even matter. It was all right in my face the whole time. I couldn't even get the girl in my own story.

CHAPTER XIX: UNDER THE BRIDGE

    I made it, but it sure didn't feel like I did. I even took the trip straight up under the Hollywood sign, but I didn't feel like a star at all. It was kind of funny because, as a kid, I'd always dreamed of going to Hollywood, where all the movie stars were made. To me, that was the place where dreams come true, but once I reached that sign across the mountain, all of my dreams were dead. Everything I hoped for felt like the same ghosts I'd been chasing all along. People say ghosts aren't real, but are dreams just as unreal as a ghost can be?

    I wondered that as I stood underneath the Hollywood sign and took my pictures to show everyone I had finally made it. From Mobile through Savannah to Maine and all the way across to California. I made it all the way, but what was I traveling toward?

This whole time I shot toward the stars, and all of those stars accumulated into one person. She was there, but she was so far away. It broke my heart leaving Vegas without telling her how I truly felt, but I didn't know how and the time just wasn't there. That million-dollar moment just didn't come, and it felt like everything had just gone away with the wind.

I made my way to Oceanside, California, the day after that, but it was so cloudy outside it seemed like the sun didn't even have the will to shine for me. I sat there on the Oceanside pier for a time as a seagull bent its neck right beside me, and I thought, *Coast to coast. I made it across the country from coast to coast. I thought it would all feel like a great thing in the end, but it doesn't. I'm still sitting here all by myself. This is what it all led to—everything. Am I always meant to just end up like this?* None of it seemed to mean anything anymore. While I sat there on that pier, I started scrolling through Facebook, and I ran across a video Brooke had posted. She was strapped up in a vest on the edge of the Stratosphere. I'm guessing it was the instructor that said, "Well, go ahead and jump."

And she did. Of course, she had bungee cables on, but in the video, she screamed so loud in terror the whole world could have heard it, but she ended it all in laughter. I thought to myself, *You have the most beautiful soul, and you have so much more courage than I could ever hope to find. I really believe in you. I really do. Not just for who you are but because you're who I've always been afraid to be. You just let it all go, and it's hard for me to let anything go, especially when it comes to love. It feels like everything I've come to love the most has already come to pass, and that's why it's so hard to let it all go. To let the past go would be letting what I love the most go, and what is still here for me, it just can't be reached. It's all out of reach, and I don't think I'll ever have it.*

After watching Brooke's video, I sat there by myself with the setting sun along that pier. It was the first time I smiled in days—

since the last time I saw her, in fact. Her joy brought me joy at that moment, but it was just another passing thing like so many others. Once the sun went down again and I drove off in the night, I was still alone. I hadn't driven into 29 Palms yet, but it awaited me the next day. I stayed in Joshua Tree the whole time, not 29 Palms, for whatever reason. It would be my father's birthday the next day. June 28 just so happened to be the last day of the trip altogether, and I didn't even plan on it. I thought to myself, *Here we go again, Dad. We're at the end of another road, and it's just me and you again. Maybe it was always meant to be that way after all.* When I woke up the next day, on June 28, 2020, it was like the words from his old boot camp letters started speaking through the air from the past. He sounded so distraught in some of them.

He said in one, *Mom, I miss you all so much. I'm not doing my best, but through the Lord, I know I'm going to do better. It's just really hard here, harder than I ever thought it would be. All the sergeants tell me that I'm the worst recruit that they've ever seen. I don't know how I'm going to make it, Mom, but I know that I can. I'm just going to keep praying as much as I can, and through the Lord, I know that I'll do better. I can do it; I know that I can. Through the Lord, I can do anything.*

He would sound so letdown, but he'd always pull through in the end when he'd say, *Guess what, Mom? I did it. I can't believe I did, but I really made it. I'm so good with a rifle now they even put me in a special class. I bet you would've never thought you'd have a son that was one of the top elite riflemen in the world, huh? I'm so proud of myself! Private Robert Thomas Smith, one of the top elite riflemen in the whole world, who would've ever thought? I really made it, Mom! I really did it. I hope all of you are really proud of me!*

He ended up being so proud of himself, and during his time in boot camp, he was completely in love with my mom. Maybe that's what pulled him through all along. He'd say stuff in his letters like; *I'm so very proud to be in love with someone like you. The* high that comes from love is just unexplainable and incredibly beautiful. It can only be encountered by two that are dedicated to one another to the utmost and are truly in love. I wrote this for you, Kim:

Like a bird soars high, may our love always fly

From mountain tops to early dawn, may our love flow like a song

Our love grows in increasing commitment, as we are faithful & intimate

May our love always grow strong, & our lives blessed together to be long

For we were meant to be, as we both can now see

It was made at the beginning of time that you'd always be mine

He'd write his poems for her, and then he'd go on to say, *That's how you make me feel. You make me feel taller than the biggest mountain and that I can overcome any problem that I might face. You are my everything. You just make my heart sing.*

His heart would just fill with joy when she sent him a letter back. Even if his heart were full of doubt, he'd say, *I received your card today. It was so very beautiful, and it really touched my heart; thank you, baby! I loved your letter with it too. I know you really care. You're my real-life angel! You have strength and determination, but yet can be so sweet all at the same time. Have you ever heard this song Hold On to the Night by Richard Marx? It makes me think of you every time I hear it. I'll try to keep playing it back so I can quote the words right.*

After quoting some lyrics, he'd say, *What do you think, Kim? Do you like it? That's how I feel about you.* With those old letters I'd read so many times going through my head, I thought to myself, *That's exactly how I feel about Brooke, but I just don't think she feels the same way about me. I'd do everything I could to give her all of her dreams on a silver platter if I could, but I still wouldn't know. I wouldn't know if she wanted me or not. Ever since we parted ways in Vegas,* we still hadn't really talked. She sent me a picture of a sunset over the Grand Canyon she had taken, but I still sensed there was an overwhelming distance between us. I couldn't help feeling it. There was some sort of wall Brooke had built back up, or maybe it was from something her grandmother had said.

Nevertheless, it was there, and I felt empty. I still sent her a sunset when I was at Oceanside and even the waterfall when I visited Taquitz Canyon, but I knew deep down inside the battle was already lost. I'd go back home, and it would be the same as it was just before. I'd have to go right back into the dark.

I finally reached 29 Palms after I'd went through Joshua Tree Park. I felt so much of my sadness blowing through those trees, but once I saw the sign that read *Twentynine Palms a Desert Oasis*, things started to change. I thought to myself; *Today isn't a regular day. Today it's the eighties all over again—like when my dad used to live here. It's his day today, after all—* even if it was just for a moment. That's why all those old songs remind me of him because those were the best times in his life and I always feel closer to him through them. I went to my mom and dad's old apartment, which just so happened to be there still, and that's the last place I blessed my amulet. I thought to myself, *This is where it all started, but the journey ends here. Or maybe this is where it all begins again?*

I just didn't know. After I cruised around 29 Palms all day, I decided to end the day in the desert. It just seemed like it was all meant to be—out there in Indians Cove.

An old boy-scouts trail was at the beginning of the road, and it led out toward two massive juggernaut heaps of rock calling to me. After all, the sun set between them. I hiked all the way out there. It had to be about a mile or so, and I climbed the giant rock closest to the trail to watch the sun go down, and that's where I started to break down. It's like my thoughts possessed me.

29 Palms

Here I am. 29 Palms. It took so long, like forever, to get here, but I'm still all alone. I'm out in this desert all alone, and I don't have anybody. But then the all-too-familiar voice said, *You're not all alone; you have me.*

It felt annoying, and it made me feel crazy to have something around I couldn't touch or see, but it was someone—something to talk to. Maybe I was crazy when I said out loud, "You say that you're here, but you're not. You always say that. I'm not sure what you are, and I don't even know if you're my father, but I'm still here all alone." I dropped my face into my hands and said, "You're not here, and this is all just another fantasy."

But the all-to-familiar voice continued on, *You're wrong. I've always been here, Hawke. I've been with you through all of your journeys. Even through the dark waters. You knew it when you wrote of the boy and the broken mirror. You're the one that hasn't been paying attention. You're the one that has denied me.*

I couldn't take it; the word denied. It felt like I had never denied anyone, but I knew all-too-well how rejection felt. All-too-well how denial felt. I said, "Denied? The whole world has denied me. All I've ever felt in this life is rejection."

My tears started to flow evermore as if rain had finally hit the desert floor. The all-too-familiar voice sounded so much like my father, and I could feel his presence with me more than ever. I couldn't help spilling my heart out to him as if he were there. "I felt so alone after you left me. I saw you dying. You couldn't talk to me—we just couldn't—we couldn't ever fly kites together anymore. You said that we would fly together forever, but you left me here all alone."

But then the all-too-familiar voice said, *That's what you don't realize, Hawke; I never left you. I've been here this whole time. You've just been too distracted to see it.*

I've always felt a presence near me, but I always tried to keep myself occupied so I didn't have to deal with all of the things going on on the inside. It felt so dark in there. I said back, "I wish that I would've just died so I could've stayed with you. I never wanted to be here. Sometimes I wish I would've run out there to try and save you, and if it all didn't work out, we would've gone to heaven together. I haven't been able to find my place in this world since I lost you. It's like I became a ghost at the same time."

It was true. After the year 1999, the world died to me because everything that came after was a world he wasn't a part of. The desert wind started to blow like a typhoon all around the desert canyon that lie all around me as the all-too-familiar voice said, "Heaven isn't what you think it is. It's paradise, don't get me wrong, but what is paradise? Paradise is love, and the greatest of loves is unconditional. It's something in the heart and heaven—all of it can be experienced through the heart."

I couldn't help but hear the voice of my father out there as that sun set across the canyon. I felt like I finally got him back and I could truly spill my heart out to him when I said, "You know when I was a little boy, you were the reason why I read books. In those worlds, I could always escape this one and picture you as the hero all over again bound to save everybody, but I didn't know in most of the stories the hero dies. I'd get you back, only to see you die all over again. I saw you die a thousand times in my dreams. It's like we're on a chessboard at opposite ends, and I'm just pushing past all of the pieces just to get back to you. When I run toward you, the checkered floor starts falling to pieces into the sea below, and just as soon as my hand reaches yours, you fall too."

The blood of my heart rained upon the deserted ground as I continued evermore, "It's like once you fall into those dark waters your hand is still in mine, but you're drowning. I've seen your face beneath those waters so many times, but no matter how hard I try to pull you up, I'm just not strong enough. I try to save you. I try to do everything I can. I scratch and claw at your arm to pull you back up as the floor caves in, but it's never enough. I scream at the top of my lungs that you can't leave me, but it's never enough. You always die. My hero always dies at the end of the story, and I can never save you. What kind of hero does that make me?"

Sand blew everywhere, and the winds rumbled through the sound of my cries. I went on evermore, "I wish I could've been strong enough. I wish I could've saved you. I wish I would've run out there that night so we could've just died together. You were my hero. You were my safe place. I'd do anything to have one more minute with you, even if it was just a hug and for you to tell me that you loved me. I love you, Dad. I really do, and I just don't understand how this world can still turn without you. I don't want to go on without you, but I'm still here. What am I supposed to do? I traveled the whole country for true love because that was a dream of yours too, but it never came true. I wanted to find it for both of us. During this whole trip, I could feel you right alongside me the entire way, like you were really there. I've felt closer to you this entire time more than I ever have throughout all of these years without you. Is it goodbye after this? Are you just going to go away again?"

Through the desert winds, the all-to-familiar voice spoke, "Letting go doesn't mean forgetting. You can still feel the breadth of what you truly love without letting go. If it lasts, that's how you know it's true. Feeling love in your heart is always a pure thing to do. Follow that even if it doesn't make any sense; that's what the world is truly built upon. Your biggest problem is that you fear yourself too much. Never be afraid to love. A heart in a cage is cheated, but an unbridled one can lead you anywhere. Go where your heart leads you."

29 Palms

    I still felt so frustrated. I understood, but I didn't. I lamented across the canyons, "In this world, it feels like a heart like mine doesn't have a place. I've tried so many times to connect with other people, but it's like none of them want anything to do with me. It's like—the world doesn't like people like me. Everywhere I look, people are too afraid to love. It's either because they're afraid to get hurt, or they just don't want to feel anything at all. I've wondered so many times if this is the part in the world's story where love truly dies. It's like people just don't want it anymore, and passion for anything has become a sin. I feel like the world destroyed you because of the heart you had. You died with a broken heart. Am I going to die with one too? If there is a place for me in this world, where could it be?"

    The wind raged throughout the desert, blowing sand and shrubbery every which way. *Why was it so windy out?* I couldn't understand, but the all-too-familiar voice replied, "Hardships are what condition a heart. As you pass through each, the capacity for love grows. The hardest of paths tend to lead toward the greatest of things, but it is your choice where that path ends. Your biggest problem is that you try to conform to the ways of others and not the ways of your own heart. You keep who you truly are on the inside hidden from the others out of the fear of being rejected. You try so hard to obtain validation from them, but all you need in the end is yourself. All the rest will come along the way. You've heard it all before, but you didn't want to see it. All of what is outside of you is in constant flux, forever changing. Not one soul could ever hope to control it. The only thing you truly have control over is yourself. Tend to the garden in your own heart, and it shall flourish. Share your fruits with others unheeded. Have faith Ahnzerah. Have you ever thought that an open heart is the key to the world?"

    The words of the all-too-familiar voice ebbed through and around me. The dashing of the wind penetrated my heart through the mystic glowing rays of the twilight sun. I could feel the death of something old and the birth of something new. The name Ahnzerah is a mystery to even I. It was a name I merely stumbled across in my dreams, but it feels all so true. This is the first time I've ever revealed it to anyone. My higher self was with me; I could feel it all.

I could feel my father with me. He was there, and even still, the drums of doubt had quieted, and I could feel my love for Brooke there too. I could feel my love for my family, my friends; it all felt like the greatest source of joy imaginable in that flicker of a moment, and out there too—I saw my little boys again.

I tried as much as I could to keep them out of my mind because the thought of all the pain they could be going through without me was just too much for me to bear. I focused on my trip and a dream. The dream of finding true love in a forever moment that maybe—just maybe—could've last forever. This whole time I'd been chasing true love and I already had it. I've felt true love for my father, my mother, all of them, and especially for my sons. The love I have for them all in my heart, even for those who have hurt me, it was the truest love that could ever be hoped to find. The love I have for them is unconditional, and it's truly the only thing I'll ever experience that will last forever. Something that stands outside of the world that is always in constant flux and forever changing. I knew in that moment the type of love I hold in my heart isn't of this world. Nothing could ever change how I feel about the people I've truly loved. They could die, they could betray me, they could put me through the worst type of things, but the people I've truly loved—I'll love them forever. Nothing can change that, but I still wondered evermore what would it feel like to get that type of love back?

EPILOGUE: LIFE IS BUT A DREAM

The trip back home wasn't half the ride that it was on my way to California. In fact, you couldn't even call it a ride at all; I ended up flying back.

Of course, the old angry bald guy did fix the cooling system in the '69, but that was all that he fixed—the electrical system was still screwed and the exhaust system was in shambles, so I had it towed back to Alabama. I was tired of the road anyway. In a way, I was ready to go home even if I'd still have to face the pain of not getting to see my kids all over again. I knew I had family that had come down from Ohio to greet me when I got back, and I was really looking forward to that. I thought to myself, *Well everybody won't be there, but there's still people back there that really love me that can't wait to see me.* I couldn't wait to see them either. My heart was still beating for Brooke at the same degree it had been the whole trip, and I knew back in Mobile was where she was, and the mere thought of getting to see her again made my heart soar to the same heights it always had. I wasn't ready to give up on being with her. If now wasn't the time, maybe it would happen later.

After I got settled back in and went over the whole trip with family, I started texting Brooke again. Our texts became a lot shorter after we met up in Vegas, but I didn't allow the fear of her not ever giving me a chance cripple me. My heart desired her too much to give up. I knew she loved traveling, so I tried to come at her from that angle. All I could do was hope she wouldn't close the door on me again. I texted her, *You planned your next trip yet?*

My next trip is Europe. Eleven months away.

She was still being really short with me, and I wasn't sure why. She told me her grandma spoke to her about what I said, but I didn't understand how that could have hurt anything. What I said was true and it was all how I really felt. I guess she got this idea in her head I planned my whole trip around her plans to go to Vegas for some reason. Of course part of what she thought was true. Out of everything in the country, she's what I wanted to see the most. I told her when I booked for Vegas I wasn't sure when she would be there, but I hoped it was around the same time she was going because I really wanted to see her. I didn't ever get a reply from her after that, but I didn't want to give up. She was the only girl that ever came into my heart in the way she did, and out of all the girls in the whole world, she was the only one I truly wanted. I responded, *I have a few side excursions planned if you would like to come along.*

I'm really trying to save for Europe, so it just depends where.

My heart leaped up in my chest. *Would she really go somewhere with me?* Something seemed really different, though, I could feel it. She was getting ready to shut the door on me again. I still replied anyway. I didn't want to face it. *What about Savannah? I want you to go back there with me; you don't have to worry about the money or anything.*

I didn't get a reply from her after that text. I could feel my greatest fear approaching head-on like a subway train shooting right toward me, but the thing was—I was already tied to the tracks. I started to lose hope of ever seeing her again, so I did what I never should have. I acted out of desperation and sent her another text. *I never wanted anything out of you like most guys. I just know that you like to see different places, that's why I wanted to take you along. I guess I messed up because I really feel something toward you now. You're apart of one of the biggest stories of my life whether you like it or not. At this point, you're going to be one of the greatest girls that ever got away. I'll change your name in the book if I have to, but I'd really like your help writing it.*

I get you've never wanted anything out of me "like most guys" but you still have yet respected the fact I don't want a relationship and I don't want to be intimate with a guy right now. Taking those trips with you would be a bad idea, because you do have feelings for me and in a way you think that'll bring us closer. This story you are writing is yours to write. Only you can be the author; everyone else is just characters. I am so flattered by the way you think so highly of me, but I really cannot get close to you because I do not want to get your hopes up or give any one-sided expectations. I don't mind being here to help you with advice, but I can't be more than that. I hope you understand and respect my wishes.

There it was. She wasn't going to give me a chance. After all of it, she was going to close the door on me all over again. *But what about all of this love I have for you? Doesn't it mean anything? It has to. It all has to mean something.* I knew the battle was lost. So I admitted it. I admitted everything I wished I could have told her in person. *I* have gotten my hopes up about a relationship with you, I'm not going to lie. It's like that song goes "if I had to walk the world to make you fall for me, I would." One of the reasons why I traveled so far was to impress you. It's fine if you don't want me, but I can't help myself caring about you. That's just how my heart works. I've wondered if it would have been easier if I'd never met you, but in my heart, you're someone that I'll carry forever. It's just who you are; I can't help it Brooke. You can do your own thing, it's whatever. My heart is full of you, though; I just can't help it. I didn't try for that; it just happened.

I couldn't help letting it all spill out; I just couldn't take it anymore. I got tired of hiding how I truly felt about her. I was sitting alone all over again though, with the songs still singing within my heart that she had placed there. I thought to myself, *If she could only read what's on my mind and in my heart; maybe she'll understand then.* So I took the love that I couldn't show and I put it into a book. I started writing immediately, but meanwhile something unexpected happened.

A call came from an unknown number, only three days after I got back from the trip; it was my ex. I guess she got the "kiss my ass" message loud and clear. She told me a time and place, and I gunned my truck, Trusty, to pick up the boys.

They were so happy to see me. The baby looked shocked, but Robbie was all smiles. He knew in his heart his daddy was back and the dark times were over because it was time to have adventures together again. Azariah wouldn't say a word, though. It took him a while, but when he said those words—when he called me daddy again—it almost made me break down in tears. I scooped that little boy up into my arms and told him I loved him.

"I love you both with all my heart. I really do," I said to them both. They're not only my legacy, but my father's legacy. They're a part of both of us and a testament we were here and our story really means something. Robbie and Azariah's story is going to be so much better, though.

Things aren't going to be a tragedy for them, and I'm going to do everything I can to help them build their own tale as special as it can be. We're going to build great memories together, and I'm going to make sure they laugh more than they cry without a shadow of a doubt. I guess that's a way I can believe in myself the most. I never want to let them down.

The custody battle continued for months, though. Their mom ended up keeping them from me after the court date got pushed back again, but when the moment of truth came, justice won. I got full custody of my boys. A bolt of lightning struck me on that day and it was so shocking, I couldn't even fathom it at the time. It was just like magic you could say. I could finally make the story I always wanted to make with them. Their home was with me, and I became their safe place. It's funny how it all rolls back around. My dad was my safe place to me and I'm the same to them, but it makes me scared because if history repeated itself that way, I really hope it doesn't repeat itself in another. My son Robbie asked me on one occasion, "Daddy is it going to stay like this?"

I didn't know what he was talking about, so I replied, "Like what?"

Robbie looked at me and smiled, "Me and you everyday, daddy. Is it going to last forever?"

I lied to him and told him it would. I couldn't break his heart and tell him nothing lasts forever. He's going to have to find that out on his own. I'm going to make it last for as long as I can though. I can at least promise that.

With great things come terrible things, unfortunately. My grandpa, Gene St. Clair, died at eighty-eight years old just before I got custody. Even though I passed by his room at my uncle's so many times without saying a word, I was ready to bring my boys back up to Ohio to visit with him, but I never got the chance.

I felt terrible for walking past his room like I did. He couldn't carry on and talk with me like he used to, and I'd get bored. I was so used to him always being there; I thought he'd live forever, but like so many other things I was wrong. I should've known he wouldn't. After my dad died, Grandpa and my Uncle Gary were the father figures I had in my life. Every morning would start with Grandpa, though. He'd take me to school and pick me up every day. We'd start the morning talking with one another, and we'd end it all the same way, every day for years. He was one of my greatest heroes after my dad died, and I lost him.

It was kind of crazy to me that back in his day, Grandpa Gene had been all over the states too and seen it all just like I had. I remember him telling me, "Hawke, I've been everywhere. Across the seas and to every state in the country."

I thought that was so amazing. I said to him, "Really grandpa? What's it like out there?"

He told me, "Beautiful, that's all I can say. Korea was always the prettiest to me."

He was such a hero and an inspiration to me and he always will be. I smiled and said, "I'm going to see it all someday just like you grandpa."

At one point, he even ended up on a chain gang in Mexico or somewhere somehow, but nothing could hold that guy down. He ended up breaking out and smuggled his way back into the States toward freedom. It always sounded like a crazy story to me, but those scars he had on his ankles came from somewhere. He was sort of like Lincoln Clay back in his day you could say. One of my greatest dreams is to make his story into something, a book maybe. That would be my cousin Gab's job, though. She'd do it a lot of justice. *The Legend of Gene St. Clair.* Now that would be one hell of a story to tell.

I'm going to be the carrier of legacies, however which way it goes, though. With my father, he taught me how to dare to love and Grandpa Gene solidified that, not with words but from that old radio of his. I'd hear those songs and think to myself, *What a dream. I want to know a love like that someday.* Grandpa taught me a lesson of his own, though, that didn't have anything to do with my father and that was daring to live. Dare to love and dare even more to live through it all. I've been blessed with the most wonderful people a heart could ever hope to find. I just don't want it to be lost to time. I want to find a way to make all those I love live and last forever. The only way I know how to do that is through stories.

Holding onto forever is hard, though. When I heard my sons sing me happy birthday together on my twenty-eighth, I wished that moment could've lasted forever. In a moment, where they love me without a shadow of a doubt in each of their hearts, but even still, in that moment, I still thought about her. I couldn't forget about Brooke. My heart still longed for her so much.

It's like my heart is missing something no matter what I do. I still loved Brooke, and I didn't know what to do. I was lost for a while; the whole time I wrote this book in fact, but then she texted me right after I finished the first draft at the beginning of November in 2020. Strange, to say the least.

Apparently, it was a lot for her to handle, you know, me traveling across the country and all in the name of true love. It was something she definitely didn't expect to ever happen. I love catching people off guard though. You gotta do what you can to keep things interesting right?

It brought tears of joy to my eyes when I saw that message from her. I thought to myself, *She didn't forget about me after all and now I have this amazing story I can share with her.* I felt so lucky, but see the thing is she beat me to the punch. She shared her story with me before I even had the chance to share mine. Her tale was one full of hardships and disappointment too. A lot of people let her down over the years, but she was still lucky enough to have her warriors in the storm it seems. It's incredible everything she's overcome and I hope she finds the courage to write her own book one day. Whether she does or not, her story is already my favorite.

After hearing it, I told her, *The ones who suffer the most, the broken ones, I believe have the greatest treasures of happiness waiting in the winds. The thing is to just make it out of that storm and as another comes—they always do—its up to you to see to it that your sails are strengthened and are stronger than they ever were before. True happiness can only be known through the greatest of sufferings and love is the only way to nurture the wings to soar towards the heights of the heavens. Your on your way to doing that. It makes a lot more sense now with this strong energy I've always felt off of you. Its like just for the couple of glimpses that I have caught inside of your eyes I could tell pain had been there, but that it wasn't anymore. I saw a person filled full of the love of life. You have the frequency of an angel its sort of hard to explain or put into words. Thats why I've always told you that your unforgettable. Your one of a kind. Theres so much more that I could say, but I'll leave it at that. Thank you so much for sharing your story with me.*

We weren't just "pen pals" either, thank god for that. The texting bullshit was getting really old; texting is such a crippled form of communication. It's much better to get the full experience of someone in person. After I sent her the second draft of this book, we ended up meeting up for some coffee.

We sat in a square in downtown Mobile getting lost in one another's words. Our conversation didn't miss a beat and she loved the book as fractured as it may have been at the time. While I sat on that bench talking with her, I could feel my cheeks getting so red and I felt so warm inside. I thought to myself, *There she is. The girl I'd walk the world for. Is this really life or is it a dream?* I wanted so bad to scoot over and hold her close to me, but she was still on the friend thing. I thought, *Your killing me softly with this friend zone shit man,* but then another dream came true, we sat under the stars together.

It was the night of the Great Conjunction, when Jupiter met Saturn to produce the Bethlehem Star. It was sort of funny how it all happened because before she came over to my house I was gunnin' it down the road in the '69 singing along to the old tune of "Sunshine of Your Love." I thought about her the whole time and how I'd love to sit under the stars with her that night. I hit her up, but she damn near invited herself over. Which I really didn't approve of at all. She had to get past an insurmountable amount of resistance on my part for it to even happen, but I eventually gave in.

It was absolutely breathtaking though. She sat there with my pea coat wrapped around her and talked the night away with me. That's the thing, there's never anything awkward between her and I; like we're both just right where we were always meant to be. I listened to her talk about what she thought of things, and I heard her even more. Not with my ears, but more with my heart.

She stared up in the night sky with me, and she got so excited when she said, "Look at that shooting star! Did you see it?"

The truth is I didn't see it because I was looking at her. That shooting star passed right by me because everything I'd ever hoped for sat right beside me; I didn't care about the stars anymore. The one star I've always searched for was already there.

While I sat there gazing upon her I thought to myself, *Two flames of the same fire nothing ever felt so true. We're right for one another me and you.* I wanted to reach my hand out to her and pull her in closely. I wanted to lift her chin up to where our eyes could meet and tell her, "You see that sky up there? It's full of lights and dancing stars, but the moon is still and the heart of the sun is beating. You wanna dance with me or somethin'? Let us be the sun and the moon of tonight."

It would've been just like that song "In the Still of the Night" from grandpa's radio, but you have to be more than friends to do that. I mean if I'm dancing, I'm gonna do some kissing to after all.

Brooke loved the '69 too by the way. I tapped the hood and laughed, "It's still hard to believe I traveled across the whole country in this car. Sort of nuts, right?"

Brooke just looked at me and smiled. Then she looked back towards the '69 and said, "It was definitely a crazy thing to do."

After talking damn near the whole night away, I walked her out to her car and she gave me the weird, awkward friend hug unfortunately. My heart was beating like a tambourine as I thought, *Everything about tonight was great, but there's so much more I want with you.* As she was pulling out of our hug I held on to her still, and popped back a little to see if I could catch a glimpse of something more stirring there. I probably looked about half nuts to tell you the truth. I wasn't sure to be honest though. I didn't want to ruin it by ending it all with her saying, "I'm just not ready." Like she had so many times before.

That night under the stars with her was fantastic, but I felt like I had to constantly hold myself back because I was afraid of ruining it. I tried to get her to be with me so many times before. I mean traveling across the whole country alone to show someone that you mean what you say and your different than all the rest, is a big move to make. On top of that writing a book about it all. That's a one in a million thing right there. All she had to do was take my hand and say yes and I'd give her the world. Every time I'd always try though it would always end the same, "I'm just not ready."

I could understand to a degree why she wasn't. I mean I do have two kids, but I have them handled fine on my own and they're as happy as can be. Not everyone can handle that though. Kids tend to freak folks out when it comes to dating, plus there's the treacherous gossip circles to worry about, you don't want those fiends at your back. Brooke still tried to hang out with me anyways though. She told me once, **I tried to stop thinking about you, but I can't.**

I replied, *I feel the same way.*

I know, but I'm scared to be anything more than friends right now. I have all these plans that I want to do and I'm just afraid that they won't come true.

I understood what she meant, but I wasn't sure what she was so afraid of; it just hadn't dawned on me yet. I told her, *Brooke I don't think it really matters what either of us do we're going to keep crossing each others paths. Everything that's happened since we met has just been so strange and unbelievable. It's like I didn't even write the book. It's more like fate did.*

I meant every word that I said, but I couldn't accept that she just wanted to be friends. I felt way to much passion for her to just be that. I never meant to cause her heart any trouble and it hurts me even more that I did. You see, she tried to see me a few times after that, but I pulled back because I wanted more.

All this time I preached unconditional love, but my love for her had conditions. I traveled across the whole country and wrote a book about it to get her to fall for me, but she still wouldn't have me. I felt rejected by her and it made me feel like I wasn't good enough. So I pulled away from her. I wasn't as responsive to her because I didn't get what I wanted, but see the thing is, her not taking my hand didn't have anything to do with me. She just wanted to live out her dreams and make her own story. So she made that choice in the end. She chose her dreams over me. I can't blame her honestly.

    I wish I would've just listened to her, before she disappeared on me. She got on this weird kick that she didn't want to be on social media anymore and one of the last things she told me was that she was suppose to go to Michigan for some seasonal work. After that the line went dead. Her number isn't even the same anymore.

    When I found out she was gone, I'm not sure if I've ever cried like that before; not even in the desert. It went on for days. It's still going on in a way. To know true love, is to know true pain. The inside crashes and at the stake your burnt to ashes. You scream in the dark and the scars make there mark. When it all finally hit me after my return to that town with all the lights, I shattered. I was broken in Las Vegas all over again.

    When Jay Gatsby says,"It's so hard to just make her understand. I've gotten all of these things for her, all of these things and she just—now she just wants to run away." Then Nick Caraway says, "Jay you can't repeat the past."

    "Can't repeat the past? Why of course you can—of course you can." I could feel those words all to much in that moment. It's like Gatsby's words and feelings were my own especially when he said,"If I could just get back to the start— if I could just get back to the start, I could— I could find it again."

    It seems like I've been trying to just get back to the start my entire life. Back towards something—something that I don't quite even understand. The majority of my life has been spent chasing whats left and now that Brooke is out of my life, it's like she just turned into another ghost out there.

I can't spend anymore time chasing ghosts though. I've already spent to much time chasing the ghost of my father. I have to let her go because I love her that much. If you want to know what true love is it's not a game for the faint of heart. It's a match for mountains that can play their part no matter what the conditions are. Will I truly love Brooke always and forever? Yes I will. No matter what. Always and forever with all of my heart. I can truly say that now, but I can't say I won't cry about her from time to time. After all, when the winds blow and the colors of beauty flow, it all still reminds me of her. I really do miss her. More than words could ever say.

So what becomes of the broken hearted? I sure hope something does. I still want to write a real love story and travel the globe with my one true love. I thought Brooke was the one, but if she was, I don't think it would be this hard. Maybe that's the purpose of this book after all. It's like a message in a bottle cast out to sea. Perhaps someone will pick it up and fall in love with me.

So until then, what will the next step be? I like the idea of building an empire; that sounds about right to me. After all, who wouldn't want to be rich? Either way, I don't really care. My heart is already so full of riches, and that's all I really need to take me anywhere; it's already taken me so far. With an unbridled heart and not a fear in the way when it comes to love—I do believe I'll go quite far. I'm not sure what to do next, but learning how to fly seems like a good next step.

I'm serious; I met this guy that has a plane and he's going to teach me how to fly the thing. It's a propeller airplane—by no means a jet, but it seems like a good start. I talked with my brother about it the other day. I asked him, "Hey, man, do you think I could fly a propeller plane all the way across the Atlantic to Europe?"

"Fuck no, are you crazy? There's no way you could do that."

I wasn't quite convinced, "I don't know about that, man; I mean Amelia Earhart did it, didn't she? I think I could probably do it."

My brother looked at me like I was completely insane, "Hawke, Amelia Earhart is fuckin' dead, man! It's not going to work!"

Nope, still not convinced. I replied, "Well, we won't know unless we try."

And so that settles it. I'm going to be the next Iceman of the sky shooting through the air *Top Gun* style. Of course a propeller plane isn't like one of the *Top Gun* jets, but I'll get there.

I already planned my next trip too. I might be a single dad, but a trip every once in awhile never hurt anybody. I figured forty-two days across Europe would be pretty fun. At first, I wasn't sure where I wanted to go next, but this old 80's song kept going around in my head called "99 Luftballoons." Some chick from Europe sings it. I have no idea what the fuck she is talking about in the song, but it's gotta pretty catchy tune to it. I don't know; it just got me thinking about Europe I guess. Might as well head that way, why not? As for the next step after that, who knows? There's only one thing I know for sure. Time tells everything.

www.ingramcontent.com/pod-product-compliance
Lightning Source LLC
Chambersburg PA
CBHW032146080426
42735CB00008B/599